One Hundred Masterpieces
from the Hermitage

One Hundred Masterpieces *from the Hermitage*

Impressionist and Avant-Garde Works at the Scuderie Papali al Quirinale

Electa

Cover illustration
Henri Matisse
La Danse, 1910
The Dance
(no. 69)

Translated from the Italian by
Felicity Lutz, Mark Eaton, Paul Metcalfe
for *Scriptum*, Rome

© 1999 by SIAE
Pierre Bonnard, Maurice Denis,
André Derain, Maurice de Vlaminck,
Fernand Léger, Henri Manguin,
Albert Marquet, Pablo Picasso,
Georges Rouault, Ker Xavier Roussel,
Louis Valtat, Kees Van Dongen,
Edouard Vuillard

© 1999 by SIAE - H. Matisse Inheritance

© 1999 by Electa, Milan
Elemond Editori Associati
All rights reserved

Under the auspices of
the President of the Italian Republic

One Hundred Masterpieces from the Hermitage. Impressionist and Avant-Garde Works at the Scuderie Papali al Quirinale

Rome, Scuderie Papali al Quirinale
22 December 1999 - 11 June 2000

This exhibition has been supported by
Prime Minister's Office
Ministry of Foreign Affairs
Ministry of the National Heritage
Ministry of Education
Ministry of Higher Education and Scientific and Technological Research
Rome City Council
Ministry of Culture of the Russian Federation

This exhibition has been promoted by
Hermitage State Museum, St. Petersburg
Rome Agency for Jubilee Preparations
Mondadori

Scientific Director
Mikhail Piotrovsky
Director of the Hermitage State Museum

Scientific Committee
Claudio Strinati
Director of the Rome Department of the Artistic and Historical Heritage
Bruno Contardi
Director of the Milan Department of the Artistic and Historical Heritage
Maurizio Calvesi
Professor of Art History, "La Sapienza" University, Rome

Exhibition organized by
Albert Kostenevich
Curator of the Western Art Department, Hermitage State Museum

Rome Agency for Jubilee Preparations
General organization
Rita Cassano, Emilio Melli
Organizational Secretariat
Alexandra Andresen
Press Office
Nino Criscenti

Rome Department of the Artistic and Historical Heritage
Claudio Strinati
Director
Exhibitions Office
Morena Costantini
Mario Di Bartolomeo
Conservation of Works
Immacolata Affan de Rivera Costagutti

Production and Organization
Elemond spa

Organizational Secretariat
Tomaso Radaelli, Simone Todorow di San Giorgio

Electa Press Office
Flavia Fossa Margutti
Sveva Fede

Gratitude is expressed to
Federica Baioni
Fabrizia Casagrande
Stefania Di Gioia
Virginia Massimo Lancellotti
Diamara Parodi
Valerio Pozzi
Dario Tagliabue

Exhibition planning and coordination
Designers
Gae Aulenti
with Francesca Fenaroli
Graphic layout
Pierluigi Cerri
with Dario Zannier
Lighting
Piero Castiglioni

Transport
Alitalia, Hepry, Propileo Transport

Insurance
Progress Insurance

Ticket and Booking Office
P.B.S. srl, Milan

Internet: www.ticket.it/100capolavori

Technical sponsors

official carrier

Il Messaggero

PROGRESS
INSURANCE BROKER

The emotion that many will feel on looking through the One Hundred Masterpieces from the Hermitage *catalog is wholly justified. The exhibition for which this publication provides a critical commentary and overview presents a whole series of acknowledged masterpieces, and is unquestionably one of the most important cultural events of 2000. In the year of the Jubilee, Rome and Italy can take pride in being able to offer visitors from all over the world an exhibition of extraordinary quality made possible by the cooperation of St. Petersburg's Hermitage Museum and the Russian Ministry of Culture, by private sponsors, and by the Rome Agency for Jubilee Preparations, all of which we thank. In the rooms of the Scuderie Papali al Quirinale, a new venue for culture, we can thus trace the roots and evolution of the language of contemporary Western art through celebrated works that have played a substantial role in the development of the European visual alphabet. A process that started in France with Impressionism and has continued through Gauguin, Matisse, the* Fauves *and Picasso up to the present. This alphabet still helps citizens to form their own viewpoint with respect to reality and its interpretation, in a word to interpret life itself. Thanks to the far-sightedness of a few great collectors and patrons, as well as a whole series of chance events, visitors will be able to undertake an exceptional exploration of the most important works of an extraordinary museum by artists such as Monet, Renoir, Degas, Sisley, Cézanne, Rousseau 'le Douanier', Matisse, Gauguin and Picasso. And it is not only the importance of the painters that acts as a magnet. Some of the works exhibited are images that form an integral part of the symbolic universe of the West. Suffice it to mention Matisse's* The Dance. *The works are also all in excellent condition thanks to the care lavished on them by one of the world's most important museums. In a country like Italy, where the cultural scene is dominated by memories of the ancient past and there are few examples of Impressionism, providing an opportunity such as the one represented by this exhibition also means allowing citizens to expand their knowledge of the languages of contemporary art, increasing their awareness, and bringing them closer to the values of the millennium that is now ending. This is an opportunity for extraordinary cultural growth that will delight not only the specialists but all those who look to art for answers, meaning or even just emotions. I am sure that it will prove a great success.*

Giovanna Melandri
Minister for the National Heritage

The history of the cultural links between the Hermitage and Italy stretches back over a number of centuries. The buildings forming the premises of this great museum were also the work of various Italian architects - Rastrelli (the Winter Palace), Quarenghi (the Hermitage Theater and the Raphael Loggias), Rossi (the General Staff building) – who linked their lives to Russia forever. The Hermitage Museum's collections include immortal works by Raphael and Leonardo da Vinci, Titian and Caravaggio, Tiepolo and Giorgione. Our museum has held various exhibitions of works by contemporary Italian artists, and works from the Hermitage have been displayed on numerous occasions in museums and venues in Rome, Florence, Venice and other Italian cities. This time the Hermitage is presenting an extraordinary exhibition of works by the greatest French artists of the late nineteenth and early twentieth centuries at the Scuderie Papali in Rome. The paintings and drawings by Monet, Renoir, Cézanne, Gauguin, Bonnard, Matisse and Picasso will undoubtedly contribute to the success of the exhibition with Italian art lovers. The exhibition thus seeks to develop the traditional ties between Russia and Italy, and between St. Petersburg and Italy, and paves the way for their continuation in the twenty-first century, the new millennium.
I wish all the organizers and creators of the exhibition the greatest success and am sincerely delighted that visitors will have an opportunity to make the acquaintance of these splendid and indeed sublime works of art from the Hermitage.

Vladimir Egorov
Minister of Culture of the Russian Federation

At the beginning of the year 2000, an extraordinary new exhibition center, the Scuderie Papali al Quirinale, inaugurates its activities by displaying one hundred masterpieces from the Hermitage Museum in St. Petersburg.
After nearly three hundred years this splendid Roman palazzo, which is part of the property attached to the Presidency of the Italian Republic and joins Palazzo della Consulta to complete the extraordinary setting of the Piazza del Quirinale, takes on a new role as a major international cultural center.
Innocent XIII commissioned Alessandro Specchi to build the Scuderie to house the papal stables and carriages at the beginning of the eighteenth century, but the work was actually completed by Ferdinando Fuga for Clement XII.
At the end of the 1930s the horses and carriages were replaced by automobiles, first those of the Italian Royal Family and then those of the Presidency of the Republic. With its surface area of thirty thousand square meters, the Scuderie has remained unused for the last twenty years.
The Presidency of the Republic has granted Rome City Council permission to use it temporarily as a center for art exhibitions during the Holy Year.
The conversion of the premises, which was facilitated by the enormous size of the stables, was a very demanding technical feat involving complex operations to ensure the best possible use of the display areas while guaranteeing the necessary conditions of safety and environmental control.
The restoration work was planned by the architect Gae Aulenti and directed by the Rome Superintendency of the Environmental and Architectural Heritage.
For many centuries Rome has been regarded as the world's leading city for art. At the beginning of the third millennium, its universal role is further enhanced by the inauguration of this ultramodern exhibition center.
The Rome Agency for Jubilee Preparations, which has been assigned responsibility for managing the Scuderie during the year 2000, has been able to organize the One Hundred Masterpieces from the Hermitage *exhibition thanks to the assistance of the Mondadori-Elemond publishing house. The one hundred key works drawn from the astonishing collections of the Russian dealers Shchukin and Morozov document the essential features of the crucial period in French art that stretches from Impressionism to the early avant-garde movements and thus significantly exemplify the cultural movements of the twentieth century.*
The choice of this exhibition was an easy one for the Agency to take.
The unparalleled value of the works to be admired over the first few months of 2000 at the Scuderie is the best possible guarantee of the success of a debut of the utmost cultural quality and prestige.
The Rome Agency for Jubilee Preparations wishes to thank all those who have made the exhibition possible, first of all Mikhail Piotrovsky, Director of the Hermitage Museum, Albert Kostenevich, Curator of the Hermitage's Department of Western Art, and the architect Gae Aulenti, who is responsible both for the refurbishment of the building and for the design of the exhibition.

Luigi Zanda
President of the Rome Agency for Jubilee Preparations

The first spark was struck ten years ago.
On my way to visit the Morozov-Shchukin collection, I already knew it was going to be something extraordinary, but the emotion I felt was far beyond all my expectations. Only true lovers of art can understand the joy of the magic moments offered by your first encounter with a masterpiece. And I was faced not with one masterpiece, but a never-ending series of marvelous works, namely the Impressionist and Post-Impressionist paintings collected with extraordinary intuitive taste by Ivan Morozov and Sergei Shchukin at the beginning of this century.
On leaving St. Petersburg, I promised myself that one day I would succeed in sharing this experience with the greatest possible number of people by bringing those masterpieces to Italy. Now that this promise has been fulfilled and what I like to describe as the "impossible" exhibition, something never managed before, has become a reality, I should like first of all to express my gratitude to all those who have worked alongside me, starting with Mikhail Piotrovsky, the Director of St. Petersburg's Hermitage Museum.
The turning point in the project came when Piotrovsky and I decided to initiate a long-term agreement between the Hermitage and Mondadori for the purpose of organizing various cultural initiatives, first and foremost the presentation of the Morozov-Shchukin collection in Italy.
All of this has come about, and the masterpieces of the Hermitage Museum have finally arrived in Italy.
I thank all those who have made this exhibition possible. Particular thanks go to the Rome Agency for Jubilee Preparations, which has made available the Scuderie Papali al Quirinale, specially restored for the occasion by Gae Aulenti, who also designed the exhibition; the Wind Corporation, a firm believer and investor in the project from the very outset; Alitalia, which organized the airlift to transport the works between St. Petersburg and Rome; the newspaper Il Messaggero; *the Ministry of Culture and the Ambassador to Italy of the Russian Federation; the Rome Department of the Artistic and Historical Heritage; and the Italian Ministry for the National Heritage.*
Their cooperation has made it possible to organize this memorable exhibition and thus ensure Italy's leading position on the circuit of great international cultural and artistic events during this Jubilee Year.

Leonardo Mondadori
President of the Mondadori Publishing House

The Hermitage in Rome

The Hermitage is delighted to present one of its finest collections in one of Europe's best and most modern exhibition centers. The Romans and their guests will thus be able to see our splendid Impressionist and Post-Impressionist works, many of which have become landmarks in art history. Without them one can have no understanding either of the art of the period or of the works of later generations. Matisse's The Dance *has become the symbol of twentieth-century aesthetics. The Hermitage's Gauguins and Cézannes leave visitors speechless. No other museum has such extraordinary works by Derain. Today, at the end of the twentieth century, this exhibition provides an opportunity to reflect on the origins of modern art (and everything that has followed). The artistic map of the world is somewhat bizarre. Italy, the country that constitutes mankind's most precious artistic treasure, has practically no works of the French school of the late nineteenth and early twentieth centuries. What are probably the world's greatest collections were instead built up in Russia. We recall with gratitude Sergei Shchukin, Ivan Morozov and the other collectors related to them, Moscow dealers who not only loved art but were also able to identify the right artists and the best works offered by the market of the time. It is time alone that has demonstrated their farsightedness and divine gift of impeccable taste.*

Without these extraordinary collections, the extremely important Russian avant-garde movement would never have existed. Russia was indeed one of the channels through which the art of the entire world was influenced by Cézanne, Picasso and Matisse. Even during the Soviet period these works helped to make up for the conservative isolation into which our country was plunged, and to educate a new generation of great artists.

These extraordinary pages of the history of art and art collecting also relate the history of the Hermitage, a great museum where the founders of modern art have become part of a world of universal masterpieces and splendid records of Russian history. We are grateful to all those who contributed to the formation of the Hermitage's collections and made it possible to offer them once again to the public and the world. We are grateful to our Italian friends, who will, I hope, become more numerous after this exhibition. The Hermitage has come as a guest to Rome, where "all roads lead". We hope that once visitors have made the acquaintance of the Hermitage, they will also want to see the other sections of our vast museum.

Mikhail Piotrovsky
Director of the Hermitage Museum

The Wind Corporation and Culture

The Wind Corporation has worked with conviction and enthusiasm to bring about the exhibition One Hundred Masterpieces from the Hermitage. Impressionist and Avant-Garde Works *at the Scuderie Papali al Quirinale for three essential reasons. Firstly, because of the extraordinary nature of this cultural event, which will give the Italian public and the visitors pouring into Rome for the Holy Year an opportunity to admire key works in the history of modern art, many of which are on display outside Russia for the first time ever. Secondly, because this exhibition inaugurates the new season of the Palazzo delle Scuderie al Quirinale, a building of incomparable beauty restructured by Gae Aulenti on behalf of the Presidency of the Republic to form a splendid exhibition center. Thirdly, because we have worked together with the Rome Agency for Jubilee Preparations to organize an event distinguished not only by its cultural quality but also by the quality of the service offered to visitors.*
In this connection, the Wind Corporation has provided its know-how in the telecommunications and multimedia field to enhance the information made available to all concerned, to ensure that visitors encounter minimal inconvenience, and to enable them to enjoy their participation in the event to the full. We are convinced that telecommunications can assist the world of culture, and especially those responsible for managing Italy's immense monumental and artistic heritage, in their progress towards greater dissemination, efficiency and closeness to citizens. For this reason we are committed to assistance in innovative cultural initiatives. In this way we can also put into practice the Wind Corporation's key watchwords: "to surpass existing reality" by helping artistic creativity to express itself and spread also with the aid of new information technologies; "to work as a system", because great cultural events can only be the outcome of effective cooperation between numerous bodies; "to focus on human beings", who can rediscover in the sharing of great cultural values a strong identity capable of combining the memory of the past with a desire for the future.

Tommaso Pompei
Managing Director of the Wind Corporation

Contents

27   Impressionist Themes
Claudio Strinati

32   Paris, circa 1910
Bruno Contardi

36   French Painting from Impressionism to the Avant-garde
Maurizio Calvesi

44   French Artists and Russian Collectors
Albert Kostenevich

91   Illustrations

237   Descriptions of the Works
by Albert Kostenevich, Asya Kantor-Gukovskaya

Impressionist Themes

Claudio Strinati

In addition to the unquestionable intrinsic value of the individual works, which truly exemplify Impressionist and Post-Impressionist art, the masterpieces on display in this exhibition make it possible to identify a whole series of themes and issues for the benefit of the attentive viewer.

Impressionism is, in fact, often seen in terms of pure formal language, and within certain limits this is both right and necessary. On such an occasion as this, however, it may be possible to put forward some further observations, without in any way altering the consolidated ideas on the basis of which the question is normally addressed. If we accept the view that Impressionism forms the starting point for any discussion of the frameworks of contemporary art, we cannot fail to note that a crucial element lies precisely in the clean break that Impressionism – drawing unquestionably on ideas that had developed at length over the years preceding 1850 and culminated in Corot – makes with the iconographic tradition that had prevailed until a short while earlier, including its rich output of landscapes. There can, however, be no doubt that Impressionism clearly brought out the crisis point reached by modern consciousness in its determination that the importance of the subject matter represented should no longer be regarded as guaranteeing the excellence of the result achieved.

Impressionism thus saw the consolidation of an idea formulated in precise theoretical terms nearly a century later by T.W. Adorno in the second part (1945) of *Minima Moralia*: "Bad painting (...) imagines that the dignity of a work and the glory it merits depend on the dignity of the objects, and that a representation of the Battle of Leipzig is worth more than a chair seen at an angle (...) It is always the same bad ingenuousness." Here Adorno was summing up a historical process that had begun with the 1855 Universal Exposition in Paris and culminated in the irreversible crisis of the identification of aesthetic relevance with importance of content, thus arriving at Impressionism and the very roots of the contemporary world.

Adorno's view is thus perfectly in line with the conscious stance adopted by Courbet when he exhibited *The Artist's Studio* at the same Exposition, without initially provoking any particular reaction. The idea clearly expressed in this memorable work, namely that pure inspiration "signifies" as such and as such reflects the purity of the mind seeking truth, did however gradually penetrate. The nude figure of the woman contemplating the artist at work was thus intended to merge the two concepts of *nature* and *truth* into a single whole.

This is certainly one of the major premises of the history of Impressionism, which was from the very outset a trend rather than a movement.

Today, however, a long time after the period in which Adorno formulated his theses, it appears equally legitimate to examine the artistic legacy bequeathed to us by the civilization of Impressionism and Post-Impressionism also in more strictly content-oriented terms. This implies no attempt to take Impressionism back to a time and a culture to which it does not belong, but rather a desire to reconsider the deeper meaning communicated by this exhibition of a considerable portion of the Hermitage Museum's extraordinary collection.

The works were chosen not in order to prove a specific thesis but to reconstruct a sequence capable primarily of illustrating the actual period of Impressionism, definitively established by historians as running from the Impressionists' first exhibition in Nadar's gallery in 1874 to their last in 1886. This sequence is then closely linked, again in accordance with the established historical reconstruction, to Post-Impressionism and the birth of the avant-garde movements seen in terms of the Fauves and Picasso's early work.

The selection is thus characterized by certainty and the infallible identification of quality that is supreme and indeed still regarded as insuperable in absolute terms.

It is, however, for this very reason that it may be worth seeking in this exhibition not so much one unifying theme, which would make no sense, as traces of the great thematic "indicators" of Impressionism, which the modern observer does not always take correctly into account.

As regards the "content" of works of art, Impressionism was in fact the result of the necessary confluence of a whole series of elements that ripened at dizzying speed midway through the nineteenth century, and still influence our judgment of art in the overall sense as well as our aesthetic theories.

It is indeed a mistake to believe that our categories of judgment as regards the facts and things of art were transformed by the avant-garde movements of Cubism and Abstract art, and far more correct to recall that the great change, whose impact we still feel with a sense of absolute continuity, took place at the time of Flaubert and Baudelaire, Ruskin and Turner, Delacroix and Corot. When the latter, a great painter, appeared to adopt a stance at the very borderline of the concept of art as it had been delineated and addressed for centuries with his claim that what mattered in the work of art was not execution but the value determined by the identification of form in itself, the problem had arrived at breaking point. The question that still torments every art enthusiast and connoisseur, namely doubt as to the field of application of the very concept of art, was already being formulated. This is implicitly asserted by Courbet in his above-mentioned work *The Artist's Studio* when he places a child in front of the inspired artist intent on painting a landscape to indicate that it must be determined by *truth*. The child's absolute ingenuousness is the path to the understanding of art because this alone offers an *a priori* elimination of ignorant preconceptions that seek to circumscribe the artist's field of action. This is the idea expressed many years later by Paul Klee in response to someone who accused him of childishness, claiming that his work could be produced by a child: "Children can do it too, and the fact that they can is proof of wisdom."

In short, the idea of a shattering, epoch-making revolution in the artistic field took shape midway through the nineteenth century, when Queen Victoria and Napoleon III inaugurated the Universal Exposition and the French emperor proclaimed that the time had come to see Europe as one great family.

The essential impetus, which still survives today, stemmed from the official sanctioning of the old masters, who were substantially all alike in their superb skill in illustrating the great subjects and beauties of mythology. The old question of the Ancients and the Moderns thus made a sudden reappearance. The Moderns were in fact practically all "ancient" at the time, with very few exceptions including the great Millet, branded by the Director General Count Nieuwerkerke as a democrat and therefore not an artist. This dimension of democracy rekindled the dispute between Ancients and Moderns. The time had come to take up the positive elements furnished above all by landscape painters like Théodore Rousseau and to be modern. And being modern meant first of all taking control of one's own profession and following the great path traced by intellectuals like John Ruskin, ready to fight for the victory of the modern element in art against all preconceptions and platitudes.

It was, however, essential that there should be no misunderstanding of the principle formulated by Ruskin in *Modern Painters*, and there was certainly no misunderstanding on the part of the great French critics from Théophile Gautier to Baudelaire. Ruskin's principle drew strength from its elementary simplicity. It was a matter of seeing how things really are, of seeing and nothing else, and hence of restoring to figurative art its ultimate and absolute meaning. What Charlotte Brontë wrote on reading *Modern Painters* – the vast and by no means easy work written by Ruskin to defend and glorify Turner, seen as the painter par excellence, the hero capable of taking art in hand and elevating it to the everlasting glory of beauty – could stand as the emblem of the birth of modern art. As G. Leonelli recalls in his foreword to the Italian translation (Einaudi, Turin, 1998) of *Modern Painters*, after reading the first volume Charlotte Brontë remarked in a letter to W.S. Williams that it was like having her sight restored after going around blindfold. And that is precisely what it was. A few years before the fateful date of 1855, still in the first half of the century, Ruskin's defense of Turner proposed an extraordinary visual and conceptual experience, an authentic expedition into the constituent elements of art that, leaving aside any banal formalism, taught everyone that art could and must be seen in terms of progress in understanding and expressing color, light and form. The Moderns thus had every right to go beyond the Ancients, and the duty of modern art was to stand in the *avant-garde*.

This may well appear paradoxical, and an aesthetic thesis formulated in terms of progress or regress would unquestionably be regarded today as groundless and unacceptable, but the Impressionists actually did appear as soon as these concepts were put forward, as though a historic destiny had to be fulfilled and to extend to the present day, possibly to be refuted once again. And the apparently intransigent formalism also contained the seeds of the inseparable need to tackle concrete issues and content so that art might once again perform a communicative function without having content imposed upon it. The true content would come from a focus on the specific, and the most competent critics of the day began to be divided on the question of whether the work of art should be examined in *formal-structural* or *iconographic-iconological* terms, a debate that was to continue right up to the present day. It may therefore be interesting to recall how certain "formal" discoveries of the Impressionists and Post-Impressionists are closely linked to a complex dynamics of investigations on specific themes that in most cases legitimize figurative ideas in themselves and demonstrate their deep significance. The period from the second half of the nineteenth century to the beginning of the twentieth does of course see a slow change in the themes addressed, which gradually shift towards those generated by city life, but here again it is impossible to impose preconceived schemata.

While the *city* is of course the Baudelairean theme par excellence, it runs parallel to the only apparently contrasting theme of the country and the associated dimension of peace and rest.

Closer investigation reveals, however, that the real issue is not that of the city or the country, and still less the contrast between them. The basic theme remains that of *truth* and how to achieve an authentic vision capable of reflecting the living dimension of the work of art. An exhibition like this therefore enables us to establish the concrete artistic work performed in one of the greatest periods ever celebrated in the history of art rather than the differences between Impressionism and Divisionism or between the Nabis and the Fauves. Though certainly substantial and susceptible to clarification, such differences are perhaps less important today than a thorough knowledge of the period as a whole.

This knowledge is to be sought in certain themes addressed by the artists responsible for the radical break between the Impressionist period and everything that had gone before. In short, we must examine the real concerns that drove artists to undertake a largely unplanned journey, and identify the overall trends, which ultimately regard the relationship between the artists' social and existential condition and the subjects they focus on. A crucial theme in this connection is that of *comfort* and *discomfort*, the tension between art understood as the moment of verification of a state of mind that is fulfilled and truly involved, and art as the representation of conditions of discomfort and torment. The great teachings of Monet, a man deeply disturbed in his existential experience and the supreme poet of comfort as artistic well-being, thus contrast sharply with the knotty, anguished teachings of Gauguin, Cézanne and the early Picasso, whose lives alternated between hardship and sedate calm, serious concern and abundant satisfaction. In any case, and for all their differences in standpoint, the latter expressed the difficulty of life, the constant disturbance of the mind, and the disintegration of an organic relationship between man and nature.

This was the period that saw the birth of the idea of *progress* as it is still understood today. It is no coincidence that Impressionism arose in a social and cultural context that witnessed the birth of modern technology and science as well as practically all the discoveries upon which our cultural assumptions rest. Advances in the medical, economic, political, scientific and administrative fields, together with the discovery of technologies and sources of energy that are still used today, were concentrated in the period running roughly from 1855 to 1905, i.e. the period covered by this exhibition. It was then that the true question of progress took specific shape and hence the issue of artistic progress, and it still appears legitimate to see a strong reflection of this crucial concept in many aspects of Impressionist and Post-Impressionist culture. Progress is also unquestionably tied up with the dynamics of middle-class society, even though Impressionism and Post-Impressionism cannot rightly be interpreted in terms that are excessively pro or anti middle-class. Monet, a bold and intransigent revolutionary in painting, could very well be taken as an emblem of the bourgeoisie, as could Manet in certain respects, while the restless Gauguin, who was unquestionably anti-bourgeois in his behavior, produced paintings that evidently reflect a typically middle-class desire for order, peace and the simplification of discourse in moral terms.

There is, however, no doubt that the Impressionists' ideas were dominated by a literally elementary component in precise opposition to the constituent elements of the art of the past, founded as it was on obedience to rules and choices that were no longer acceptable. It is the *primal elements* of water, earth, fire and air that attract the attention of those who seek to identify the truth of perception, first with a sense of immediacy and involvement in the very life of nature, and then in the scientific and analytical sense developed by Seurat. It is because they are *vital* that the Impressionists won their battle and their enduring place in history against the opposition of those who maintain that art has no need to draw upon the true sources of life. And it is this vital sense that provides the deeper explanation of Monet's visual philosophy when he arrived in his full maturity at the great cycles of Rouen cathedral or the water lilies, when he reaffirmed the significance of changes in form generated by changes in light, thereby consecrating Corot's identification of *form* and its associated *values* as the ultimate meaning of the work of art. It is legitimate to argue that the so-called avant-garde movements changed none of the essential terms of the question constituted by the increasingly intense and involved descent into truth of knowledge that, in order to be such, eschews the schematic reproduction of what it appears to have definitively mastered. It is of course with the avant-garde movements that the problem is intensified to the point where we arrive at the question of what falls within the domain delimited by the concept of art and what necessarily remains outside. This is why the beginning of the twentieth century saw the birth of so many aesthetic philosophies (as exemplified in Italy by the celebrated work of Benedetto Croce) designed to establish precisely what could and should be defined as art in a far different fashion from the philosophical reflection of previous centuries, including Hegelian idealism. There emerged a concern to exorcise aesthetic experiences endowed with real cognitive power by declaring them extraneous to the defined domain of *art* as such.

The period that stretches from the Impressionists to the early avant-garde and up to the present obviously includes two world wars and an attempt to give concrete shape to the idea of the *European family* regarded by Napoleon III as imminent at the time of the 1885 Universal Exposition. The fact remains, however, that the contents of Impressionist and Post-Impressionist work can be seen today as precise documents of a civilization endowed with features that are immediately linked with our own, and hence form part of a historical epoch that is still unified, even though the collapse of the *belle époque* and the emergence of the early avant-garde movements were perceived at the time as a definitive watershed that relegated certain phenomena to the past and marked others with the stigmata of irreversible modernity.

This was not precisely so, however, as we realize more than ever today. Though devoid of any one overriding theme, this exhibition can therefore be interpreted in these terms, thus enabling us to recapitulate a course of events that still belongs to us.

In this way we note that certain important themes run through the entire exhibition and exemplify certain trends of Impressionist culture other than the obvious and overworked ones of *landscape*, the relationship between works produced in the studio and in the open air, and the progressive breakdown of chromatic mass and light. A fundamental role is played first of all by the contrast between the environments of city and country. More specifically, however, we note in Monet the vast amount of space given to reflection on the dialectic between images of the garden, a domestic and bourgeois place but one interpreted in terms of the free expansion of nature, and of true *natural space* addressed in terms of the ordered and rationalized standpoint of the domestic garden, in the search for a deeper meaning of the very idea of the natural place described as the supreme *locus* of comfort, joy and pleasure in the broadest possible sense. In this perspective nature is thus our home and immersion into its state of reasonable idleness becomes a glorification of the self-regenerative capacity of the senses. It is clearly the theme of *life* that runs through Monet's work and makes it the emblem of Impressionism. The supreme theme is the one that verges on the inexpressible, namely making art into a living fabric that constantly renews itself and constantly accompanies the cycle of existence. Everything passes through this gigantic filter of vision, and it appears impossible to ignore the influence of the idea of the Zen garden as mediated by a knowledge of Japanese art, a blend of nature and artifice but reinterpreted here in the perspective of a mind that is both rational and emotionally involved.

Alongside the great theme of nature is that of the *city*, which constitutes a figurative personage in the densely crowded meditations of Pissarro and Sisley, but once again in the Impressionist perspective of the living fact. The city is alive, but in a very different fashion from the natural context, in accordance with the belle époque's idea of constant, never-ending movement. The theme of the city passes through the most disparate experiences until it arrives at the concept of an enchanted space, as in Marquet, or of life concentrated within the closed environment of a home inhabited by infinite echoes, as in Bonnard. In its constant focus on the great theme of comfort and discomfort, Impressionism is of course also the painting of people who move between the comforts and discomforts of the city, splendid though it may be, and between the pleasures and relaxation of life in the country villa. The boredom and fear dreaded by Baudelaire often creep into the interstices of a world that feels the weight of the void of awareness and the loss of identity, and memorable examples can be seen in the works of Rousseau 'le Douanier' and also Vlaminck. This progression comes to a sublime and agonizing climax with the early Picasso, a savage and hypersensitive poet truly suspended over the gaping abyss opened up before the belle époque as though to foreshadow the tragedies of solitude and make-believe in the metaphor of the circus and stock theatrical characters. A supreme peak is reached here with the great theme of mirroring and reflection. While Cézanne experienced this with the harrowing impression of a single form of matter substantiating all things and people, Matisse is the great lyricist of this trend. It is remarkable to note his glorification of the dance, which was in fact to prove one of the most powerful aesthetic media at the beginning of the new century – suffice it to recall the extraordinary achievements of Diaghilev – in a period that invoked the power of art understood as movement.

The theme of Matisse's *The Dance* is the theme par excellence with which the new century opens. While the evocative power of ancient myth persists and again finds its way into the meditations of such chosen spirits as Debussy, Maurice Denis and Odilon Redon, we also see the reappearance of the dialectic between Ancients and Moderns, which seemed to have settled for the moment into definitively established positions.

This is a question that reappeared yet again after the end of World War II, and makes it possible for all of us to regard ourselves as the legitimate heirs of the great period of art known as Impressionism.

Paris, circa 1910

Bruno Contardi

Exhibitions are normally arranged and presented to the public in rigorously chronological order. Whether they are monographic exhibitions focusing on a single artist or encompass broader artistic trends and phenomena, temporal narration seems to be the only way to do full justice to the historical course of events and the unraveling of the artistic problems and episodes. This exhibition, which focuses on one hundred masterpieces of French Impressionist and Post-Impressionist art from the Hermitage Museum in St. Petersburg, is likewise organized along a temporal axis from Monet to Renoir, from Sisley to Pissarro, from Gauguin to Cézanne, up to Matisse and Picasso. The visitor is thus provided with an anthological but orderly overview of the leading figures in French art over a period stretching more or less from 1870 to 1914.

While the exhibition can also be seen as tracing the intellectual and ultimately existential adventure of the two extraordinary Muscovite collectors Sergei Ivanovich Shchukin and Ivan Abramovich Morozov, as Albert Kostenevich suggests in his essay in this catalog, the succession of the works exhibited in no way reflects the formation of their collections. There is, however, nothing to prevent visitors from using the catalog to view the works not as they are displayed in the Scuderie Papali al Quirinale but in the order in which they were actually purchased by these two exceptional figures. This would make it possible to trace the changes in their taste and their conscious participation in the artistic discussions and developments taking place at the time in Paris as part of a relationship that can only be understood as a sometimes intense dialectic between painters, dealers and collectors. I would instead advise the reader to visit the rooms of the exhibition almost in reverse order and start with two of the (chronologically) last paintings exhibited in order to reflect on a crucial moment in twentieth-century art. Let us therefore begin with Paris around the year 1910.

In the extraordinary collection of works displayed in this exhibition, one painting stands out by virtue not only of its quality but also of the importance it has had in the general culture of this century. Matisse's *The Dance* is unanimously recognized as an absolute masterpiece precisely because it somehow mysteriously encapsulates the doubts, demands, thoughts and feelings of an era. Unlike practically all the other works on display, this exceptionally large canvas, measuring nearly four meters in width and over two and a half in height, has the particular distinction of having been not simply purchased but also specifically commissioned by Sergei Shchukin. This extremely rich Russian merchant wanted Matisse to decorate the staircase of his Moscow residence, which already contained many extraordinary works by the artist, all bought in Paris by their owner after painstaking selection. Matisse himself suggested the subject of *The Dance* (together with its great companion piece *Music*, also held by the Hermitage but not included in the exhibition in Rome). As he stated in an interview, the work was conceived as part of a triptych depicting different states of mind that produce an immediate echo in the viewer: "*J'imagine le visiteur qui vient du dehors. Le premier étage s'offre à lui. Il faut obtenir un effort, donner un sentiment d'allégement. Mon premier panneau représent la danse, cette ronde envolée au dessus de la colline. Au deuxième étage on est dans l'intérieur de la maison: dans son esprit et son silence, je vois une scène de musique, avec des personnages attentifs; enfin au troisième étage c'est le plein calme et je peins une scène de repos: des gens étendus sur l'herbe, devisant ou rêvent. J'obtiendrai cela par les moyens les plus simples et les moins nombreux, ceux qui permettent pertinemment au peintre d'exprimer toute sa vision intérieure.*"[1] Matisse thus proposed a great decorative scheme capable of acting upon the mental state of those entering the house.

It was only after some misgivings, and above all after seeing the watercolor sketch (*Composition no. 1*, now in the Pushkin Museum in Moscow), that Shchukin accepted the proposal. The three scenes suggested by Matisse were, however, reduced to two. The commission was confirmed in a letter sent from Moscow on 31 March 1909: "*Je trouve votre panneau la danse d'une telle noblesse, que j'ai pris la résolution de braver notre opinion bourgeoise et de mettre sur mon escalier un sujet avec le nu. En même temps il me faudra un deuxième panneau, dont le sujet serait très bien la musique.*"

The commission was therefore of the utmost prestige and certainly lucrative (Matisse received 15,000 francs for *The Dance* and 12,000 for *Music*). Its importance for the painter's future career can hardly be overestimated. Shchukin was in fact the greatest collector of Matisse's work, and his purchases alone made it possible in 1909 for Matisse to rent, and four years later to buy, a house and garden at Issy-les-Moulineaux with room for a studio large enough for the huge canvases produced in those years. The fact that the house in Moscow was much frequented by painters and connoisseurs, constituting a sort of museum open to artists, meant that Matisse's works would be practically on "public" display. For this very important opportunity, Matisse proposed a subject he had already tackled on various occasions. Female figures joining hands and dancing in a circle also appear, in fact, in the very famous and carefully thought-out work *Joy of Life* (Barnes Foundation, Merion), exhibited for the first time to great controversy at the Salon des Indépendants in 1906. This is a sort of dreamlike and mythical evocation of the golden age (past or future, but in any case lying outside history), where nature and the human figure are not only equivalent but actually appear to merge in a kind of mystic union. As is known, *Joy of Life* is the canvas with which Matisse proclaims what were to be the aims of the Fauves in open contrast to Signac's scientifically oriented Pointillism. The latter was indeed one of the painting's harshest critics: "Matisse, some of whose works I had appreciated, appears to have taken a completely wrong turning. He has filled a canvas with strange figures with outlines as thick as your finger, and covered it with flat, sharply delimited slabs of color that, although pure, produce the most appalling effect."[2] The luminous, expansive, pure color is not restrained but enhanced by sinuous black contours. The different hues harmonize with and sustain one another to attain their maximum chromatic value. In the same way there is reciprocal agreement between the distinct individual episodes. The arabesque line traces the figures of musicians, naked lovers embracing, and young girls picking flowers or lying softly on the grass. In the middle of the composition, acting both as a visual fulcrum and as a distant backdrop, a group of six girls dance in a circle on the beach beyond the trees of the clearing and on this side of the shore.

The image added to the others in 1906 to evoke a mythical golden age took on a life of its own in the following years, almost as though it were growing mysteriously within the artist's imagination. The individual elements present in the great canvas – the musician, the group of girls on the grass, the figures dancing in a circle – reappear on more than one occasion between 1906 and 1909. In 1909 Matisse produced the first version of the Hermitage painting (now in the Museum of Modern Art, New York, and in turn reproduced as the background of a still life on display in this exhibition entitled *Fruit, Flowers, Panel "The Dance"*). When he suggested dance as the subject of the decoration in Shchukin's house in Moscow, Matisse evidently intended to produce a more mature treatment of a theme that had interested him for several years. Comparison of the girls dancing on the beach in *Joy of Life* with those in the Moscow painting does, however, reveal many significant differences. First of all, Matisse reduces the number of figures joining hands from six to five. The reason is clear: the elimination of one figure disrupts the regular circular movement of the dance and transforms it into pure rhythm. In order to close the circle, the figure in the foreground reaches out in a sort of diagonal towards the outstretched arm of the one on the far left. The two hands do not touch, however, and this minute hiatus gives birth to the juxtaposed intersecting diagonals, the taut, elastic, bow-like curves, and the antithetical forces. All these elements serve to create the constant and almost urgent rhythm that pervades the entire work with its alternation of speed, tension and gravity. Moreover, while the vegetation in the *Joy of Life* is still naturalistic (including trees, a stretch of grass, a beach, the sky and the distant sea), in the Moscow *Dance* nature is wholly eliminated through reduction to its essential primordial elements of sky and earth, represented respectively by blue and green. Together with the red of the nude bodies, these are the only colors applied to the canvas. Serving to represent the essence of the elements, color thus goes far beyond any form of naturalism to become solely symbolic and constitute the quality of things. In a letter, Matisse recalls that he wanted "for the sky a beautiful blue, the bluest of blues (the surface is saturated with color to the point where blue, the idea of absolute blue, finally emerges), and the same goes for the green of the earth and the vibrant crimson of the bodies". The painting thus becomes a representation of the universe reduced to its essential elements of sky, earth and human figures that beat the ground to break free of it, that animate the air by plunging into it, running through it and shattering its compactness to such an extent that Matisse places a more transparent layer of cobalt blue over the matte ultramarine in order to accentuate its depth.

Painting, or art, thus intuitively reveals the deepest essence of the world and becomes pure decoration, i.e. something that is radically different from nature, rational knowledge and interpretation of reality. It uses rhythm, line and color to create another reality, another nature that has nothing to do with sense experience. Even the sublime beauty of the figures has none of the naturalistic "appeal" that derives from sensory experience. In his greatest masterpiece, and one of the greatest works of our century, Matisse thus offers a highly lucid exposition of his conception of art as experience that is solely aesthetic and as such structurally different from other forms of human activity.

This clearly developed view, which even goes beyond what Matisse himself had produced during the previous years of hard work, is necessarily defined also through polemical contrast with other equally lucid but sharply divergent choices that appeared to have come out on top in 1910, first in Paris and then in Moscow.

Shchukin's letter acknowledging receipt of Matisse's two large canvases, which had come in for harsh criticism when exhibited at the Salon of 1910, contained a prediction that is certainly colored not by hypocrisy but by the irony of fate: "The public is against you, but the future is on your side." This prophecy was indeed to prove singularly false as regards Shchukin's own choices, but probably also in more general terms. Although Matisse followed up *The Dance* and *Music* with other exceptional masterpieces, Shchukin fell suddenly under the spell of the young Spanish artist Picasso, and in the very short space of time between 1910 and 1914 an entire room of his mansion was dedicated exclusively to his work and filled with over fifty paintings, including some of the most important. The future was to be on the side of Pablo Picasso, even apart from the personal taste and choices of Shchukin, who soon added works from the Blue and Rose periods to the Cubist works in an effort to record the artist's evolution as completely as possible. The collector himself gave the following confused account of his overriding compulsion to buy Picasso's works in telling Nikolai Preobrazensky of the irreconcilable contrast between the first canvas by the Spanish master to enter his collection and the rest of his paintings, despite their excellent quality: "One day I was horrified to feel that, despite its lack of a subject, the picture (the first painting by Picasso to hang in the Moscow residence) had a core of iron, solidity, strength. I was horrified because all the other paintings in my gallery suddenly seemed to lack that core, to be made of cotton wool. And the worst thing was that I no longer wanted to see them. They had lost all interest and meaning for me." Even if only at the intuitive level, Shchukin perceived the absolute lack of any links or possibility of reconciliation between the solidity of Picasso's Cubism and the decorative approach theorized by Matisse, which he had been fascinated by and still continued to love. Although it is uncertain whether the first Picasso bought by Shchukin can in fact be identified as the *Seated Woman* now in the Hermitage (painted in 1908, the year in which Shchukin became interested in Picasso's work), this painting easily explains the collector's consternation. Volumetrically armored like an African idol, the *Seated Woman* has an unparalleled inner strength in comparison with which the works of Matisse, and indeed all other contemporary works, really do look as though they are "made of cotton wool".

Here space is not built up around form. Form becomes space and space coagulates into form. The different successive planes are not arranged in a spatial sequence, i.e. they are not embedded in a pre-existing space, but are themselves space and functions of space. This is demonstrated by the asymmetry of the woman's shoulders. While the right is rounded as the arm turns to hold the fan, the left is straight through its formal connection with the outstretched arm. X-ray examination has revealed an earlier version where the woman's face is turned towards the viewer. The change, which embeds the face more deeply in a closed form, emphasizes the absolute independence of form with respect to any preconceived idea of space. The face is almost seen from above, the torso frontally, and the hand holding the fan practically from below. The object is built up (not presented) in accordance with its essential, intimate, inner form. In the *Seated Woman* even color is a function of space and volume. There is none of Matisse's extreme accentuation of pure color through juxtaposition with the other colors, but a variation on light shades of brown and gray because the volumes and spaces are created in terms of the different chromatic planes distinguished by the light.

In Shchukin's Moscow residence, and now in the Scuderie al Quirinale, the two great canvases, Matisse's *The Dance* and Picasso's *Seated Woman*, exemplify two diverging approaches that foreshadowed the future right back at the beginning of the century. While *The Dance* delineates an art that is solely aesthetic experience, Picasso struggled in the same years to establish an art that is knowledge, creation and interpretation of the world. The extraordinary weightlessness of the dance on the hill has its historical counterpoint in Picasso's earthy and immensely solid woman, in the "iron core" that so impressed Shchukin. For all their divergence, however, both Matisse and Picasso are direct descendants of the revered master Cézanne, whose great exhibition in 1907 had an extraordinary impact on contemporary art. While the *Joy of Life* was ultimately a critical reworking of *Les Grandes Baigneuses*, and through this of the mythological paintings of the Renaissance, the *Seated Woman* is inconceivable without the Provençal portraits, one of which – *The Smoker* – is shown in this exhibition. Through the chromatic structure of Cézanne's paintings, however, Matisse links up with the Impressionists, with Monet's transformation of pure sensation into color, and is equally interested in Gauguin. Picasso, instead, seeks to go beyond the synthesis of color, space and volume achieved by Cézanne and solidify the image in a "thingness" belonging to the object and not to the image.

Leaving aside their common ancestry and cultural development, we can say that around the year 1910 two artists in Paris and one collector in Moscow traced the course of two paths that were to run through the entire century. The twentieth century was to be divided between the ideas stemming respectively from Matisse and Picasso of art as pure aesthetic experience or as a form of knowledge, between an artistic experience that is detached from the world and one that is driven by moral needs to seek commitment in the world. Art will thus be myth or history; it will emerge from the disconcerting abysses of the subconscious or from the lightning flash of knowledge. Where Matisse founded art as the expression of a reality existing prior to awareness, Picasso redefined modernism in the sense in which the concept is used today, e.g. by Clement Greenberg and in Timothy J. Clark's recent *Farewell to an Idea*.

At the end of the century we can only reflect once again on a story that has still not come to an end.

---

[1] "I imagine the visitor arriving from outside. The first floor opens up before him. It is necessary to obtain an effort, to give a feeling of relief. My first panel represents the dance, the flying dance in a circle up on the hill. On the second floor we are inside the house, inside its spirit and its silence. I see a musical scene with engrossed figures. Finally, on the third floor, everything is calm, and I shall paint a scene of rest with figures lying on the grass and thinking or dreaming. I shall obtain all this with the fewest and simplest means, those that enable a painter to express his inner vision to the full." H. Matisse, 'Entretien avec Estienne. Des tendances de la peinture moderne', in *Les Nouvelles*, 12 April 1909.

[2] P. Signac, letter to Agrand (14 January 1906), quoted in *Matisse, his Art and his Public*, A. Barr, The Museum of Modern Art, New York, 1951, p. 82.

French Painting from Impressionism to the Avant-garde

Maurizio Calvesi

Monet and Impressionism
"Where do we come from? Who are we? Where are we going?" The Impressionists were certainly not tormented by the questions Gauguin posed in a celebrated work painted at the turn of the century, at least not at the time of their first flowering in the 1860s and 1870s.
Monet painted *Lady in the Garden*, the splendid work that opens this catalog, in 1867. As an interpreter – albeit daring and largely unappreciated – of optimistic middle-class society, he knew or thought he knew where it was going and where it came from. It came from the liberal and civil ideals of the French Revolution, from history and historical progress, from the conquests of democracy, science, industry and art itself. It was heading towards a future that was bright with new goals. His painting was itself a conquest, an opening up of new horizons. No one before him had succeeded in capturing the natural splendor of light with equal truth and intensity, in pinning down sensation in such absolute terms, in imposing duration upon its fleeting mobility in such a way as to convey the explosive sense of life and the very essence of vitality and joy. Such results were made possible by a technical discovery that took its place alongside other breakthroughs of the modern age, namely the discovery of optical mixing. The eye's ability to blend colors placed one beside the other in short brushstrokes meant that it was no longer necessary to mix them physically on the palette, thereby dimming and sacrificing their *éclat*.
This happy illusion was short-lived. The radical programs put forward by the most advanced wing of the middle class had made it appear that the disinterested ideals that inspired the Impressionists and their belief in progress also in social terms were actually shared by the bourgeoisie in general. This had made it possible for the Impressionists to feel harmoniously integrated with that class despite their rejection in terms of taste. The full and disturbing impact of the failure of liberal and radical projects was, however, soon to become clear. Friction with the working masses led the ruling class to ally themselves openly with the conservative forces and jettison the enlightened principles that had optimistically been thought compatible with prosperous development. The middle class began to show intellectuals and artists the cynical narrow-mindedness that would lead the latter to rebel and take up arms against them.
In this light, the Impressionists' primary goal came to look like a sterile reduction of art's spiritual and cognitive ambitions to an unproductive and dissatisfying cult of pure phenomena and sensation devoid of depth and critical bite. The apparent social harmony had allowed artists to mirror themselves in a world of day-trippers and tutu-clad ballerinas, but such carefree description had now entered a state of crisis and the need to go "beyond Impressionism", albeit without going as far as political commitment, led to the quest for a more problematic approach to reality.
This was the climate developing in the 1880s, but the other work by Monet displayed in this exhibition, the *Pond at Montgeron* painted in 1876, already shows some change with respect to the canvas of ten years earlier, the introduction of some sort of doubt. It is no longer the serene beauty of nature that Monet's eye celebrates, but its mystery, profundity and melancholy anguish that grip his soul. The female figure half-hidden by the branches is dwarfed in a relationship with the great womb or "great mother" that is no longer on an equal footing but practically one of subdued bewilderment.

Cézanne
Though they initiate different strands in what was to be the complex development of avant-garde art, Cézanne and Gauguin are, however, linked by their abandonment of pure sensation in order to introduce a mental element of reflection that lends color the strength of a plastic support while freeing it from traditional chiaroscuro.

Cézanne was involved in the Impressionists' first exhibition at Nadar's gallery in 1874 but refused to take part in the second two years later. In 1877 he gave in to pressure from his friends and took part in the third, but with little conviction. For the Impressionists, sensation was both the starting point and the goal. For Cézanne it was only a starting point to be subjected to conscious elaboration. He countered Monet's instinctive perception with a conscious, critical perception that worked back through self-analysis to achieve a synthesis of eye and mind. While Monet's harshest critics could accuse him of a sort of lack of awareness, Cézanne set himself the goal of an absolute awareness of reality, whose processes could be compared – bearing in mind the heterogeneity of the terms involved – to the interior act of "self-awareness" in Romantic-Idealistic philosophy, the act whereby ego produces non-ego, i.e. the object, nature, the world. "Little by little – as he wrote in a letter to Emile Bernard in 1905 – time and reflection end up modifying our way of seeing, and finally we attain understanding," an understanding of nature and its necessarily inner "truth". It was to Bernard that he had, one year earlier, expressed the celebrated maxim that nature should be treated in terms of the cylinder, the sphere and the cone, i.e. modeled through forms that are archetypically ideal. To continue in the same vein, we might add that it should be built up through the form of knowledge represented by the Kantian *a priori*. "There are – says Kant – ideas that do not come to us through the senses and that we find within ourselves without having formed them, although it is the senses that make it possible to perceive them."

There can be no true knowledge of the object without conscious participation on the part of the subject. The prismatic and organically structural sense that Cézanne imparts to vision, thereby "solidifying" the Impressionist impression, stems from this sort of mirroring of mental structures in nature, from this meeting between the intelligible and the sensible, between the Kantian noumenon and phenomenon, whereby the phenomenon becomes absolute and the noumenal absolute becomes relative. Once embodied, the geometrical models thus take shape and crumble like friable objects in an interlacing of vibrant shadowless colors and variously oriented open and closed planes. This compositional pattern is then reproduced in every area of the painting through a dynamics of brushstrokes each of which identifies not the vibrating point of light of pure Impressionist painting, but a plane of rotation, an invisible seam of the great prism, an instant of the great duration.

By yoking the appearance of the real world to the datum of consciousness, Cézanne forms a link between the ideas of the nineteenth century and the explorations of the avant-garde in the new century, especially the "mentalization" of Cubism. This also accounts for the immense interest taken in Cézanne by the protagonists of these explorations when a great exhibition of his work was held in Paris after his death in the Salon d'Automne. The "knowledge" of nature to which the artist aspired through the reciprocal interference of eye and mind was best appreciated by Picasso: "In 1906 Cézanne's influence penetrated everywhere. The art of composition, of the contrast of forms and the harmony of colors, spread rapidly. I was faced with two problems. I understood that painting had an intrinsic value independent from the real representation of objects. I wondered whether things should not be represented as they are known to be rather than as they are seen."

Gauguin and Symbolism
If we are to understand how the revolutionary world of Picasso and the avant-garde context came into being, however, the influence of Cézanne must be seen alongside at least two other components, namely Primitivism and Symbolism. This brings us to the second of the two masters mentioned above, Paul Gauguin.

While for Cézanne awareness takes the form of elevating perception to "intellective perception", for Gauguin it is directed towards Romantic sentiment and a quest for the original, the mythical, the deep, ancient and universal sediment within man. All of this dwells in the "depths" of each and every one of us, in a "mysterious center of thought" that was not felt by the Impressionists, who – he writes – "seek around the eye and not the mysterious center of thought".

In May 1886 Gauguin took part in the Impressionists' eighth exhibition, but with works that already showed a tendency to subject the naturalistic vision conveyed by his companions in the free flow and merging of short brushstrokes to a framework of lines that break the canvas up into areas of color but are endowed with a greater communicative intensity that produces the inner echo of a state of mind.

Gauguin again sees sensation as the starting point but not the goal. The external generates inner resonance. Color begins to be used as a "symbol", as a link or bridge between the real and the spiritual, between the meteorology of the elements and of the soul, between perception and "mysterious thought". In Cézanne (whose handling of volume was, however, the object of Gauguin's attention), form was instead the link with the intellect, between perception and thought that was not mysterious but more rationally lucid.

Gauguin found the social context surrounding him unbearable. In 1886, the very year of Van Gogh's arrival in Paris, he expressed his rebellion by abandoning the capital in July to take refuge at Pont-Aven in Brittany for three months. Almost wild in its bleakness, covered in prehistoric megaliths and lashed by a raging sea, Brittany suited the painter's impetuous spirit and his hatred of the sophistication and hypocrisy of Parisian society. This was the first of the "flights" that were to take him to Panama and Martinique in 1887, back to Pont-Aven, Arles and Le Pouldu in 1888-1890, to Tahiti in 1891-1893, back to Le Pouldu and Pont-Aven in 1894, and to Papeete, Tahiti and the Marquesas Islands from 1895 until his death in 1903.

He hoped to find peace through contact with primitive societies, to grasp the real meaning of life, to capture in an archaic people uncorrupted by civilization the authenticity of a relationship with nature at its uncontaminated source. Jean Jacques Rousseau's views of man as naturally good but spoilt by progress and of nature as a benign maternal force were widely accepted at the time.

Painting aspires to the purity of poetry. "Forms and colors harmoniously arranged are themselves poetry," Gauguin wrote. "I dream of powerful harmonies in the midst of natural perfumes that make me inebriated (…) what is ancient, sublime, religious (...) the veiled image of the invisible enigma (...) I dream in the infinite space stretching out before me."

While Cézanne produces volume through a sort of inner growth from the luminous pregnancy of forms that are squarely arranged and fueled with color, Gauguin uses chromatic surfaces that extend in the two dimensions of the canvas alongside others that tend towards the compact and unwind in space, sharply delineated, almost like pigment-soaked slabs adorning volume.

As a result, the space of the painting is a continuous field furrowed by arabesques of the depths that interweave with those of the surface, a synthesis of aligned, simplified and defined planes that release ("symbolize") the blue reveries of a dreaming spirit, feelings of innocence and purity, crimson messages of love, messages of time, atmospheres of holiness and mystery. This constitutes Gauguin's "synthetism" and his "symbolism", which parallels that of Van Gogh, but while the latter expressed a hallucinated and desperate thirst for light, Gauguin assuaged his anxieties and found a model of catharsis in the nirvana of painting.

While Cézanne's way out of naturalism was through the mental domination of sensibility, Gauguin's lay in a use of color capable of transcending the perceptual datum to enhance its expressive power, as exemplified by the *Yellow Christ* depicted in a stark primitive style against a line of red trees.

Gauguin addressed the theme of religion as a manifestation of the sacredness of life instinctively perceived by primitive peoples. He combined the Oceanic cults with the Christian subjects of the Passion as he had contemplated them in medieval works in Brittany, labored Calvaries and clumsy Stations of the Cross expressing an archaic and pure form of popular devotion.

Gauguin's other gifts to his most immediate followers and most distant successors include the symbolic function of color, a cult of the primitive that was to extend in the new century to the appreciation of African idols, a rediscovered approach to religious art, and a celebration of innocence that opened up a path towards a taste for the simple, popular, and even childlike. All these elements were to fuel the explorations of the avant-garde.

Rousseau 'le Douanier'
The path of popular and childlike *naïveté*, often combined with the exotic, was pursued furthest by the painter Henri Rousseau, known as 'le Douanier', a namesake of the great French philosopher who proclaimed man's original goodness and advocated a childlike approach to nature.

For Rousseau, however, the exotic that Gauguin pursued in his travels as far as the antipodes was the horizon of a flight that took place only in his imagination. In order to account for his visions of tropical forests, he let it be believed that he had spent a few years in Mexico (Gauguin had spent his early childhood in Peru), perhaps not realizing that there are none in that country. He was actually an avid reader of botanical works and books of popular science, like the then celebrated *The World Before the Creation of Man* by Camille Flammarion, and invented landscapes that pushed the quest for the "original" back into eras even prior to mankind. He would collect vast assortments of leaves and twigs in the woods to take back to his studio and copy with minute care. In transferring them to paper or canvas, he superimposed them to form interwoven fans of petals and ferns, or thinner fringes of elongated vegetation charged with a secret serpentine energy. He thus filled the whole surface of the painting, leaving a glimpse of light blue sky above the modulated mass of greens, ranging from the lightest to the darkest hues and animated by bright flashes of pink, yellow, white or red to mark flowers or fruit. Grays, browns and tawny hues also appeared to mark the noble savages inhabiting the jungle or felines giving vent to their stealthy and guiltless predatory instincts. A world governed by the most elementary laws of nature, an unperturbed and innocent world moved in its shimmering light by a vividly delicate force, a world in which even evil is not such but the manifestation of an enchanted "ecosystem", as we would call it.

The delicacy of the chromatic harmonies creates an inexpressible beauty of vibrations and movements of color orchestrated with exquisite musical sensitivity. The plate on Rousseau's door read "Lessons in elocution, music, painting and musical scales". The innocence of the natural spectacle reconstructed by the painter in his imagination corresponded to the innocence of his spirit, which was not actually ingenuous but innocent, and was expressed through an appropriately childlike form of draftsmanship. It is true that Rousseau, having missed out on an academic training, was not a deft and "professional" draftsman in the academic sense, and that his childlike style was also the result of this condition. He was, however, able to make this into a choice, the invention of a new way of painting fully in line with the "flat" vision that was gaining ground in the new symbolist and primitive painting and expressed new and genuine values in opposition to bourgeois taste, not least in its *naïveté*. Rousseau's work marked the poetic legitimization of childlike virginity in front of a world that regained the same virginity in the fanciful evocation of the exotic and primitive.

Though among Rousseau's most successful subjects, equatorial forests are by no means the only ones depicted in his work from about 1891 on. But also in the other paintings – very often landscapes, views of small towns or parks peopled by little men in contact with the silent expanses of sky and greenery – the naïve stylization frontally aligns the elements of a delicately cadenced representation with the same innocent simplicity and the same chromatic delicacy.

The Nabis

While the Polynesia of Gauguin gave way to the fantastic jungles of Rousseau, at Pont-Aven, the scene of the master's first flights and his initial experiments with Synthetism, the latter, with all its symbolic implications, found followers in a group of painters gathered around Emile Bernard, including Sérusier. A friend of Gauguin, Bernard produced a "synthetic" form of painting (*Cloisonnisme*) where subjects of a religious or spiritual nature were depicted by means of flat stylized areas of color bounded by dark outlines resembling medieval stained glass. Sérusier gave the name "Talisman" to a small landscape painted as an almost abstract pattern of colors in accordance with Gauguin's symbolist ideas, and took it to Paris to show to Denis, Bonnard and Vuillard, his young fellow students at the Académie Julian. The *Talisman* and Bernard's ideas led to the birth of the Nabis group, founded in 1888 by Sérusier and Maurice Denis together with Bonnard and Ranson. "Nabi", a simplified form of the Hebrew word *nebiim*, means seer or prophet.

Prophets of a sort of New Age, these painters formed a community. They wore special ceremonial garments, set up a "temple" in Ranson's studio, and adopted a hieratic and precious form of language. They shared a loathing of the bourgeoisie, their shallow ideals of contentment and their conventions. Like Gauguin before them, they loved Japanese prints and popular art. Denis and Sérusier dreamt of a return to the original sources of Christianity and pre-capitalist medieval society. While Denis's celebrated dictum may suggest an anticipation of Abstractionism, it is actually a call to give precedence to the formal and "decorative" concision of Synthetism over its illustrative aspects: "Remember that a picture, before being a war horse, a nude woman or some anecdote, is essentially a flat surface covered with colors arranged in a certain order."

The arabesque plays a dominant role in the group's painting, which constantly strives for transparent spirituality of content despite its varied evolution. The works displayed at the exhibition are on religious subjects (*Mary's Visit to Elizabeth*, *Martha and Mary*). The figures are set with all the lightness of apparitions in space that is tapestry-like or two-dimensionally dissolved in the evanescence of light.

In *Sacred Spring in Guidel*, the water scooped up by the pilgrims in their white bowls evokes an ideal of purity that is reflected in the spring landscape.

Bonnard and Vuillard, the two most distinguished members of the group and very close friends, actually part company with Denis on the question of spiritualism, which they regard as a superstructure, and the symbolic use of color. They return to themes of modern life, and in some respects to the "impression", but this is enclosed within the cocoon of intimist sensibility and relished with a sort of emotional lingering.

They are painters of outstanding quality that blooms and ripens like a sensuous hothouse flower or the soft flesh of fruit, protected from the Impressionists' sudden bursts of light. It is no longer exteriors, dazzling boulevards or sweeping landscapes that predominate but interiors, their private domestic world tinged with a Proustian evocation of sensation re-experienced. Denis and Sérusier's particular love of "decoration" is transferred from the structure of the painting to the ornamental detail, the soft patterns of the wallpaper and carpets that delimit the internal space and enrich it with their cozy bustle.

In Vuillard we find neither the broad chromatic fields of the Symbolists and Synthetists nor the very short brushstrokes of the Impressionists, but rather a delicate ferment of colors clotted into dense but friable patches of color that crumble and mix in the no longer point-form but gently trembling vibration of light. In his work, each pulsation running through the pictorial organism is, however, an undercurrent that leaves the uniform silence of the rooms intact.

In comparison, and for all the considerable affinity between the two painters, Bonnard's sensuous eloquence appears more intense and vital, and replaces the hint of melancholy that surfaces in Vuillard with a quiver of joy. Bonnard combines the theme of the interior, the "casket" safeguarding the jewels of intimacy, with forays into the open air, scenes of modern life in places of entertainment and promenades, expansive approaches to landscape, a dynamic interest in action, and a taste for the nude that is not chaste but softly intriguing. His brushstroke is as textured as his friend's, but somehow more sumptuous, prehensile and richer in annotation, just as his broader vision encompasses massive depths of color with gentle shudders of pink, gray-tinged blues, pale greens or crackling reds.

As regards Vallotton, another Nabi with a more sharply isolated profile, we shall pause only to draw attention to the importance of his attempt to reconcile the arabesques of Synthetism with a return to a lucid handling of volume, and his reinvesting of Rousseau's chromatic delicacy in a plastic vision that is not dimmed by Impressionist blurring. Similarly, we have not paused to discuss other figures who are present in this exhibition but play a less central role in the developments we are tracing in an attempt to identify their "main paths".

The Pointillists

While the absence of Van Gogh constitutes a gap that must be filled mentally, it perhaps weighs less within the economy of the overview the exhibition seeks to present of French painting from the Impressionists to the avant-garde. As is well known, the main influence of the "northerner" Van Gogh is projected above all into the violence of Expression, although he does also play a marked role alongside Gauguin in the evolution from Symbolism to the Fauves, whose debut we are now approaching.

The further absence of Seurat will have to be compensated for by examining the work of his follower Henri Edmond Cross, who applied the principles of Seurat's Pointillism. This movement was only apparently free of the reservations expressed by the culture of the 1880s and 1890s with regard to Impressionism. While recognizing the scientific interest of its intuitions, the Pointillists felt that these should be thrashed out in terms of a rigorous "system". To this end, they replaced the improvisation and irregularity of the Impressionist brushstroke with a construction of colors broken down into uniform dots (reminiscent of the "screen" of photomechanical reproduction). These were aligned in a rationally organized and geometrically defined scheme making it possible to use the borders between the different chromatic areas to suggest linear elements, and to invest both these and the colors with "symbolic" values based on empathetic psychological principles (as lines and shades that convey a sense of elation and joy or withdrawal and sadness). Seurat thus combined Cézanne's call for mental control over sensation with Symbolism's introspection in a wholly different and original form – and with extraordinary results – and found a gleaming point of equilibrium that flaunted its own origin in a scientifically analytical process.

In his *The Church of Santa Maria degli Angeli near Assisi*, Cross arranges his dots to form a geometrical interlocking of vertical and horizontal elements with an orderly vibration of light capable of inducing a feeling of calm.

Matisse and the Fauves
The painting described above brings us up to 1909. A number of bombshells had burst over the four previous years. Outrage had been caused at the 1905 Salon d'Automne by the optical violence of the works exhibited by painters such as Matisse, Vlaminck, Derain, Marquet, Van Dongen, Vallat and Manguin, who used pure color freely applied over large surfaces. So violent were the results that the critic Vauxcelles was prompted to call these painters "*fauves*", i.e. wild animals. We shall examine the oldest and greatest of them, Henri Matisse, the movement's acknowledged guiding spirit. On looking at his paintings and those of his companions today, we would indeed be hard put to find anything wild, even in the least restrained works of the Dutchman Van Dongen or Vlaminck, a radical admirer of Van Gogh. There is, of course, an insistence on the use of glaring color.

What we find in Matisse is instead a well-bred sensitivity that had already gone through a politely but not dogmatically Pointillist phase as exemplified by the work *Luxe, calme et volupté* exhibited at the Salon of 1905. This Baudelairean title was both provocative and programmatic: a (flaunted) luxurious and serene delight in color, pleasure with no feelings of artistic guilt. Applied in spaciously distanced dabs, the color is no longer arranged in terms of a geometric pattern, but outlines the gentle, pleasing curves of the landscape and the figures. By now the work's only aim is poetic. There is no plumbing of inner or mental depths, analysis of language, exaltation of the primitive, or insistence on symbol. The latter, understood as correspondence of line and color to internal resonance, lives on affably as the echo of a harmonious disposition of the spirit towards a disinterested delight in art. The "primitive" is an ideal model of simplicity. As with the Nabis, the taste for the exotic implies no yearning for a different society but simply an appreciation of sophisticated oriental arts ranging from Persian carpets to Japanese prints and their exquisite sensitivity towards decorative surfaces.

Matisse evolved towards an increasingly absolute liberation of color and its way of presenting itself to the eye. In front of the again significantly entitled work *Joy of Life* (now in Copenhagen), "Color!" is the only exclamation possible. Delightful swirls of red, violet, cobalt blue and light green meander between slabs and wedges of color constituting variations on the same hues and fill the canvas without smothering it. On the contrary, they celebrate an airy, spacious freedom and pour forth all their joy in almost musical fashion. The rigid pole-like structures of Pointillist painting are like masts that have been rigged with sails and are now bending in the breeze of fancy. The optimism of the Impressionists is back, but is now directed at art itself and its function of creating joy, no longer at society.

In the years immediately after 1905, the period in which he produced the ten magnificent paintings exhibited here, Matisse forged ahead in his research to achieve the most complete expression of his artistic vision. Color invades the canvas to cover the surface with huge tilted planes that reduce any suggestion of depth to the bare minimum and flaunts itself in their rampantly flagrant light. The figures, plants and objects resting there, enclosed in light, fluid outlines, again strike notes of pure color in a pattern dissolved into musical echoes.

In *The Red Room* the wall and table merge to form a single continuous red plane. The angle between them disappears and they can barely be perceived as two distinct elements. The flower motifs of the paper or fabric covering the walls are echoed by similar shapes on the table, thus making it possible to mistake the bowls of flowers for patterns in a rug.

The space that holds the chair placed next to the figure is cancelled out completely. The result is a delicate and agile upward movement of "Japanese" arabesques echoed from the window by the flat lobes of the small oriental-looking trees, whose whiteness creates a dreamlike rather than perspective sense of distance and lightens the visual weight of the red.

The light, fluid outlines suggest the movements of a dance, which was indeed one of Matisse's favorite themes, as in the celebrated masterpiece *The Dance* of 1910 exhibited here. The circular movement of the ethereal dance depicted in blazing color against the blue and green depths of the background becomes the symbol of a happy time rotating around the albeit brief moment of youth. The hint of incipient nostalgia ("Gather ye rosebuds while ye may") does not, however, cloud the artist's serenity because joy is prolonged in the act of creation. Matisse would not see forty again.

Picasso
At that time Picasso was not yet thirty. His appearance on the Parisian scene at the same time as the birth of Fauvism had a more brutal impact, and his probing of reality was conducted with often ruthless penetration. *The Absinthe Drinker* of 1901, belonging to his so-called Blue period, shifts the focus of attention sharply from nature – a domain loved not only by the Impressionists – to man. Among others, Toulouse-Lautrec had already chosen to depict dancers and prostitutes, people hovering on the fringes of middle-class life and the world of the poor and outcast, the haunts of sin, but did so with the cheerful complicity of a fellow creature of the night. Picasso instead observes the *Drinker* with detachment. He appears to offer her his sympathy, but above all lays bare her downfall. The color, which conjures up impending gloom, neither reabsorbs the drawing, as it does in practically all the artists we have discussed, nor bends it to form a linear comment, but grasps the figure and squeezes it to mold its boundless solitude.

The social aspect of Picasso's interests, which was to manifest itself later in outspoken political commitment, may appear to clash with the more clinically cognitive stance of Cubism. The two are, however, linked by a lucid spirit of investigation, as exemplified in Cubist vivisection.

After definitively settling in Paris in 1904, Picasso embarked on his Rose period, with paintings like *Boy with a Dog* (1905) and *Nude Boy* (1906). The colors are softer and the outlines vibrate with subtle and almost classical incisiveness, as though the artist were using his extraordinary mimetic talent to win the approval of his new and sophisticated public. But in 1906, responding to the "uncivilized" challenge of the Fauves, he showed his true colors and seemed determined to surpass everyone else with his barbaric power.

He came to know African sculpture through some pieces Matisse had given to the Stein family, or perhaps directly through Matisse himself, as Max Jacob recounts: "Matisse picked up a statuette of black wood from a piece of furniture and showed it to Picasso. It was the first piece of African sculpture. Picasso kept hold of it all through the evening. When I arrived at the studio the next morning the floor was covered in sheets of Ingres paper. On each sheet there was one large drawing, practically the same in every case: the face of a woman with one eye only, an excessively long nose merging with the mouth, and a lock of hair on her shoulder."

Picasso responded to the violence of Fauvist color with the violence of lines inflicted like blows of an ax. He took up Cézanne's faceted volumes in order to overturn them in a rigid but wild tumult of sharply angled planes. In a veritable orgy of "primitivism" he combined African masks with the Iberian sculpture in the Louvre and the Catalonian Romanesque frescoes revisited in the summer of 1906.

The following year a painting initially entitled *Le bourdel d'Avignon* but then renamed *Les Demoiselles d'Avignon* (or *Le bourdel philosophique*) by André Salmon caused an unprecedented outcry. "Social" interest in the theme of prostitution was outweighed by the artistic need to break down the barriers of all pictorial convention, almost as though driven on by the subversive nature of the subject matter. Midway between nymphs and furies, the figures are stripped of all psychological traits to become possessed idols. Their angular forms clash in space in a visual tumult that goes beyond any moral consideration of good and evil and not only shakes the viewer but slaps him or her right across the face.

The *Composition with a Skull* of 1908 exhibited here combines a similarly violent arrangement with shocking reds and blues, the skull being apparently added for the faint-

hearted in much the same spirit as one might make faces at a frightened child.
Where Matisse's art is an end in itself, an invitation to sheer visual pleasure, it is free to attack and offend, but in actual fact bears the seeds of a new understanding of form.
Engrossed in the emerging problems of language, Picasso withdrew from the real world that so attracted him to pursue a vision verging upon abstraction. Emphasizing the construction of form (in post-Cézanne and anti-Impressionist terms) as the paramount problem of painting, he freed it from the relativity of appearance. Pushing color – the protagonist of Impressionist appearance – to monochromatic extremes, he restricted its function to the spatial gradation of volumes broken down into planes. This marks the birth of Cubism, where space is no longer that of Renaissance perspective or its representation on a flat surface, but takes up the para-scientific idea of the "fourth dimension" to present itself as the stratification of a temporal succession of superimposed viewpoints. It also marks a return to the scientific inclinations of Pointillism, but in an analytic process that starts from Cézanne's geometrical and cognitive demands and achieves a Cézannesque synthesis of eye and mind in a structure that is by now totally divorced from sensation.
After the shock administered by the Spanish master, the subtleties of the French tradition – already somewhat exhausted in the Nabis – began to flower once again with noble severity in sophisticated Cubist works, including those of Picasso himself and his fellow pioneer Braque, as well as in their progress towards new techniques such as collage. A great painter like Derain took the neo-Cézannesque approach as his starting point to attain the composure of a modern classicism, but the winning of new terrain for this *ésprit de finesse* had required an imported breach, a transfusion of new blood, the hot blood of a Spaniard. There is no need to emphasize the central importance assumed both by Cubist syntax in avant-garde developments extending up to Futurism, Abstractionism and Constructivism, and by its mentalism in the "anti-retinal" and conceptual assertions of Duchamp and subsequent artists in the second half of the century.
With Cézanne and Gauguin (together with Van Gogh) behind them, the Fauves and Cubists thus opened up the two main paths of contemporary art. Within Abstract art itself we find a Constructivist strand in Mondrian and a color-oriented "Orphic" strand in Kandinsky. But while the most visually gratifying innovation was Matisse's palette, inseparably linked though it was to the by now uncertain fate of painting, the most radical revolution was Picasso's structural breakthrough and his use of new materials, which also paved the way for today's widespread extra-pictorial experimentation.

French Artists and Russian Collectors

Albert Kostenevich

The reputation of the Hermitage's collection of paintings by the Impressionists and the subsequent artistic movements is such that it needs no special recommendation. Without the many masterpieces on view in this exhibition, the whole panorama of European art at the end of the nineteenth century and the beginning of the twentieth century would undoubtedly be deprived of much of its fascination.

The extraordinary collection of "contemporary French artists" attracts not only the habitués of the Hermitage, but also those who have only heard about it, those who visit for the first time, or those who come to know it at a distance, thanks to temporary exhibitions or to the museum's website. Certainly, this has not always been true. At the beginning of the twentieth century, when Impressionism was already a closed chapter in the history of world art, not only did the museum not possess any paintings from this current, but the very idea would have seemed absurd or blasphemous. At that time the Hermitage collection contained no works from the nineteenth century, and its fame was based entirely on works from the ancient world or by the European masters of the past. In reality, the original conception of the Hermitage was not bound so exclusively to antiquity: as well as Renaissance and Baroque masterpieces, in fact, Catherine II was also quite happy to acquire contemporary works. It would have been logical to expect the future acquisitions of the museum, which at the end of the eighteenth century had already become one of the best in Europe, to follow the original policy, open not only to the works of the old masters but also to contemporary art. However, while they occasionally bought modern works for their own private apartments, Catherine's heirs tended not to do so when expanding the collection of the Hermitage, which, although still thought of as their private property, was now also considered a national heritage, a cultural institution tied to the Russian empire. After its foundation, in fact, the museum quite quickly became a genuine treasure-chest of masterpieces of European art, created not only with the help of money, but also with the advice of the greatest experts and scholars. The aesthetic principles that guided Catherine and her enlightened advisors were less rigid than those of her descendants, who seemed not to trust their own tastes and did not attempt to add works of modern painting to the collection, even though they themselves appreciated it. On the other hand, we should remember that the works by contemporary French artists purchased for the Hermitage by the empress were truly *la crème de la crème*. Catherine's collections, which established the guidelines for the acquisition policy of the imperial court for the following 150 years, had thus succeeded surprisingly well in avoiding notable differences in quality between the ancient and the modern works, and had laid down extremely strict criteria of selection that would be impossible to ignore in the future. These strict criteria were also one of the reasons why even the acquisitions of old masters were subsequently to slow down.

As far as modern art was concerned, new and more significant obstacles emerged. At the beginning of the nineteenth century, traditional aesthetics was subject to a sort of alienation. Even when it proclaimed the need to draw inspiration from the classical world, the new era elaborated its own conception of beauty, which moved further and further away from the aesthetics of the artists of the past. It was now difficult to expect new works to be juxtaposed happily, as had happened until very recently, with Renaissance works. Only time softens contradictions, producing the necessary critical evaluation. And if we bear in mind the frequent tendency of contemporaries to undervalue the art that is created before their eyes, we will be less surprised by the evident diffidence towards modern painting in those who might have had influence over the acquisitions for the imperial museum.

In 1904, A.I. Somov, the director of the gallery of paintings of the Hermitage, wrote in the monumental Brockhaus-Efron Encyclopedia, the most popular Russian reference work, that the paintings on exhibit at the St. Petersburg museum "present examples of the painting of all the principle schools (Italian, Spanish, German, Flemish, Dutch, French and English) which by date of execution belong to periods not later than the beginning of the nineteenth century".[1] The term "not later than" strikes us as strange, the partial acknowledgment of a lacuna covering an entire century.

The creation of a section of art from the "century of steam and electricity", of a gallery that would be the worthy completion of the St. Petersburg museum, would not come about in the near future, but much later, during the Soviet period, thanks both to the devotion of the museum directors[2] and to fortuitous circumstances and the dramatic events experienced by the country.

The nucleus of the Hermitage collection devoted to nineteenth-century European art was to be the Kushelev Gallery, donated in 1922 by the Academy of Fine Arts of St. Petersburg. Its creator, Count Nikolai Kushelev-Bezborodko (1834-1862), while still a young man had inherited a vast fortune and a part of the collection of paintings of old masters gathered together by Catherine's chancellor, Alexander Bezborodko. Kushelev-Bezborodko set himself the task of extending the collection by acquiring contemporary works. Although he was to die young, in the space of five years he managed to put together a fully-fledged museum. It included many fashionable canvases, linked to the taste of the Academy Salons, but the essential tone of the collection was dictated by the paintings of the Romantics and the Realists. Kushelev-Bezborodko brought back works by Delacroix, Courbet, Théodore Rousseau, Daubigny, Diaz de la Peña and Corot at a time when their art was far from meeting with unanimous acclaim, and was often subject to violent criticism. He left his collection to the Academy of Fine Arts so that it would be accessible to everyone.

As well as the Kushelev Gallery, after the 1917 Revolution the museum acquired numerous paintings as a result of the nationalization of the private collections belonging to the St. Petersburg nobility. These collections included portraits executed by celebrated European artists, works of neo-classicism or romanticism in the terms admitted by the Salons, but were entirely lacking in those who had gone against the system of the Academy and its Salons. There were no works by the Impressionists or the Post-Impressionists, let alone by Matisse or Picasso. One exception was the collection of Georges E. Haasen, which was fairly modest in number, but which included canvases by Marquet and Manguin and a series of paintings by Vallotton that was unique of its kind. Haasen, who looked after the interests of a Swiss chocolate manufacturer in the pre-Revolution capital, was however not a typical figure in St. Petersburg, and was closer to the Muscovite collectors who, like him, were merchants.

The paintings of the Impressionists and the Post-Impressionists reached the Hermitage in the thirties and forties following the reorganization of Soviet museums that took place during that period. The vast majority of these paintings came from two extraordinary collections in Moscow, belonging to Sergei Ivanovich Shchukin and Ivan Abramovich Morozov.

Even today, at the end of an era that has seen many examples of great initiative in the field of art collecting, the achievement of Sergei Shchukin around the turn of the century still does not cease to strike the imagination. He belonged to an old family of Muscovite merchants. During his childhood and adolescence it would hardly have been possible to forecast such a brilliant future. No-one would have guessed that it was he who would take the place of his father as the head of the "I.V. Shchukin & Sons" firm, which played an important role in the textile market in Russia. It was to Sergei that his father would leave the family home, the former Trubetskoy Palace, an elegant eighteenth-century building. The third-born child, sickly and hampered by a stutter, he seemed the least suited to take over from his father, who was greatly respected in commercial circles. His stutter was so bad that his parents did not have the courage to send him to school, and preferred to have tutors come to their home. The circumstances in which Sergei passed his childhood and adolescence, far from the company of other children, played a large part in the formation of his character: he grew up with a very independent personality, capable of overcoming any hesitation and of taking his own decisions, if necessary going against the general opinion. His strong character, together with his refined sensibility, made him a great collector.

Sergei Shchukin's family was very much out of the ordinary. His father Ivan was famous in Moscow as a brilliant merchant, despite his modest education.[3] Through his marriage in 1849 to Ekaterina Botkina, the eldest daughter of the extremely wealthy tea merchant P.K. Botkin, Ivan Shchukin allied himself to some of the most well-known families of merchants. Thanks to this marriage, the Shchukins entered into contact with a whole series of illustrious exponents of Russian science, art and culture. Ekaterina's sister, Maria Botkin, had married the poet Afanasii Fet, and her cousin Sergei, a professor at the Academy of Military Medicine, had married the daughter of Pavel Tretyakov; her cousin Nadezhda was to marry the artist Ilya Ostrouchov, who came from a merchant background. Her brothers Mikhail and Dmitry Botkin were unusual collectors: the former collected objects of all kinds, from antique terra-cotta works to the medieval enamels of Limoges and Italian Renaissance majolica,[4] while the latter was interested in particular in nineteenth-century Western art, and could boast of the presence in his collection of artists from the Barbizon school, and works by Corot, Courbet and Millet.[5] The doors of their collections were always open to the Shchukins, as was the collection of their celebrated relative Pavel Tretyakov, long before it became the Tretyakov Gallery.

It is no coincidence that the field of activity of the Tretyakov brothers, and later of the Shchukin brothers and Morozov, was Moscow. No-one in the merchant circles of St. Petersburg could match these collectors. In their attempt to enter into contact with high society, in fact, the merchants of St. Petersburg were too obsequious to its tastes and fashions to produce a truly great collector. From around 1860, with the death of Nikolai Kushelev-Bezborodko, private collecting in St. Petersburg entered a phase of stagnation. The aristocratic families who possessed large collections added to them very rarely, generally when they succumbed to the temptation to have their portrait painted by some well-known artist from the Paris Salons. The merchants in Moscow were characterized by a much more independent and democratic spirit, and were more interested in meeting exponents of the world of science and art. From the middle of the nineteenth century, frequent meetings were held in the houses of the wealthy merchants, attended by artists, musicians and university professors. In 1861, in his *Letters on Moscow*, the perceptive St. Petersburg writer Pyotr Boborykin observed: "…mercantile and industrial Moscow is beginning to act as a *humus* for the realm of the intelligentsia".[6]

In the same period in which these words were written, Pavel Tretyakov made access to his gallery completely free. The Shchukins were still not able to compete with him, but they were beginning exactly around this time to take their first independent steps.[7]

There were probably some paintings in the Shchukin home, an integral part of the prestige and the decorum that the family was obliged to maintain. Ivan himself had no particular passion for painting. He led a very simple life and was a frequent churchgoer, but he did have a box at the Bolshoi Theater and loved Italian opera. He tried to give the best education possible to his eleven children. The two eldest, Nikolai and Pyotr, studied in St. Petersburg and in Finland.

Ivan very much wanted Sergei, too, to complete his education abroad, but the plan was initially rendered impossible by the young man's serious stutter. When Sergei reached his nineteenth birthday, his father took him to Germany for treatment. The treatment was not entirely successful, but it was sufficient to allow him to attend the Academy of Commercial Practice in the city of Gera, in Thuringia. He also studied for a while in France, and when he returned to Moscow at the end of 1878 he began to help his father in the management of the business. It very soon became apparent that the stuttering Sergei had a much greater flair for business than his more fortunate brothers. With the passing of the years, his management of production and commercial operations and his ability to find his way not only in the domestic market but also in the foreign market brought him a reputation in the world of finance as "the Minister of Trade". In 1912 he became Dean of the Merchant Board of Moscow, but much earlier than that he had already acquired fame as a shrewd, enterprising businessman, especially when, during the general strikes of 1905, as the world of business was seized by panic, he had bought up all the manufactured products available and had then raised their prices abruptly once the protest had been calmed.

It is curious that his success in business over a period of almost fifteen years did not fill Sergei Shchukin with the desire to spend money on works of art, at least no more than was expected of a solidly established merchant. His elder brothers might have served as an example. Nikolai not only bought silverware, but for three years also filled his house with paintings until he got bored with it: he did not have the true passion of the collector. This failing was more than compensated by Pyotr (1853-1912), who had begun as a young boy to collect photographs and lithographs. Later he began to hunt down antique books, engravings, documents and old Russian utensils. He was not distinguished by any particular flair. He liked to buy, and bought without thinking about it too much, and once an object entered his collection he would never part with it. Pyotr lacked the self-criticism of his younger brother Sergei. For this reason he gathered things indiscriminately: old Russian coins, wooden baskets and distaffs, Polish woven belts, Persian carpets, and so on. Although he concentrated his attention on Russian antique objects, he refused to give up any of his other interests, trying, as he said himself, "to demonstrate visually the influence exercised by the East and by the West on Russian culture".[8]

In the footsteps of Pavel Tretyakov, Pyotr began in 1892 to construct a building to house his own museum, a colossal collection that included 23,911 inventory numbers, some of which referred to whole series of items.[9] There were also numerous unequaled examples of applied art. As soon as the doors of the Shchukin Museum opened in 1895 (admission for the public was free), it began to be frequented regularly by artists. Vasily Surikov painted his studies for "Stepan Razin" here, while Apollinarius Vasnetsov found old pictures of buildings in Moscow for his historical landscapes. Valentin Serov was attracted by the Persian miniatures, which were brought back to life in his curtain for Diaghilev's theater. For having donated the museum he had created to the city of Moscow - to the Historical Museum, to be precise - the Czar awarded Pyotr Shchukin the title of Councilor of the V Class, the equivalent of the rank of general, which naturally flattered the self-esteem of the merchant's son. Pyotr, in fact, was blessed with considerable ingenuousness, which was also reflected, as we have seen, in his methods of collecting. But his character was generous, authentically Russian. The same passion that had led him in his youth to attend the lessons of the great historian Nikolai Kostomarov at the university, now made him devote every minute of his spare time to his collections: this stubborn dedication brought many tangible fruits, whose value has still not been fully appreciated.[10]

Sergei was preceded on the path of art collecting not only by Pyotr, but also by his younger brothers. Dmitry gathered together the best collection in pre-Revolution Moscow of artists of the past. In 1924 he was forced to sell 146 paintings and pastels from his collection to the Museum of Fine Arts (the future Historical Museum), where a picture gallery was being created. Fate ultimately treated him kindly, for he was appointed director of the Italian section of the picture gallery. It was a secondary office, but it allowed him to remain in contact with his paintings, for he was so attached to them that he put aside the idea of leaving Moscow despite the fact that life was becoming increasingly hard and dangerous.

Each of the brothers had found his own path in the world of art; however, while the life of the older brothers was inseparable from Moscow and work in the family business, Ivan (1869-1908), who now belonged to the second generation, was allowed by his father to choose his own path. He was able to take no practical part in the running of the business and to enroll in the Faculty of History and Philosophy at the University of Moscow. From then on, as well as his studies, he began to collect rare books and engravings. In 1893 he settled in Paris, where he wrote articles under the pseudonym Jean Brochet ("the pike"), working mainly for the influential and liberal St. Petersburg daily *Novoe vremja* (Modern Times). For fifteen years or so his Paris apartments became a sort of focal point for the Russian community. A.S. Sovorin, the editor of *Novoe vremja*, stayed there, as did the writers Vladimir Nemirovich-Danchenko, Dmitry Merezhkovsky, Konstantin Bal'mont and Maksimilian Voloshin, and the painters Igor Grabar and Alexander Benois. In a letter to his wife, Chekhov defined Ivan Shchukin as an interesting man, adding that he dined at his home every time he stayed in Paris.[11] Shchukin's home in avenue Wagram was frequented by Degas, Renoir, Rodin, Redon, Huysmans and Durand-Ruel. Ivan was flattered to be considered a Russian aristocrat: some people even addressed him as count. Above all, however, he was truly happy to take part in discussions on art and had the chance to buy the works of great artists, with whom he could even exchange a few words. Unfortunately, it is now impossible to get an idea of this part of his collection: the works were dispersed without leaving any trace. The only record we now have seems to be the splendid pastel now at the Neue Pinakothek in Munich, with the dedication "To M.J. Stchoukine. Degas". Most of the works, canvases by Carrière, Puvis de Chavannes, etc., were sold by Ivan Shchukin himself in 1900.

His collection of painters of the past was undoubtedly more valuable. We can get some idea of it from the sale in Berlin in 1907.[12] The 107 paintings consisted mainly of Dutch works, in particular those of the masters of landscape and still life: Jacob and Salomon Ruysdael, Jacob and Philips Koninck, Willem and Adriaen van de Velde, Kalf, Heda, Huysum, Beyeren, Hondecoeter, and so on. There was a small group of English portraits (Reynolds, Raeburn, Lawrence), fashionable at the turn of the century. The most prestigious canvases were Italian and Spanish (Tintoretto, Bronzino, Guardi, El Greco, Goya), including El Greco's *Maria Maddalena*, now at the National Gallery of Budapest, universally acknowledged to be the artist's masterpiece. Ivan Shchukin had always spent much more than he earned. Being permanently hard up, he sold his share of the family business to Sergei, who gave him 2,200 rubles every year. In his passion for collecting, Ivan seemed to acquire excellent paintings very cheaply. But his appetite grew more quickly than his ability to pay, and he began to telegraph his elder brother ever more frequently, imploring him to send more money. Sergei, however, did not have large sums of cash to play with, since profits were immediately reinvested in the firm. Both Sergei and Pyotr advised Ivan to sell his paintings. Being collectors themselves, they could not have failed to realize how cruel such advice was. There was no other alternative, however, even though Ivan did not want to give in. The hardest thing for him was to be separated from the Spanish works, his latest and strongest passion. Some of them had been bought on the advice of Ignacio Zuloaga, who had become his best friend. Taking Rodin with them, they traveled together to Spain. The auction in Berlin served only to delay the tragedy. No longer able to count on the help of his brothers, Ivan decided to sell the canvases by El Greco. But the experts called to value the paintings declared that they were fakes. Ivan took this verdict as a death sentence, and poisoned himself. His extraordinary library was given to the School of Oriental Languages, and for many years remained the best collection of Russian books in France; his collection, on the other hand, was sold off in great haste and cheaply. Was the expert opinion right? We now know that it was not. Obviously it is impossible to establish whether Ivan Shchukin was the victim of a trick or of an error committed in good faith by the "experts".[13] All this took place in 1908. Only ten years earlier he had been on the crest of a wave, as the first Russian not only to have begun to understand the Impressionists, but also to have risked buying their works.

His acquaintance with Paul Durand-Ruel, the dealer who had supported the Impressionists during the most difficult moments of their fight to obtain recognition, had allowed Ivan Shchukin to introduce his older brothers into that world. It was Ivan who had accompanied his older brother Pyotr, already the director of the museum he had created, to the Durand-Ruel Gallery. The result was that the museum's collection was enriched by the acquisition of paintings by Monet, Renoir, Degas, Pissarro and Sisley, later added to by works by Mary Cassat, Raffaëlli, Cottet, Forain, Helleu, Moreau and Denis.

Without the help of Ivan, Pyotr Shchukin would hardly have been able to find his way in such an infallible manner. His first acquisitions at the gallery of the old Durand allowed him to become the owner of several true masterpieces of French painting. While *Place de la Théatre Française* by the patriarch of Impressionism Camille Pissarro, fresh from the artist's studio, was one of the last testimonies of the vitality of the movement, the youthful work by Sisley, *The Town of Villeneuve-la-Garenne on the Seine*, at that time still known as *Village on the Banks of the Seine*, was a demonstration of the lively influence of the classics of European landscape on the Impressionists. The addition of Monet's *Lady in the Garden*, one of the greatest of the artist's early works, gave the small group of French paintings in the P.I. Shchukin Museum extraordinary importance.

The Lady in the Garden is still striking for the brightness of the shimmering light. How it must have astonished the visitors to the Shchukin Museum at the end of the nineteenth century! Especially because the custom at the time was to look for narrative content in paintings, entirely lacking in Monet's work. The true protagonist of the painting is the light, and here there is more light, genuine sunlight, than in any of the works of his predecessors and contemporaries. Monet has even deliberately portrayed the subject herself (a person not unknown to him, his cousin's wife) with her back turned to the viewer. The artist was not interested in her character or in the possibility of creating a narrative plot, but in the behavior of the light, which is present even in the shadows. The theme of the lady in the garden was one that he painted frequently. He had already used the motif of the woman standing in a similar pose in the visual manifesto *Déjeuner sur l'herbe* (1865, A.S. Pushkin Museum of Fine Arts, Moscow), which was subsequently purchased by Sergei Shchukin. In *Déjeuner sur l'herbe*, however, there is still a subject, however naive. In *The Lady in the Garden* the female figure is not a character around which the action is built, but merely one of the patches of color. The lady's outfit is not simply in harmony with the surrounding green. This detail might serve as a key to the understanding of the fundamental problem of Impressionist painting: the reciprocal relations between color, light and shade *en plein air*.

Another masterpiece from the first phase of Impressionism is Sisley's *The Town of Villeneuve-la-Garenne*, which followed in the tracks of Claude Monet. Painted five years after *The Lady in the Garden*, *The Town of Villeneuve-la-Garenne* maintains a closer link with tradition in all its details (the subdivision of the planes, the shaded background, the scenario of trees). The painting is very similar to *The Lady in the Garden* in the clarity of design and in the pictorial manner, in which the brushstroke follows the form of the object exactly, a technique that Monet himself had already given up by 1872, having discovered new horizons. Sisley did not have Monet's temperament and determination, but he was blessed with incomparable delicacy. In *The Town* he emerges as one of the finest painters of the beautiful scenery around Paris. The landscape is set in a dark frame of trees and foliage, which is not used simply to create a sense of depth, but allows the gentle ray of sun that floods the opposite bank to shine more enchantingly.

The way in which the canvases of the Impressionists were exhibited in the museum, mixed up haphazardly in a narrow space, like in an antique shop, may now make us smile, but there was a sort of logic in the choice. The contemporary Western European landscapes (top row) were contrasted with antique landscapes from the Far East (bottom row). The dark Persian carpets that separated the two rows had no relation to either, but together with the frames they provided these wonderfully bright "windows on nature" with an additional, opulent setting, both refined and amateurish.

As well as the landscapes by Pissarro, Monet and Sisley, in 1898 Pyotr Shchukin also acquired two paintings that were not destined to be shown to the public: Degas' *Woman Combing Her Hair* and Renoir's *Female Nude* (1876, Pushkin Museum). It was said at the time that he had acquired *Female Nude* as part of a single lot with a Japanese screen (perhaps the same one that occupied the central part of the wall, "below the Impressionists"?). By exhibiting works of this kind in his museum, Pyotr would have seriously risked his reputation. The paintings in the series to which *Woman Combing Her Hair* belonged had caused a scandal at the Impressionists Exhibition of 1886: and that was in Paris, which had long been accustomed to representations of female nudity. What would have happened in Russia, a country of much more austere traditions, conserved for centuries by orthodoxy? A few people were aware of the existence of these paintings in his private apartment, and probably considered them an excusable weakness in the old bachelor. In reality both works are among the greatest achievements of French painting, especially Renoir's *Female Nude* (also known by the title *The Beautiful Anna*).

Sergei Shchukin bought his first Impressionist paintings at the same time as his brother Pyotr, he too probably advised by Ivan. At that time he was already a fairly experienced collector. It is difficult to say exactly when he began to buy paintings, perhaps at the end of the 1880s or the beginning of the 1890s. His first acquisitions were works by the Russian realists known as the Wanderers, which he would later be rather ashamed of. His interest at that time in Russian art is indirectly confirmed by his participation in the "First Congress of Artists and Connoisseurs of Russian Art", held in Moscow in 1894. In merchant circles, as we know, those who gave financial support to artists or purchased works of art were considered art lovers. In 1896 and 1897, Sergei began to turn his attention towards Western Europe.

In 1899, evidently certain that the works in his collection would be of interest to the public, Sergei loaned two paintings by Forain, *The Races* (1888) and *The Theatre Foyer* (circa 1895), both now at the Pushkin Museum, for an exhibition organized by the journal *Mir iskusstva* (The World of Art). In this way he became known as the first Russian collector of modern French painting.

During the same period, or slightly later, Sergei managed to acquire Courbet's *Mountain Hut* (1874-1876, Pushkin Museum), which started off his collection. This painting marks a precise dividing-line: the collection of Sergei Tretyakov ended with a landscape by the most famous master of realism of the century (*Sea*, 1867; Pushkin Museum). Shortly before Shchukin had acquired a number of works by the contemporary realists of the so-called *Bande Noire*, and by realists who had managed to enter the Salon.

"Shchukin's first acquisitions at the end of the 1890s," observed the critic Yakov A. Tugendhold, a friend of the collector and the author of the first brilliant essays on Shchukin's gallery, "were landscapes by Thaulow and Paterson, Cottet and Simon and Zuloaga's *Spanish Women*, in other words a neutral art, far from the great and stormy flow of contemporary art."[14]

These paintings reflect the rather romantic banality of the average art lover. They include James Paterson's *Enchanted Castle in Scotland* (1896, Pushkin Museum), the outlines of Venice fading into the night, painted by Cottet, and the brilliant *Spanish Women on the Stage. Plaza de Toros* by Zuloaga (circa 1899-1900; Pushkin Museum), and finally the common folk depicted by Simon (*Barge-Haulers*; Pushkin Museum); this large canvas was likened by the Muscovites to Repin's *Barge-Haulers on the Volga*, which had by now become an anthology piece. The list of paintings clearly shows Sergei's uncertain tread as a collector. One Norwegian, one Englishman, a Spaniard and two Frenchmen formed a true international, despite the fact that the paintings were all purchased in Paris. In 1897 he visited the chapel of Exeter College in Oxford, where he saw a tapestry designed by Burne-Jones and made in William Morris's famous workshop at Merton Abbey. He commissioned a copy, which he initially hung in his dining-room. These works were expensive, but it was probably not the cost that kept him from making similar purchases in the future, but rather the limited creative potential of "woven paintings".

In the space of a year or two, Shchukin had decided that he ought to limit himself to a single school, that of modern French painting. But here too he did not immediately find the path that would subsequently bring him fame as an infallible collector. Who nowadays has heard of Guilloux or Maglin? Shchukin brought back works by these artists in 1898, having bought them because he was struck by their enigmatic quality. However, in the same year he was to buy a landscape by Monet at the Durand-Ruel Gallery: *The Cliffs at Belles-Isles* (1886; Pushkin Museum).[15] Although the order in which the paintings reached Moscow remains uncertain, it is important to note that these were the first. One year later, in 1899, the house in Snamenski Street would be enriched by another fine landscape by Monet, *Haystack in Giverny*. Are we to deduce that Shchukin had understood the language of contemporary painting and had learned infallibly to choose the very best? Not yet. Together with the work by Monet he also purchased several interiors by Lobre: painted under the influence of the Impressionists, they well executed in terms of the use of color, but were of secondary importance in the artistic context of the time, and did not point to significant discoveries in the future. The collection grew with the acquisition of compositions by the Symbolist Menard and by La Touche, close to Symbolism, an artist who was much in vogue at the beginning of the century, but is now forgotten. His *Transfer of the Relics*, bought at the Universal Exposition of 1900, reveals a literary attempt to convey religious ecstasy rather than genuine pictorial intuition. The colors seem shrill. It is undoubtedly not a painting worthy of Shchukin, but this should come as no surprise. In his career as a collector, Sergei underwent a period of apprenticeship, and given that he was easily hurt and reluctant to take advice, he behaved substantially as we would expect from a self-taught expert.

In the diary of the painter Vasily Perepletchikov, we read of his visit to Shchukin's house in the winter of 1900. He mentions works by Simon, Brangwyn (*Charity*, 1890; Hermitage; *Market*, 1893; Pushkin Museum), and Whistler (three small studies, now at the Hermitage), paintings with the same characteristics as the works of Cottet and Lobre. "Here is Monet," says Sergei Shchukin. "Look how alive he is. Under the electric light at a certain distance you don't notice the colors. You seem to be looking out of the window, in the morning, somewhere in Normandy, the dew still sparkles, it will be a scorching day … Look at Pochitonov, it seems black compared to Monet, I will have to have it taken down. Here is Degas, jockeys and ballerinas, and here is Simon… Let's go into the dining-room, that's where I keep Puvis de Chavannes."[16]

Eighteen months before the arrival in Moscow of the first Impressionist canvases brought by the Shchukin brothers, a great deal of interest had been raised in many art lovers by Igor Grabar's article "Decline or Renaissance".[17] The young critic had taken a violent stance against traditions that are reduced to barren repetition. He upheld the tradition of research, although fully respecting the artists of the past, and this line of thought was consequently very close to the ideas of Shchukin. He had already noticed that the artists of the Barbizon School were too closely linked to the Dutch landscape artists of the seventeenth century, and that it was not them, but the Impressionists, who were responsible for the truly great innovation in French art.

Very soon the distinctive feature of Shchukin's method of collecting was the attempt to keep "on the same wavelength" as the process of contemporary art. Initially it was a question of "tuning in to the wavelength" or, to be more precise, to the latest phase of the process. For a Russian art lover in the 1890s, this was anything but easy. For proof of this, we need only refer to the memoirs of the artist and art historian Alexander Benois, the greatest expert of the time. "Until the 1890s, Impressionism was a prevalently 'underground' phenomenon, known only within a restricted circle. An even more restricted circle was not only aware of the existence of a number of artists known as Impressionists, but also appreciated their art, considering it to be interesting and splendid. The masses only rarely heard about the existence of artists such as Manet, Degas, Monet, Renoir, and when these names were uttered or printed in some critical article, it was always with an overtone of irony or indignation. These artists, now the undisputed 'glories of France', seemed to the vast majority of people to be madmen, if not charlatans. The following, on the other hand, were celebrated as the undisputed 'glories of France': Gérôme, Benjamin Constant, J.P. Laurens, Henner, Meissonier, Bonnat, Bouguereau, Roybet, Jules Lefèbvre… Even our illustrious artist I.E. Repin, who lived for a number of years in France precisely at the time when the Impressionists flourished, had a very vague idea of them and rather looked down on them."[18]

If the Impressionists seemed to enlightened society to be charlatans, those who went so far as to collect their works must have seemed even more so in the eyes of the vast majority. In 1914, when the initial phase of the formation of Sergei Shchukin's collection had still not been forgotten, Yakov A. Tugendhold wrote: "The first landscapes by Monet brought by Shchukin aroused the same indignation as Picasso does now: it is no coincidence that a painting by Monet was daubed over in pencil as a protest by one of Shchukin's guests."[19] It is clear that this episode did not take place in the 1890s, but a decade later, when the gallery was opened to the public. From 1901-1903 onwards, the essential characteristic of Shchukin's attitude to art was not the pedantic search for completeness that characterizes "congenital" collectors (Sergei had begun too late to be able to consider himself such), but the desire to concentrate on the essential. Fascinated by the painting of the Impressionists, he reached the conclusion that the main figure in the movement was Monet. To use the words of P.P. Muratov, the author of the first essay on the Shchukin Gallery, who was probably expressing an opinion shared by the collector: "Claude Monet is the creator of the pictorial technique that came to be known as Impressionism."[20] For Shchukin, Monet and Impressionism were synonymous. He became increasingly convinced that the technique of Impressionism was mastered by Claude Monet better than by anyone else. For this reason in the first seven years (1898-1904) he bought eleven works by Monet (later he would acquire two more from his brother Pyotr), while he abstained from buying works by Sisley, Morisot, or Cassat: and he was to buy only one Pissarro, albeit of the highest quality (*Avenue de l'Opéra*. Paris, 1899; Pushkin Museum). The other Impressionists, too, remained in the shadow of Claude Monet (four works by Degas, and only two by Renoir).

At the turn of the century, Shchukin was already attracted by living, contemporary art, in which he could take an active part. He desired to buy works that were truly "fresh": in 1902 *The Town of Vétheuil* (1901; Pushkin Museum) and two years later *Seagulls* (1904; Pushkin Museum), enchanting paintings characterized by the artist's ability to create almost impalpable nuances of pure color. For Shchukin this was the highest point that Monet's painting could attain, and he did not purchase any of the artist's later works.

Towards 1903-1904, Sergei Shchukin's interests turned to Post-Impressionism. He began to look out for the most daring innovators, and from now on the development of his collection went hand in hand with the rapid evolution of French painting. Without counting his very first steps, Shchukin's activity as a collector can be divided into three phases: the first, 1898-1904, when he was interested mainly in Monet; the second, 1904-1910, the period of Cézanne, Van Gogh and Gauguin; the third, 1910-1914, linked to the names of Matisse, Derain and Picasso. This division is substantially correct, although a number of qualifications need to be made. The first canvases by Gauguin and Cézanne were bought by Shchukin in 1903, long before the artists were universally recognized in the West. In the space of a few years, his collection of works by Gauguin was to become the best in the world. In exactly the same way, in 1910 he acquired a series of extraordinary works by Matisse, including *The Red Room*.
In 1904 Shchukin purchased one of Cézanne's finest works, *Pierrot and Harlequin* (1888; Pushkin Museum), and *Bunch of Flowers in a Vase*, which had both previously belonged to the collection of Victor Choquet, the great French collector who backed the Impressionists and Cézanne. Shchukin was the first collector in Russia to buy a painting by Cézanne, *Fruit*. This still life, bought in 1903, had belonged in the past to Havemeyer, who had the best collection of Impressionists in America at the turn of the century.
Shchukin saw that Cézanne, although siding with the Impressionists and making use of their discoveries in the field of color, was doing so in a completely original way. In *Fruit*, the color of each object assumes great intensity, though this was not invented by the artist, who matched each brushstroke to the real image. The most difficult thing consisted in not diminishing the dynamic force of the color to render three-dimensionality, and at the same time in not sacrificing the depth of the space and the volume of the objects (Impressionism had a certain tendency to flatten); it was so difficult that Cézanne had to concentrate on the representation of objects with simple geometric volumes. Spherical fruit, the carafe that joins together sphere and cylinder, next to a container that represents a conic section, semi-spherical porcelain cups. The still life is constructed in such a way that each object is easily legible from any distance without ruining the overall composition, and that the whole range of chromatic juxtapositions can also emerge. The orange, for example, is represented in relation to the carafe, the tablecloth, the lemon, and the other orange.
Ten years later Shchukin acquired *The Smoker* and *Mont Sainte-Victoire* (both in the Pushkin Museum). He understood very well the difference between Cézanne and the Impressionists and, unlike Monet, Degas and Renoir, he "kept his eye on him".
In the paintings of Cézanne, Shchukin saw not only the latest word in European painting, but also felt the deep link with the bases of world culture. "In Paris," Matisse was to recall, "Shchukin's favorite pastime was to visit the Ancient Egypt section of the Louvre. In it he found parallels with Cézanne's peasants."[21]
Gauguin, too, attracted Shchukin not only because of the decorative beauty of his canvases, or the alluring exoticism of the far-off Tahiti (although as a seasoned traveler, who had been to India, the Palestine, and Egypt, he was not indifferent to this aspect), but also because of the deep links with many different strands of world culture, from medieval Europe to the ancient East. In Shchukin's mind the collection of canvases by Gauguin, which had pride of place on the main wall of the banqueting hall (a room that was around the same size as the music room with the works of Monet), was in some way comparable to the icons found inside cathedrals, as the habitués of his gallery observed.

"'As you enter a Gothic temple, you see the painting of the windows but you are at such a distance that you cannot make out what it depicts: yet despite this you are captured by its magical harmony; this is what I mean by the music of the painting," Gauguin once wrote (*Notes éparses*). These words come to my mind every time I cross the threshold of the Shchukin home and Gauguin's painting appears to my eyes, which still do not know what it depicts. It is strange, he could not have known that his Tahitian paintings would end up in Moscow, and yet how his words suit Shchukin's wall, and the very arrangement chosen by Shchukin! All their owner's taste is reflected here. The paintings are hung very close together, and at first you can't even tell where one ends and the next begins: you seem to be faced with a single, large fresco, with an iconostasis."[22]
After passing through the Impressionist school, Gauguin refused to stop here, because in

his mind this would have meant a reduction of the sphere of art, while he hoped to extend it enormously, by returning continually not only to the European past, especially the Middle Ages, but also to the various spheres of extra-European art. Gauguin's conceptions of culture were universal and all-inclusive. He had made deep studies of traditional popular art, whether it was that of Brittany or of Tahiti. His attention was captured by those eras in which artists, despite reaching great heights of spirituality, beauty and expression, were still anonymous artisans who did not yet stand out from the people. Until around 1860, European art had evolved without taking account of what was happening on other continents. Manet, Degas and Monet had learned to appreciate Japanese engravings and to put their lesson to good use. Gauguin went much further. He studied the art of the Near and Far East, native America and Oceania. Only the sculpture of Black Africa remained for him to get a complete picture of the various strands of world culture: previously unknown or ignored, it was to exercise a powerful influence on the formation of many currents of twentieth-century art.

Gauguin wanted to see in his painting a reflection of the supreme wisdom, of a universal philosophy-religion. The title itself, and above all the theme of the painting *Te Ave No Maria. The Month of Mary (May)* expresses his ambition to unite traditionally Christian themes and the pagan joyfulness of Tahitian mythology.

In all probability, it was precisely this ambition to create a form of painting full of profound inner experiences and indivisible from the mystery of religiosity that drove Gauguin to return incessantly to the theme of the evening, which also matched his predilections in terms of color. As sunset approaches, nature acquires new, extremely expressive nuances. In the paintings purchased by Shchukin, *Scene in the Life of the Tahitians*, *Idol*, in *Te Ave No Maria* or in *Women by the Sea (Maternity)*, the action takes place in the evening, from the time when the rays of the sun begin to be tinged with gold to twilight. The most beautiful evening is probably that depicted in *Women by the Sea*, a painting comparable to the best representations of peace and harmony in Renaissance art. It is thought that the painting was dedicated to the birth of his son. Even if that were true, Gauguin would not reduce his work to the representation of a real situation. The Tahitian woman breastfeeding a new-born baby is a synthetic, sublime figure, comparable to an image of the Madonna. In spirit the whole scene resembles pictures of the Adoration of the Magi by the great masters of the past, except for the fact that the role of the characters in adoration is assigned to several young women. The characters in the painting have also been compared to the Three Graces. As always happens with truly great works, the content of this "icon" of the contemporary era has various layers of meaning; it does not merely recount the reality of the artist's life in Tahiti, but contains links with numerous sublime artistic images of the West and the East.

After Gauguin came the turn of Van Gogh. In 1905 Shchukin's home welcomed *Spectators in the Arena in Arles*, then *The Thicket*, and in 1908 *Memory of the Garden in Etten* (all now at the Hermitage) and *Portrait of Doctor Felix Rey* (1889; Pushkin Museum). Only four paintings, but each was a unique work, a fundamental example of its kind, so that it would be impossible not to acknowledge that Shchukin's choices were extraordinary. The addition of the canvases by Cézanne, Gauguin and Van Gogh to the paintings of Monet and of the other Impressionists made the collection one of the finest in Europe. Sergei Shchukin inevitably began to think of turning his collection into a fully-fledged museum.

The sudden death of his wife Lydia, to whom he was deeply bound, drove him to act with greater decision. During the night of 4 January 1907 he drew up a will according to which the collection was to go to the city - to the Tretyakov Gallery, to be more precise. The series of tragic events that had befallen Shchukin (the death of his son Sergei, who had thrown himself in the Moskva one year earlier, and that his wife, the suicide of his brother Ivan and that of his youngest son Grigorii) would have distressed anyone. All this brought a great change in Shchukin's conscience and in his devotion to art. He opened his gallery to visitors, regularly and free of charge. Some artists had had the chance to visit even in the past, but now the doors of his house were thrown open every Sunday for anyone who wanted to come.

The influence of the gallery soon made itself felt. As early as 1908, when it had still not taken its final form, nor acquired its most radical works, P.P. Muratov rightly commented: "S.I. Shchukin's gallery of paintings in Moscow belongs among the finest Russian collections. For some time now it has enjoyed wide and justified fame among artists and among enlightened art lovers. The gallery has also had a decisive influence on the development of Russian art in the last few years. It was destined to become the most powerful vehicle in Russia of Western artistic currents, so vividly expressed in the works of Claude Monet, Cézanne and Gauguin which belong to it."[23]

At the time these words were being written, Shchukin was establishing a special relationship with Matisse. The echo of the scandal that had accompanied the participation of the Fauves in the 1905 Salon d'Automne had already reached Russia. But the first Russian Revolution was in progress, art lovers had other things on their mind, and it was some time before these echoes were heard. Sergei, however, kept up with what was happening. In May 1906 he asked Vollard for Matisse's address.[24] Soon after the artist informed Manguin that he had sold Shchukin a large still life, which he had found on the mezzanine floor of his atelier.[25] Together with the American Stein family, who had settled in Paris, and the German Osthaus from Hagen, the Russian collector was immediately convinced by Matisse's work. Thanks to Shchukin Russia became the first country to begin to "import" the artist's works. In 1908 Shchukin had already acquired several extremely important works: *Game of Bowls*, painted very recently, and a whole series of still lifes from different periods; he commissioned *Statuette and Vases on an Oriental Carpet* (1908; Pushkin Museum), and arranged to reserve *Harmony in Blue* for himself. These commissions meant that Shchukin had become Matisse's patron. It would be no exaggeration to state that the union between the artist and the collector was what allowed many exceptional works to be produced. For Matisse the consolidation of his relations with Shchukin was all the more necessary in that his financial situation, as in the early 1890s, threatened to become critical, for Leo and Gertrude Stein, who had acted as patrons and possessed some of his most significant works, had begun to distance themselves from him.

It required great audacity, in 1908, to show *Game of Bowls* in his own home, and even more so, knowing Matisse's conceptions of art, to commission a "decorative *panneau* for the dining-room, as *Harmony in Blue* was described. Shchukin needed this "harmony" because blue went well with Gauguin's yellow-gold tones, which dominated the room. It is no coincidence that when *Harmony in Blue* was destroyed, it was replaced by *Blue Conversation*. By repainting the "blue harmony" in red, Matisse obtained an effect that perhaps even he did not expect. It comes as no surprise to learn that he was afraid that the Russian collector would react badly, because such a quantity of red paint, especially red paint of such dynamic character, had never been seen in European painting. Although it might have been easier for a man familiar with the scarlet surfaces of antique Russian icons to accept such a profusion of a single color. The painting challenged all previous artistic conventions, but it was not painted to cause scandal, but to find a harmony of an absolutely unprecedented type, matching the spirit of the new century. And since the harmony was miraculously achieved, the painting became the manifesto of the new art. In this sense *The Red Room* has greater significance that the other great works that Shchukin had purchased previously, such as Monet's *Déjeuner sur l'herbe* (1866), Gauguin's *Ruperupe* (1899), both at the Pushkin Museum, or Van Gogh's *The Thicket*.

No-one apart from Shchukin, perhaps, could have appreciated *Game of Bowls*, one of the first and most audacious examples of primitivism in European painting, so soon after its appearance. It was the Russian collector who immediately shared Matisse's interest in art from outside the sphere of the European culture that had developed from the Renaissance onwards, which seemed by the end of the nineteenth century to have exhausted its resources. The primitivism of Matisse's painting is linked prevalently to themes that transported the artist back to the primordial past of mankind, to the legendary time when art had only just been born. *Game of Bowls*, part of the golden age cycle, is entirely devoid of the idyllic tones that generally characterize titles of this kind.

The figures in *Game of Bowls*, like those in *The Dance* and *Music* later, both resemble real people and differ from them. The young characters are absorbed in the game, like modern youngsters; it seems as though they are really playing *pétanque*, the form of bowls popular in the south of France, but at the same time their gestures and poses are almost ritual. Matisse's characters are not enjoying themselves, but are involved in the "game of life". The extremely stylized landscape becomes part of the action, for it matches perfectly the austere, enigmatic symbolism of what is happening: the stretch of water on the horizon (the sea or a river) is not perceived so much as an element of the rural landscape, but as a symbolic environment, for since ancient times the river and the sea have been felt as a sort of metaphor of the dialectic unity of life and death.

There is a subject in the painting, but in the absence of any psychological explanation, and in the presence of the general simplification of formal means, it is transformed into allegory. The number of characters is symbolic (three, the chosen number in folklore). It is no coincidence that the number of bowls is the same. The whole scene is reminiscent of an act of prophesy. What might seem to be a superficial theme unfolds in a solemn, even dramatic manner. Surprisingly at first sight, though deeply justified on reflection, the range of colors used contains no sign of joy. The green of the grass is the expression of the life-giving energy of the earth, though not only of this. The Egyptians painted the figure of Osiris green, the divinity of the generative energy of nature and the lord of the underworld. The symbolism of colors is not univocal but antinomic, for it is intuitive rather than literary in nature. Matisse represented the golden age in a broad and contradictory way, as we see in *Game of Bowls* and also in another painting in the cycle, *The Nymph and the Satyr*. Here, using the composition of the ceramic panel he had worked on almost two years earlier, the artist raises the level of emotive perception of the theme. The ceramic triptych was purely decorative: it lacks completely the background landscape, though there was a stylized border of bunches of grapes. In the canvas painted for Shchukin, Matisse not only maintains the mythological elements but also invests the whole scene with an archetypal symbolic significance that combines the concepts of destiny, life, and sex, allowing us to place the work on the same level as *Game of Bowls*, *The Dance*, and *Music*.

The Dance and *Music* were the most powerful and accomplished expression not only of the painting of Matisse, but of the whole of the *fauvisme* movement. While in *The Red Room*, and then in *The Conversation*, the artist had unexpectedly revealed a grandiose, eternal element in the theme of the interior, in the even more marked simplification and monumentalism of *The Dance* and *Music* he goes even further, breaking for good the threads that tied him to the tradition of genre painting.

Both panels were composed on the basis of a solid tradition, which had given new fruits in the Symbolists. In them the round-dance became an obvious, repeated theme, whose plastic potential was in keeping with the tastes of the *fin-de-siécle*. The theme found its natural expression in the enclosed form, so highly cherished by the supporters of Art Nouveau: it was, in fact, easy to draw from it the ductile, curved lines without which Art Nouveau would be unthinkable. It is no coincidence that in their representations of dances the Art Nouveau artists preferred female figures. Matisse accepted the rules of the game, but his *The Dance* can be considered a caricature of the representations of the same theme at the turn of the century, for his whirling dynamism is the antithesis of the fragile elegance of the dances of Maurice Denis and other similar painters. At the same time Shchukin too, by commissioning *The Dance*, was attracted by the desire to show the whole of Moscow and his friend and rival Ivan Morozov, whose guests reacted with enthusiasm to the series of panels by Denis entitled *Story of Psyche*, how far avant-garde painting could move forward in decorative works.

At this time the eternal themes of music and dance were even more widespread due to the growing influence of Nietzsche, who believed that these two artistic genres contained the "eternal truths, belonging to Apollo and Dionysus". No other work of contemporary art matches the definition of music and dance given by the German philosopher better than the panel commissioned by Shchukin. The characters are lost in dance and music, with the sense of self-oblivion typical of the act of creation. We might describe the theme of the work as the relation between man and life resolved through art.

In the work of the painters of the past, as in that of the painters tied to the Salons around the turn of the century, it is normally possible to recognize idealized representations of their contemporaries in the figures dancing or playing music. But we would hardly be likely to say of the protagonists of *The Dance* and *Music* that they are contemporaries of Matisse, or that through them he represented his idea of men of his time. They are not only without clothes, but also without any temporal attribute, if we do not count the antique flute and the violin of a more recent age. They are not conscious of their nakedness; they behave, that is, not like the characters of a historical era, but like those of mythology. They have sometimes been taken to be primitive men. But this interpretation leads nowhere, because Matisse's painting had nothing in common with the "historical" canvases of the Paris Salons, where the life of savages was reconstructed and viewers were faced with dances in costume on an archaeological theme. However, those who saw *The Dance* and *Music* would have found them hard to accept even if they had been told that Matisse's characters belonged to a symbolic rather than a historical order, for the Symbolists had accustomed them to allegories of a completely different kind.

The simplicity of the artistic structure of both panels hides a content that is far from simple, in which we can sense both a premonition and a reflection on the prehistoric past, and at the same time a reflection of the artist's individual impressions. "I love dance," Matisse said. "Dance is an extraordinary thing: life and rhythm. It is easy for me to live with dance. When I had to paint a dance for Moscow, I simply went one Sunday afternoon to the Moulin de la Galette. I watched how they danced. In particular I watched the farandole... The dancers, holding hands, run through the whole room, enveloping the rather disconcerted audience like a ribbon. When I got home, I composed my dance on a surface of four meters, humming the same tune I had heard at the Moulin de la Galette, so that the whole composition, all the dancers moved with the same rhythm..."[26]

It would be naive to explain *The Dance* only through the artist's impressions of the farandole at the Moulin de la Galette or of the sardana at Collioure. The farandole had provided the necessary tone, but the meaning of the work is more profound and important than it might appear at first glance. By transporting the action to the mythical distance of the dawn of mankind, Matisse created a figurative structure full of extremely profound meaning.

Primordial dances are substantially a magical phenomenon, an ancient act of creation, the visible triumph of life over death. Scholars of the symbology of ancient cultures have observed that dances performed holding hands signify the union between the earth and the sky. Thanks to art (whether it be dance or music), man becomes part of this union. In Matisse the earth and the sky do not act merely as a background. They are, rather, the protagonists of the action. This is why it was necessary to intensify and simplify their colors. The tonality of the panels contains within it a dense symbolic content. The single range that stretches over the whole surface is not motivated only by the desire to achieve decorative coherence. The chromatic affinities of the two works echo the cosmogonic aspect of the theme of the earth and the sky. In both works the action takes place on a hill. The hill or the mount, too, traditionally symbolized the union between the earth and the sky, and for this reason were related to the theme of elevation to the realm of the spirit. Taken separately, the panels *The Dance* and *Music* do not express completely the creative intention of the artist. Together, in their great dialectic contraposition, they mean incomparably more. According to some philosophical notions that appeared around the turn of the century, woman in the compositions is the bearer of unity, while man is the principle of division and individualism. The two sexes are antagonists, and seek union. Ultimately *Music* is as static as *The Dance* is dynamic.

Speaking of the two works, Matisse underlined the fact that their content and meaning could not be compared simply to the purposes of decorative or monumental painting. The Moscow panel," he wrote, comparing Shchukin's *Dance* to the later variation painted for the Barnes home in Merion, "still meets the requirements of a painting, that is of a work that can be placed anywhere. And this is quite comprehensible, because I had no idea of the place they would occupy, or the stairway for which they were destined."[27] In actual fact the landing of the stairway in Shchukin's home did not prove to be the ideal place for the panels, for it was rather narrow and dark, although even there they produced a powerful effect.[28]

The arrival in Moscow of *The Red Room*, *Game of Bowls*, and *The Nymph and the Satyr* had already turned Shchukin's gallery into a mouthpiece for the latest and boldest achievements of the European avant-garde. *The Dance* and *Music* were the culmination of the collaboration between the painter and his patron. The creation of this complex, a milestone of great importance in the history of European art, should not be considered the merit of Matisse alone, but also of Shchukin. When the artist's son Pierre, the greatest dealer of his time, was later asked whether his father would have painted such large canvases without Shchukin, he replied simply: "And who would he have painted them for?"[29] I clearly recall the sincere veneration with which Pierre Matisse spoke of

Shchukin, standing in front of the famous portrait in pencil done by his father.[30] He underlined not only the audacity, but also the delicate sensibility of his father's patron, who never tried to impose his ideas on the artist, or to interfere in any way in the creative process. And yet the idea for important works such as the "Sevillian" or "Spanish" still lifes, or the *Family Portrait*, was suggested by Sergei Shchukin. The evolution of Matisse's art, from the first still lifes to *The Red Room*, then to the symbolic-decorative canvases (*Games of Bowls*, *The Nymph and the Satyr*, *The Dance*, and *Music*), and finally to the Moroccan cycle, inevitably had considerable influence on Shchukin. The development of the collector's tastes was determined by his attentive interest in the various phenomena of contemporary art, and in this sense his contacts with Matisse played a far from secondary role: Matisse, in fact, undoubtedly became the most "Shchukinian" artist, present in the gallery in a more complete and varied form than anyone else. Shchukin was not afraid that buying many of Matisse's works, most of them very large, would create an imbalance in his collection.

He was occasionally "taken in" by a painting by a "second-rate" artist, such as the small *Mill on the Marne* by Herbin, but in the last phase of his activity as a collector this happened only rarely. He was not interested in extending his collection in order to make it complete, but rather in the latest developments. His intuition told him (now we all know this, but things were very different at the time) that genuine developments, and not just yet another pseudo-original novelty, could only be expected from Matisse and Picasso. The artistic discoveries of these Titans filled him with enthusiasm. After receiving *The Arab Cafe*, Shchukin wrote to Matisse to inform him that he looked at it every day for at least two hours, and that he liked it more than anything else.[31] This does not mean, however, that the painting was placed forever above everything else. In his letters to the artist, Shchukin pointed out on several occasions that he felt close to all his paintings and admired them every day.

The following is an observation of a different kind, taken from a letter informing Matisse of the arrival of *The Dance* and *Music*: "Your panels have arrived and are hung. The effect is not bad. Unfortunately, under the electric light in the evening, the blue changes considerably. It becomes dark, almost black. But all in all I find the panels interesting and hope that one day I will like them. I have complete confidence in you. The public is against you, but the future is yours."[32] Behind this considerable praise there seems to be a struggle between the mind and the heart. The phrase "I find them interesting" conveys a certain sense of doubt, a divided judgment, but from experience Shchukin knew that the aesthetic sense, when it is alive, does not remain unchanged. Despite his doubts, he trusted Matisse, because he was sure that the French artist's painting constituted one of the main paths of contemporary art.

As soon as the Shchukin home opened its doors to anyone who wanted to visit, in 1909, it immediately became an art museum, a launch-pad for works of art, since some paintings came directly from the atelier, and also a sort of arena for young artists. Mostly pupils of the Institute of Painting, Sculpture and Architecture, these young artists became the museum's most assiduous visitors. The teachers at the school, like Valentin Serov, occupied a more avant-garde position compared to their colleagues at the St. Petersburg Academy of Fine Arts; despite this, there was some conflict between pupils and teachers, stoked by the examples the young artists found and assimilated at Shchukin's gallery. Much later one of Serov's former pupils, K.S. Petrov-Vodkin, wrote that: "The contagion came from Znamenski Street, from Shchukin."[33]

The young Muscovite painters, who were soon to join together in the "Jack of Diamonds" group (whose first honorary member was Shchukin himself), were influenced strongly by Shchukin's works, as we can see quite clearly in the works of Mikhail Larionov and Natalya Goncharova. Larionov's *Lilac* (1904) is based on Monet's *Lilacs at Argenteuil*, while his *Soldier Smoking* (1910-1911; Tretyakov Gallery) is an exact copy of the pose of Cézanne's *The Smoker* (Pushkin Museum). Goncharova produced a number of variations of Gauguin's *Sunflowers*. And it would not be difficult to find many other examples. Here, however, it was not merely a case of imitation.

What makes them similar is the essential, the common perception of the natural, primordial power of primitivism. This is not a case of primitiveness or simplification, as many people believed: primitivism is felt as the quickest route to the heart of things, as the attempt to discover the truth despite the artificiality introduced by every school. The artists of the "Jack of Diamonds" group exalted forms of popular, traditional figurative art (signs, trays, *luboks*, etc.). Like Kandinsky or Malevich, Larionov felt himself to be a primitive of modern art, and followed the lessons of popular figurative culture in order to learn to draw on the deepest essence of things. Shchukin's attitude towards non-professional, "non-erudite" art was the same. There was very little sculpture in his collection. He had no interest in classical statues, nor did he appreciate Rodin's current. Yet he did bring some sculptures back from Black Africa, and was the first in Russia – and one of the first in the world – to exhibit them in his gallery. The important thing is not that it was Matisse or Picasso who inspired this interest, but that next to their works these sculptures constituted a wonderful testimony of the universality of human values and artistic techniques.

Shchukin was the first of the great collectors to begin to buy the paintings of Rousseau 'le Douanier', which struck even the most enlightened admirers of his collection as strange.[34] But Shchukin, being himself self-taught in the field of art, appreciated genuine talent rather than diplomas, and also had strong belief in his own judgment. He realized that 'le Douanier' was not a "Sunday painter", and that his unusual sense of color and arabesque gave him the right to hope for a place in history. The seven paintings by Rousseau which Shchukin collected between 1910 and 1913 form a group that is unique of its kind.

Shchukin was soon to discover the prophetic significance of the art of Picasso. It is generally thought that they were introduced by Matisse, who accompanied his Russian patron to the Bateau Lavoir in September 1908.[35] A record of the meeting can be found in the memoirs of Fernande Olivier, Picasso's mistress at the time. Fernande describes Shchukin as "a small pale, wan man with an enormous head like the mask of a pig. Afflicted with a horrible stutter, he had great difficulty expressing himself, and that embarrassed him… He bought two canvases, paying what were very high prices for the time (one of them was the beautiful *Woman with a Fan*), and from then on he became a faithful client."[36]

This caricatured description of the collector, who was actually far from resembling a pig, was almost certainly based not on a real-life encounter but on a rather poisonous sketched portrait by Picasso, in which Shchukin is depicted as a pig (the drawing is now owned by the heirs of the artist).[37] At the beginning of 1906, the dealer Ambroise Vollard had quite a large group of works by Picasso. Every time Shchukin stayed in Paris he paid a visit to the Vollard Gallery, where he regularly bought paintings. It is very unlikely that he did not notice the works by Picasso: rather, the "spark" was simply not lit the first time he saw them. Unfortunately the caricature is not dated, so we do not know the exact period in which Shchukin first became acquainted with Picasso's art. Zervos, the author of the *catalogue raisonné* of the artist's paintings and drawings, dates the sketch 1905, but it is more likely to have been done in 1906, as Richardson suggests.[38]

Shchukin undoubtedly saw the paintings of Picasso at the home of Gertrude Stein, whose opinions on contemporary art he greatly respected. He first visited the Steins' home in December 1907. Gertrude herself would tell of when Shchukin, almost in tears, had commented on the appearance of *Les demoiselles d'Avignon* with the words: "What a loss for French art!" He was probably expressing genuine regret: he would subsequently come to appreciate Cubism, but the American writer was clearly embroidering the episode here. Despite the strength of his feelings, Sergei Shchukin was not a man to shed public tears for art. *Les demoiselles d'Avignon* was painted in 1907. Shchukin saw it some time later: it is difficult to say exactly when, but in any case not before his visit to the Bateau Lavoir in September 1908.

At that time Shchukin still didn't possess any paintings by Picasso, although he was undoubtedly keeping an eye on him. In the lengthy essay on the Shchukin gallery published in August 1908, Pavel Muratov makes no mention of works by the Spanish artist.

Which *Woman with a Fan* was Fernande Olivier referring to? The title has been attributed to a painting belonging to the Pushkin Museum. This work, however, could not have been bought in 1908, for the simple reason that it did not yet exist: it was painted in 1909, and Shchukin acquired it in the autumn of the same year. In October 1911 it was published in the Moscow journal *Zerkalo* (The Mirror). In a letter to Gertrude Stein in mid-September 1909, Picasso wrote: "Shchukin bought a painting of mine from Sagot, *Portrait with a Fan*."[39] He had just moved to his new home in Boulevard Clichy, and hastened to make the fact known, for it was undoubtedly important for him, not only because of the reputation as an illustrious connoisseur of avant-garde art which Shchukin enjoyed, but also because the Russian collector had always 'backed' Matisse, who Picasso saw as his main rival. *Portrait with a Fan* is sometimes thought to refer to the *Woman with a Fan* in the Hermitage. Richardson, and Rubin after him, believe that it refers to the *Woman with a Fan* in Moscow; they are probably right in this, for this painting, unlike the one in the Hermitage, was - despite the attraction exerted by Cubism - the depiction of a real woman, Etta Cone. We might even suppose that it was precisely this circumstance that convinced Shchukin to buy the painting as a refined figure, "sculpted" by the artist. He still did not understand the essence of Cubism, but very much wished to do so.

One of the habitués of the gallery, Nikolai Preobrazhensky, wrote down the collector's account in his notes: "I didn't like this artist and I didn't buy his paintings. I had a big collection of many artists, but I didn't have anything by Picasso. My friends told me to buy at least one canvas to complete my collection, but I couldn't make my mind up. But somehow they managed to convince me, and there was also a painting by Picasso for sale at a good price. When I brought it to Moscow, for a long time I didn't hang it. I realized that there was nothing else I could place beside, it clashed with everything and created a strident note of dissonance in the whole collection. In the end I placed it near the entrance, in a dimly-lit corridor where there were no other paintings. I passed through this corridor every day to get to the dining-room. And as I passed the painting, I would involuntarily cast a glance at it. After a while it began to become familiar, and I began, still unconsciously, to look at it every day. A month or so went by, and I began to notice that if I hadn't looked at the painting I would feel uncomfortable at lunch, as if something was missing. So I began to look at it more carefully, with the sensation of swallowing splinters of glass. And at the same time I began to look at it not only as I was going to lunch, but also at other times.

And then it happened that one day, I was horrified to feel that, despite its lack of a subject, the picture had a core of iron, solidity, strength. I was horrified because all the other paintings in my gallery suddenly seemed to lack that core, to be made of cotton wool. And the worst thing was that I no longer wanted to see them. They had lost all interest and meaning for me.

I bought a second painting by Picasso. I already felt that I couldn't do without them. I bought others.. It began to take over me, and I bought one painting after another, no longer looking at any other artist. Eventually there were 51 paintings by Picasso in the gallery, much more than by any other artist." After noting these words, Preobrazhensky added: "When he spoke about Picasso, Shchukin didn't say that the artist's works aroused his enthusiasm, or that he was better than anyone else. No, he said that Picasso had taken over him, exactly like a trance or a spell."[40]

When he first bought paintings by Picasso, Shchukin was probably going against himself in some way. It is no coincidence that a few years later Tugendhold wrote that: "For now we follow the example of Shchukin, who even when he doesn't understand Picasso says 'he's probably right, not me…'."[41] *Woman with a Fan* was very soon followed by other Cubist paintings (now at the Hermitage). Increasingly conscious of the importance of Picasso's art, Shchukin decided to fill in the "gaps" and also bought early works, something he would never have done for a lesser artist. Thus in 1911 he bought *Absinthe Drinker*, and in 1913 *Portrait of Benet Soler*; probably during the same period he also bought *Boy with a Dog*, and in 1914 *Nude Boy*.

In *Absinthe Drinker* Shchukin had been fascinated not only by the phenomenal virtuosity of the twenty-year-old artist, but also by the unrepeatable dramatic quality of the figure. A figure that undoubtedly combines disparate elements. The whole physiognomy of the subject conveys the lonely wait of a person forgotten, marginalized in a literal and metaphorical sense. The dirty red tones of the wall do not only reproduce the atmosphere of a cheap bar, but also create a sad, restless background which underlines the desperate life of the drunk, alienated woman. The depiction of an unknown drunk woman becomes a picture of human tragedy, full of pathos, although the subject is of the lowest social class. We need only leaf hurriedly through the luxurious painting albums of the official Paris Salons at the beginning of the century to understand how great a challenge this painting must have been at the time. Shchukin, whose gallery also constituted a challenge to the universally accepted artistic conventions, bought the painting because it had still not lost its aesthetic freshness, even though the artist had long moved on from this phase. Shchukin was also attracted irresistibly by his works from Picasso's Blue period, in which the monochromy, symbolic and essential by nature, conveyed sadness and compassion in a profound, simple manner. It is precisely the deliberate emotive use of color that explains the concentration of different shades of blue in *The Two Sisters* or in *Portrait of Benet Soler*. In these paintings, the natural power of blue is affirmed as the only ideal substance, capable of making everything submit to it. By immersing his characters in this element, the artist obtained an effect of catharsis, of spiritual purification through compassion. The Blue period, with its aesthetics of universal, unifying pain, seemed to be unsuitable for portraits, yet Picasso often turned to this genre. Whoever the subjects may have been, all the characters seem to be the members of a single family: each is absorbed in increasingly similar reflections. The blues that dominate do not express the individual psychology of the person portrayed, but the artist's mood. Everything we know about the vain tailor Benet Soler, who would have liked to seen himself as a patron but actually remained a second-rate character, has little in common with the great depth that Picasso confers on him.

A hidden sadness characterizes *Boy with a Dog*, which already belongs to the Rose period, one of the most moving figures in all Picasso's works. Just a few months later his figures had acquired a more muscular quality. The fragile *Boy with a Dog*, linked to symbolism, was followed by the *Nude Boy*, which reminds us of the statues of Greek *kuroi* and Cézanne's bathers. Picasso felt a strong need to find support in the classical world.

Why, we might ask, had Shchukin never bought Picasso's pre-Cubism works, which were more comprehensible, before 1909? He could not have failed, in fact, to appreciate the merits of the works from the Blue and Rose periods. In the absence of documents, the question is difficult to answer. One explanation might be the fact that after 1900 he had stopped buying paintings that were not French, although he had previously taken an active interest in English and Spanish painting, and had always considered Picasso a Spanish painter, even during the Rose period. The years that had gone by since Picasso's definitive move to Paris led Shchukin to change his mind, until the beginning of Cubism when the artist quickly became the dominant figure in the most innovative, avant-garde group.

The first Cubist canvases acquired by Shchukin convinced him of their strange, paradoxical closeness to reality. He knew Fernande Olivier, and could sense that *Woman with Fan* was a reworking of a representation of her. Through his acquaintance with Gertrude Stein he was able to meet the Cone sisters at her house; contact was also possible through Matisse, whose art the sisters were deeply attached to. This was precisely how he had acquired *Woman with Fan* in the past. There is nothing surprising in this sort of initial approach to Cubism. Ivan Morozov, another extraordinary collector from Moscow, behaved in the same way: although disliking Cubism, he purchased one of its masterpieces, *Portrait of Ambroise Vollard*, probably because he knew the dealer well.

At the beginning of the century, Shchukin's collection of Picassos was rivaled only by that of Leo and Gertrude Stein, later dispersed. It was from the Steins that Shchukin bought *Three Women* (1908; Hermitage Museum), perhaps the best Cubist painting, whilst his rival Morozov bought the best Rose composition, *The Young Acrobat on a Ball* (1905; Pushkin Museum). Kahnweiler, the main dealer of Picasso's works, considered Shchukin the only great connoisseur of the avant-garde painting of his time. There was one episode in particular that he would recount; after receiving a supply of paintings by Picasso, he telegraphed Shchukin straight away, and the Russian collector rushed to Paris as soon as he could. The episode may well refer to the *ensemble* of works from 1908, for there are more of these early Cubist works in Shchukin's collection (and now in the Hermitage) than anywhere else.

When buying so many Picassos, Shchukin seemed to have forgotten that space in the gallery was already tight. There was clearly no room on the walls for the new canvases. Arranged in two or three rows, frame to frame, right up to the high ceiling, they filled a room of modest dimensions. Shchukin's methods of hanging paintings certainly belonged to the nineteenth century, and differed relatively little from the practice of his predecessors the Tretyakov brothers. These methods are alien to modern exhibition criteria, but we should not infer from this that Shchukin did not care about how the canvases were arranged. From time to time he would make changes. Sometimes he didn't think it necessary to place the paintings of a particular artist in the same place; it was possible, in his view, to put paintings from the same movement together, especially if they were based on the same decorative principles. Yet in the Picasso room everything seemed to be mixed up in a whirl of forms that clashed with each other – Blue period, Rose period, Cubism, without any chronological order – the terrifying faces of men and things crammed into a single cage.

This sensation was reinforced by the presence of African sculpture. We do not know whether Shchukin had seen Picasso again after his visit to the Bateau Lavoir in 1908. He had, however, undoubtedly talked to Yakov Tugendhold about his visit to Picasso's atelier, and the artist was certainly aware of the friendship between the critic and the collector: "I admit that I saw a rather unexpected environment for a painter: in the corner black idols from the Congo and masks from Dahomey, on the table bottles, cuttings of wall-paper and newspapers in the manner of a still life, on the walls strange models of musical instruments, cut out in cardboard by Picasso himself; and in all this a feeling of austerity, without any comforting picturesque note. And yet in this studio of black magic one could sense a workshop of creativity, an atmosphere of serious work that knew neither measure nor rest in its spirit of investigation."[42] Tugendhold wrote that Shchukin had acquired examples of African sculpture under the influence of Picasso. It is quite possible, however, that he was already familiar with these works before meeting the artist. He could have talked about the originality of African sculpture with Matisse, with whom he had a close friendship, for Matisse had begun to appreciate it before Picasso. And he would also have had the chance to see examples during his trips to Egypt. It was, however, Picasso himself who persuaded the collector to buy a number of extraordinary statuettes, which he exhibited in his gallery next to the artist's paintings.

In the first guide to the Shchukin gallery after it was nationalized by the Soviet authorities, Pyotr Perzov, a contemporary of Shchukin, wrote: "The secluded Picasso room also serves in its own way to understand this type of art, just as the spacious, bright, elegant dining-room suits the elegance of Matisse. In this room one immediately feels transported beyond the confines of all other art… One is faced with something strange, unusual and frightening, which at first one even hesitates to recognize as art. In any case it is an unusual art, out of the ordinary, which breaks up and negates itself. The Russian writer Sergei Bulgarov likened Picasso's art to the speech by Svidrigaylov, in *Crime and Punishment*, on eternity represented through the metaphor of a narrow *izba*, full of spiders. And this room does, in fact, represent something similar to that *izba*, and a 'spidery' impression arises from the lugubrious dark, or reddish, paintings hung on the walls, in which what strikes us before anything else is the long, sharp lines of the drawing."[43]

Shchukin saw Picasso as the antithesis of Matisse not only in terms of artistic form, but also from an emotional and psychological point of view. Matisse brought joy and peace. Picasso revealed to the eyes of the collector, and of those people who were spiritually close to him, a vision of hell, eternal anguish, an inevitable tragedy, but also offered catharsis or purification through compassion.

After the personal tragedies he had experienced (the death of his wife, the suicide of his son and then that of his brother Ivan), Shchukin did not fear allusions to death; in fact he sought such allusions, acquiring Picasso's *Composition with a Skull* and also the preparatory drawing, as well as Derain's *Still Life with a Skull*. As he passed to Cubism from the Blue and Rose periods, Picasso gave up all narrative or psychological undertones. By reducing the multiform variety of the world to essential geometric forms, in paintings such as *Seated Woman, Cottage in a Garden*, or *The Brick Factory at Tortosa*, he highlighted the impersonality and anonymity of the age, its hostility to nature, and consequently did not reject the tragic but transposed it to a different level.

In *Violin and Guitar* the customary appearance of the instruments is completely overturned, using the various elements to create an arbitrary composition. However, the arrangement of these elements is subject to a complex, intuitive rhythm, through which the general architectonic structure of the canvas is also formed. The emergence of this rhythm may be brought about by the imaginary oscillating movement assumed by the violin and the guitar hanging on the wall. Like the details of the instruments, the decorative flourishes of the wall-paper also play an important role in the painting. They are drawn in an almost naturalistic way (and could be replaced by cuttings of real wall-paper, as sometimes happened), for their ornamental motif is rather abstract. The purpose of the plastic construction is the creation of a network of contrasts and similarities (between, for example, the curls of the border of the wall-paper and the design of the handle and the S-shaped cuts in the violin), in other words the creation of a new structure that has no match in real nature.

Picasso's still lifes, from *Composition with a Skull* to *The Tavern* and the compositions with "cut pears" (1914), do not aim so much to capture the reality of objects; they are rather acts of profound faith. Even the most commonplace everyday objects, caught in an austere inevitability, are filled with solemn gravity. Impressionism had been the final stage in the evolution of nineteenth-century painting, its fundamental discovery. In the paintings of Cézanne, who had distanced himself from Impressionism, there are as many contrasts as there are affinities with the movement. In Picasso's first Cubist still lifes, the best of which had been bought by Shchukin, Impressionism is not corrected, as in Cézanne, but completely negated. The airiness, the vibrations of the light, and the complex modulations of color were all rejected in decisive manner. The break with the nineteenth century is particularly evident in the deformations, much more premeditated than in any previous artist. What objects are made of is often of no importance to him. It is simply a question of material, as hard as stone, primordial, freed from the power of time. Equally primordial and eternal are the forms of the objects, called on to render the idea of the simplest form, absolute and immutable.

The small still lifes of 1908 convey a powerful effect of monumentalism, unknown in the previous century. They clearly resound with the theme of destiny, of life and death, but they do so not through a scene or description, but in an abstract way, through the play of forms and colors, similar to what happens in relations between musical sounds. *Pitcher and Bowls* and *Green Bowl and Black Bottle* matched Shchukin's state of mind. He was familiar with the latter through the Stein collection, and when Leo Stein sold it to Kahnweiler he was quick to acquire it for himself. Kahnweiler wrote to Picasso in July 1912 that Shchukin had been very keen to purchase *Composition with a Skull*, which the dealer did not want to sell, until he gave way to an offer of 10,000 francs – a very high price for the time. If Shchukin had insisted so much, he must have had very good reasons to overcome the dealer's reluctance (Kahnweiler knew that Picasso preferred his works not to leave Paris). Shchukin had been struck by the overwhelming power of the work, but the most evocative *memento mori* of the beginning of the twentieth century also served him as a reminder of his own personal tragedies.

No less austere than the still lifes were the *La Rue-de-Bois* landscapes. It is hard to believe that these represent the Ile-de-France, the cradle of Impressionism, although from Picasso's paintings, too, we realize that this is a very green area, and it is even possible to make out the varieties of trees. Picasso also maintained the detail of the tiny cottages that were typical of this village. *Cottage in a Garden* is born of a clearly anti-Impressionist conception of painting, from the rejection of "painting that depends on what the weather is like", to use the artist's words. The bright whirl of tiny, dynamic brushstrokes that characterized the Impressionists is replaced by the "radical" language of forms "carved in stone" that also mark the figurative compositions of this period.

In each of the most important canvases from 1908 (*The Two Friends, Seated Woman, Dryad, Woman with a Fan*), new problems of form are resolved. It is significant that all these paintings depict a female nude. The choice of this genre clearly expresses the polemical harshness of Picasso's art, for no other figurative genre had been rendered so sickly and vulgar by the painting of the Salons, which had by no means surrendered at this time. From time immemorial, in fact, the genre had played an important role in painting. It also proved to be important for Cubism during its early days. Everything that makes the female figure attractive was eliminated. Picasso achieves an extreme degree of dynamism, using very clear outlines, poses full of tension, and very little surrounding space, thus giving the figures an aggressive quality.

The masterpiece of the Shchukin collection, *Three Women*, is the blazing Gothic of Cubism. In a world full of turmoil, this painting expressed a nostalgia for harmony. The pyramidal construction of *Three Women* is the formula of solidity consecrated over thou-

sands of years, but in Picasso it functions paradoxically as an element of dynamism. At the same time as the theory of relativity, he united that which had always been thought to be irreconcilable. *Three Women* made its appearance in Shchukin's gallery at the end of 1913 or the beginning of 1914. As soon as he found out that Gertrude Stein was selling the painting, he made sure he would not let the opportunity slip. From this time up to the middle of 1914 he bought twenty paintings by Picasso. Certainly, he would not have stopped there. On 18 June 1914, Kahnweiler wrote to offer him nine Picassos. But this time he was unable to set out straight away, and soon after the First World War broke out, marking the end of his career as a collector. Even during the war, the gallery continued to remain open to the public, and if we look at many of the works by avantgarde Russian artists dated 1915-1917, we cannot fail to be reminded of one or other of the masterpieces in the collection of Sergei Shchukin.
In the last years of the gallery's existence, Picasso's Cubist works formed the main touchstone for visitors. Although Shchukin did not understand everything about this evolution, he followed all its phases carefully, and bought the artist's latest works in the summer of 1914. He did not attempt to embrace the whole of Cubism, and was not interested in imitators, but the enigma of Picasso's art and personality fascinated him. In his personal copy of the catalog of the gallery,[44] the latest acquisitions, added by hand, are mainly paintings by the Spanish artist.
The remarkable decorative invention of Picasso's works from 1914, in which he used the strangest materials, not just cardboard and paint but also collages, wall-paper, and even shavings, as in the two versions of *Still Life with Cut Pear*, must have appealed to a "professional" connoisseur of materials, and therefore of decorative arts in general, as Shchukin would always remain. What was even more fascinating, however, was the phantasmagoric quality, so suited to the mood of Russian and European society on the eve of the First World War.

In 1914 Shchukin owned the best collection in the world not only of the works of Matisse, but also of those of Picasso. The author of the first guide to the Perzov Gallery rightly observed that: "To discover the latest word uttered by European painting, one has to go and study it in the far-off capital of the East."[45] Shchukin's activity as a collector progressed in waves that were not determined only by his own personal views. The waves were moved by the impulses that guided the evolution of both Russian and European culture. He was not happy simply to possess canvases of great artistic quality. The paintings also had to influence the artistic conscience of Russian society, and Shchukin hastened to bring to Moscow works that pointed towards new horizons, that inspired fear and fascination.
Shchukin always bought his works in Paris. For some reason he was not interested in what could be acquired in Moscow or St. Petersburg, at the exhibitions that traveled from abroad. He liked to discover paintings by himself, and also loved to shock people. Nobody in Moscow would know a painting dug out in Vollard's basement or in Matisse's atelier, while everyone would be talking about an exhibition coming from abroad.
The only purchase made in Moscow was, however, of extraordinary importance: the canvases of the Impressionists belonging to his brother Pyotr. The sale, in 1912, seemed to Muscovites to be a natural piece of family business. As Ternovez wrote, "I heard that the works were sold for a ridiculously low price, 10,000 rubles."[46] These rumors were, however, inaccurate. The details of the deal were so secret that even the usually well-informed director of the museum of "modern Western art" remained in the dark for a whole decade.
In 1907, having decided to marry at a late age, Pyotr had to leave his French mistress and send her home, after compensating her generously. After a while legal proceedings were begun against him in Bordeaux, for mademoiselle Bourgeois thought her endowment to be insufficient. The problem was overcome, but in May 1912 she began to make even more exorbitant demands. Since he did not want the matter to become public knowledge, Pyotr decided to give in and sell his French collection to raise money. Wishing to avoid a public auction, he turned to Sergei for help.
Sergei wrote to his elder brother: "I will be in Paris at the beginning of July, and I will certainly speak to Durand-Ruel, Bernheim, Druet etc., about your paintings. On the other hand I very much regret that such beautiful works should leave Russia, and for this

reason I would be very happy to buy 8 or 10 paintings. As you know, I have left my collection to the city. You have some interesting pictures, which would suit me very much. And then, above all, I know that dealers begin to squeeze the seller when the time to buy approaches, claiming that it will not be easy to sell them again, and that the price should be lowered, and so on. I will pay you the right price, and I am ready to take Degas, Renoir, Monet, Sisley, Pissarro, M. Denis, Cottet, Forain and Raffaëlli…"[47] The result of the subsequent negotiations is noted in a further letter from Sergei, written in June: "…We will reach an agreement in any case, for the 6 paintings and Denis I will give you 100,000. Keep the other paintings for now."[48] Thus he did not pay "a ridiculously low price", but ten times as much. The Parisian dealers were offering much less.

Since Shchukin was spending his money at this time on works by avant-garde masters, he was forced to restrict himself to buying only the most important paintings by Monet, Sisley, Pissarro, Renoir, and Degas. Denis's *Spring Landscape with Figures* was discussed separately. Although Sergei regarded Denis as being of historical rather than contemporary interest, he made an exception for this canvas. When the Pyotr Shchukin Museum closed, "the other paintings" went to the Historical Museum; they remained there until 1922, when they were transferred to the Morozov section of the Museum of Modern Western Art.

Immediately after Sergei and Pyotr Shchukin, or at the same time as them,[49] Mikhail Morozov began to take an interest in modern French painting, thus smoothing the way for his younger brother Ivan. Belonging by birth to the second generation, their family history was, to say the least, unusual.

Their ancestor Savva Morozov, a serf of Count Ryumin, had received his master's permission in 1797 to open a silk ribbon factory. The initial capital consisted of the five rubles of his wife's dowry. By 1820 he had accumulated 17,000 rubles to buy his freedom and that of his family, and seventeen years later he purchased a piece of land near Orekovo (now Orekovo-Zuevo) from his masters, and moved his factory there. Savva and his sons were so successful that by the end of the century the numerous family was one of the most powerful industrial and commercial dynasties in Russia.

During this period the Morozovs were generous patrons of the arts. The grandson of the progenitor, named Savva in his honor, achieved considerable fame. Backing Konstantin Stanislavsky, he helped found the celebrated Moscow Arts Theatre and became its patron. His brother Sergei financed the journal *Mir iskusstva*, and founded the Kustarniy Muzei (the Craft Museum, now the Museum of Folk Art). In the other branch of the family, which ran the Tver Manufacturing Company, "the women enjoyed particular fame, not the Morozovs by birth, but the wives of the Morozovs… Varvara was a typical example of a liberal Muscovite benefactress".[50] The father of Varvara Morozova owned numerous paintings and a remarkable collection of old Russian manuscripts, which would later become the main nucleus of the manuscripts section of the Historical Museum of Moscow. After the death of her first husband, Abram Morozov, she married V.M. Sobelevsky, editor of the remarkably popular liberal newspaper *Russkie vedomosti* (Russian News), with whom she had two children. Her position in society, however, was inevitably at risk. Civil matrimony (a church marriage would have deprived her of the colossal inheritance) was a trap in which it was difficult to find a balance. Varvara Morozova sought it in her libertarian views on women's equality, serving as President of the Moscow Women's Club and devoting herself to charity and social work. She left much of her patrimony, a majority share of the Tver factory, to her workers. Her house became a sort of literary and political salon, frequented by Chekhov, Korolenko, Gleb Uspensky, Bryusov and other writers. Her relationship with her three sons from her first marriage, Mikhail, Ivan and Arseny, was difficult, sometimes approaching open conflict. The boys learned at an early age to despise the liberalism of their teachers and the "political meetings" at their mother's house, for their political leanings were quite different. The reason may well lie not so much in convictions but in a conflict of characters, which on both sides were strong and unwilling to tolerate objections.

The brothers were very different from each other, and took very different paths. The youngest, Arseny, refused on principle to buy paintings, for he did not wish to resemble Mikhail and Ivan: it was, he would say scornfully, a "vacuous" occupation. He did not skimp, however, on the decoration of his opulent mansion on Vozdvizhenka Street in

"Moorish style". Not far from the Kremlin, the building became one of the exotic curiosities of Moscow.

The most eccentric of the Morozov brothers was Mikhail (1870-1903), an eccentric even by the standards of Moscow, which is renowned for people of this sort. A history scholar, journalist, expert on Romance culture, collector, *bon vivant* and gentleman, he was blessed with remarkable energy; he was capable of squandering enormous sums of money, and at the same time of haggling over pennies simply because buying cheaply was a matter of principle. His energy would have sufficed for several people, yet he often wasted it.

Mikhail Morozov "showed great interest, from a young age, in science and in art, and since he did not wish to enter the world of commerce he was given the opportunity to choose his own activity freely".[51] Until he came of age, however, Varvara kept her son in check by granting him only 75 rubles a month, which greatly exasperated the young student at the Faculty of History and Philology.

When he reached twenty-one, however, he inherited his share of the paternal fortune, and his life changed completely. He bought a house with marble columns at the corner of Boulevard Smolensky, where the innumerable guests invited to his Sunday lunches entered the luxurious apartments through the Egyptian-style main entrance, and where next to the telephone there was a genuine Egyptian sarcophagus with a mummy. The guests were offered the most expensive champagne and the best brands of cigarette. The story of the night at the English Club when he lost the incredible sum of over one million rubles at cards went round the whole of Moscow. He was so well-known that he even became a literary hero. His contemporaries had no doubt that Rydlov, the hero of Yuzhin-Sumbatov's play *The Gentleman*, was based on him: in any case he was always known as "Gentleman". "…I can be a critic, a musician, an artist, an actor, and a journalist. Why? Because I am a natural Russian talent, though blunted by civilization. I have just one problem, the fact that things attract me one after another, due to the excessive energy I feel."[52]

Despite becoming fabulously wealthy before he had finished university, Mikhail maintained his interest in history. For a while he wrote articles for the press on art exhibitions. One of his friends called him the "rogue-critic". He evidently enjoyed "denigrating" well-known artists, like Valentin Serov, though not to the point of breaking off relations with them. He also tried his hand at "high-flown" literature, writing the novel *In the Shadows* (1903): the entire print-run was, however, destroyed on the orders of the Cabinet, for it was easy to identity the high-ranking figures behind the fictional names. He donated large sums to shelters and hospitals. For a while he served as Treasurer of the Moscow Conservatory. He also quite frequently organized concerts at his home.

More than anything else, Mikhail Morozov was fascinated by painting. Like his younger brother Ivan, he had drawn a lot since a very early age. Twice a week for two years he had taken lessons from the young Konstantin Korovin, a student at the Institute of Painting, Sculpture and Architecture, and he subsequently kept up his friendship with the first Russian Impressionist. Later, running from one sphere of activity to another, Mikhail gave up painting (Ivan continued, as a student in Zurich, to paint landscapes "for my own soul"), but he did like to take part as an arbiter in debates and conversations on art. From 1893 a lively circle of artists, including Korovin, Vrubel, Serov, Vinogradov, Ostrouchov and Apollinarius Vasnetsov, began to gather at Morozov's mansion: he was happy to buy their works, turning the old winter garden into a picture gallery. Often Surikov too made an appearance. At the same time canvases by Western artists also began to appear in the house on Boulevard Smolensky. "I remember the famous merchant Mikhail Abramovich Morozov, his house in Moscow, fine halls and rooms in different styles, and many paintings, old, brown, dark. When showing a painting, the owner of the house would usually shrug: 'They say it's Raphael or Murillo, who knows? Or Titian perhaps, but the figure on the left, the child, they say it's not by him, but by Correggio. It's all a mystery to me…"[53]

An eloquent quotation. A jumble of names that is bound to arouse suspicion. None of these "many paintings" is the subject of this study. But it is not difficult to imagine the situation. The former student of history, who from an early age had assimilated veneration for the masters of European painting, had hastily bought some "well-known names" and was already looking forward to the reaction of those whom he wanted to impress as the owner of masterpieces by Raphael or Titian.

He naturally soon got rid of these canvases, and never spoke of them again. His first experience had taught him that buying paintings required both sound knowledge and a natural gift. The best school, he believed, was contact with the best-known artists in Moscow and St. Petersburg. Especially with those in Moscow, not only because they lived in the same city, but also because they were closer to him in spirit. His brother Ivan also "took lessons" in the same school; every time he came up from Tver, he made sure that he did not miss the "meetings" at Mikhail's home. From now on Mikhail would only buy "on sight", from the artists themselves, in order to avoid mistakes. With his convivial spirit and his generous hospitality, he did not find it difficult to deal with them, especially since most of them were of the same age, like Vinogradov, or slightly older, like Serov and Korovin. Of the previous generation only Serov was recognized, alone among the founders of the Society of Itinerant Art Exhibitions. Very soon visitors to the mansion on Boulevard Smolensky could admire masterpieces by Vrubel, such as *The Fortune-Teller* and *The Swan-Princess*, and the portraits of his son and his father by Serov, Mika Morozov, and Mikhail himself.

In his obituary of Mikhail Morozov, Sergei Diaghilev wrote: "His collection, created in the space of around five years, was enriched every year by important works imported from abroad or purchased in Russia… One can easily imagine that a great gallery would have been born from his collection, if death had not interrupted these excellent initiatives."[54] In actual fact Morozov spent not five, but at least eight years putting his collection together, although it was in the last five years of his life that it began to take real shape. Although Korovin had painted a "decoration in the style of Corot" for him in 1895, this type of painting belonged more to the decoration of the mansion than to the collection. A series of excellent Russian paintings still did not form a collection. The situation changed when Morozov began to bring works from abroad.

"Mikhail's first purchases, in 1897, were Bernard's *Fantasmagorie Intime* and Weber's *Women Fighting*. His tastes rapidly changed 'leftwards'; most of his early acquisitions returned to Paris, to be replaced by the finest exponents of Impressionism: Manet, Renoir, Degas and Monet; typical of his audacity and perspicacity was the acquisition of Gauguin and Van Gogh, artists who were still not appreciated at this time."[55]

Intimate Phantasmagoria, which had caused such a stir in the French capital (Diaghilev even recalled it in the obituary), was his first great coup as a collector. Morozov was particularly flattered to own a painting that "all Paris" was talking about. In the absence of written records, it is difficult to say much about how these purchases took place. It would be logical to assume that he first showed interest in the Impressionists, and only later in the artists of the next phase. In actual fact this is not necessarily true, for in the Vollard and Bernheim-Jeune galleries that Mikhail frequented he could have found the works of both groups.

In his obituary, Diaghilev wrote that shortly before his death Mikhail "had become the only person in Russia to own works by artists like Bonnard, Vuillard, Denis, Gauguin and others, whose works were not properly appreciated even in Paris."[56] This statement is not entirely accurate: the Shchukin brothers already possessed works by Denis, and Morozov had nothing by Vuillard (initially Russian art lovers often confused Vuillard and Bonnard). But Mikhail was the only Russian collector to own paintings by Gauguin and Bonnard (and also Vallotton, we should add). And he was the first art lover in Russia to appreciate the painting of the Nabis, verging on *intimisme*, despite the fact that it might seem rather unsuited to the collector's fiery temperament.

Mikhail probably discovered Gauguin even before Sergei Shchukin. If we are to believe Konstantin Korovin, he bought four paintings at the exhibition held immediately after Gauguin's death. "He winked at me and added proudly: 'I showed them to my brother. Go on, have a look! He looked and looked, and in the end he said: There is something. Of course there is. They are not Impressionists, after all!'"[57]

The European section of Morozov's collection can conventionally be divided into three groups: The first consisted of artists who were not French, the Scandinavians Thaulow (*Night*, mid-1890s; Hermitage), Munch (*White Night*, circa 1899; Pushkin Museum) and Gallen-Kallela (*River*, 1896; Pushkin Museum), and the Spaniards Gandara and Anglada. These mostly tended towards symbolism and Mikhail was the only collector in Russia truly to appreciate the appeal of this current in Western Europe. Morozov's *ensemble* of symbolist paintings grew further with Carrière and Denis. Shchukin, too, initially collected canvases by these two artists, but it was a secondary interest, while for his emerging rival this was clearly not the case. The second group was of modest dimensions, but was formed of unquestioned masterpieces of Impressionism. The third group consisted of the Post-Impressionists, and included not only works by *les Nabis*, but also by Van Gogh and Gauguin.

Perhaps the finest canvas in the collection of Mikhail Morozov was Renoir's *Portrait of the Actress Jeanne Samary*. It had been painted when the artist was particularly hard-up, and his hopes for the Impressionists' exhibitions were not being fulfilled. In 1879 he had decided to try once again to obtain recognition at the Salon, where he had not been admitted for several years. As Renoir wrote: "There are hardly fifteen art lovers in Paris capable of appreciating an artist without the approval of the Salon. On the other hand there are eighty thousand people who will buy nothing if the artist is not admitted to the Salon... My participation in the Salon is for commercial reasons alone. In any case, it is like those medicines which, while they may not do you any good, don't do you any harm either."[58] Renoir placed his hope in *Portrait of Madame Charpentier and Her Children* (1878, The Metropolitan Museum of Art, New York) and in *Portrait of the Actress Jeanne Samary*. The success of the former finally marked a turning point in his career. *Jeanne Samary*, on the other hand, was hung in a dark corner just under the ceiling, and was hardly noticed. Only Huysmans realized that "the eternal and intolerable smile of the actress is well rendered".[59] For many decades, the portrait would arouse conflicting feelings in historians of Impressionism and would sometimes be taken as a concession to the art of the Salons. Renoir, however, had not attempted at all to follow the yardsticks of the Salons. In the portrait of Jeanne Samary, which Mikhail found twenty years later in Paris, there are many conventional elements, but there is not the slightest trace of the mannerism and the pomposity that were characteristic of the Salons. It is only recently that the critics have acknowledged the painting as one of the most remarkable works of its time.

In terms of quantity, the Western art section of the collection is not very large, but the quality of the works has assured it an important place in the history of Russian art collections. In the light of his increasingly dynamic success before his premature death, we can justifiably state that Russia had lost a collector of the stature of Sergei Shchukin.

After Mikhail's death, his collection was inherited by his wife, Margarita Kirillovna (1873-1958), whose role in Moscow society was no less important than that of her mother-in-law. "For Margarita the death of her husband was the start of a new era; in the past she had been rather bored with life, while subsequently she became an active pupil of Scriabin in Switzerland, to some extent even his successor (though only for a while). On her return to Moscow she was always busy, on the lookout for new ideologies, often absurd but often also colorful; Nietzsche, Kant, Scriabin and Vladimir Soloviev combined in her in the most absurd ways... Searching for an identity and uncertain which direction her interests should take (towards art, philosophy, society) she invited incompatible personalities, who would never have met outside her house, to 'friendly' tea parties with music and conversation."[60] Thus wrote the poet Andrei Bely, an assiduous frequenter of Margarita's social evenings who at one stage was also in love with her.

Between 1903 and 1917, Margarita's life was full of countless occupations and was characterized by a desire to contribute to the improvement of society. She financed publications on art and philosophy (especially through her own publishing house "Put" [The Path]). Her musical and social activity was intense. She was an excellent pianist, but only played in her own home. Her teachers were Alexander Scriabin and Nikolai Metner (for many years she also gave Scriabin financial help).

In March 1910, Margarita Kirillovna donated sixty of the eighty-three paintings in Mikhail's collection to the Tretyakov Gallery, presenting the gesture as the execution of her husband's will.[61] In actual fact there is no mention in Mikhail's will of the destination of his collection, although we cannot rule out the possibility that he expressed the idea verbally. It is more likely, however, that the donation to the Tretyakov Gallery was Margarita's initiative. She chose the most important works, all the paintings from Western European and most of the Russian works, keeping the family portraits and a few paintings she was particularly fond of.⁶²

Mikhail's brother Ivan (1871-1921) began to form his own collection later than others in his circle, despite the fact that he had long been familiar with art. "Ivan Abramovich seemed to his mother to be the most suited to manage the business. He was, in fact, born for this sort of activity. He completed grammar school in Moscow and was then sent to Zurich, where he graduated in Chemistry..."⁶³ In Zurich Ivan Morozov actually attended the Polytechnic, where as well as Chemistry he also studied Engineering. When he graduated in 1892, he moved to Tver to manage the family business, returning to Moscow only in 1900.
Shortly before his return he bought an enormous old house in Prechistenka Street. From 1904 to 1906 the interior of the mansion was renovated to allow the best possible exposition of the paintings.
Back in Moscow, Ivan Morozov followed the example of his elder brother and began to acquire paintings, initially only by Russian artists. The "first stone" was laid with the purchase of a landscape by M. Ch. Aladzhalov at the Wanderers' Exhibition in 1901. Then came the turn of far more significant artists: Vrubel, Levitan, Korovin, Serov, Golovin, Benois, and Somov, all of whom had also been collected by Mikhail. Ivan was especially attracted to the work of Serov and Levitan, and like his brother abandoned the first generation of the Wanderers, making no exception even for Surikov. In time the list grew, and was joined by younger artists such as Kuznekov, Mashkov, Larionov, Goncharova, Kuprin, Konchalovsky, and Chagall, though not Kandinsky or Malevich: Ivan Morozov drew a halt when it came to this "left-wing" fringe. When he eventually stopped, his Russian collection consisted of 303 paintings and seven sculptures (most of these are now in the Tretyakov Gallery).⁶⁴
Following his brother's example, Ivan decided to branch out to foreign artists. One of the first works was probably a landscape by the now-forgotten Russian-German Ducker, *Sea-Shore* (1875; Pushkin Museum). Later, in around 1903, he bought two striking Spanish canvases: Sorolla's *Preparing the Raisins* (1901; Pushkin Museum) and Zuloaga's *Gathering Before the Corrida* (1903; Hermitage). These were both at the same level as Anglada's *Spanish Dance*, acquired a few years earlier by Mikhail, typical examples of Spanish virtuosity.
It is widely believed that he began his most important collection, that of works by French artists, with the acquisition in 1903 of Sisley's landscape *Frosty Morning at Louveciennes* (1873; Pushkin Museum). His initial steps in the Paris art world were rather uncertain. He was helped by his brother's old advisor, the painter Vinogradov. On his recommendation, in 1904 Morozov bought Pissarro's *Ploughland* (1874; Pushkin Museum) from Vollard. During the same period he visited the Durand-Ruel Gallery, where he bought Sisley's *Hoschedé Garden* and *Spring Landscape*, although he soon returned the latter. Like Sergei Shchukin, he came to an agreement with dealers that allowed him to return a painting if it did not fit in with the rest of his collection.
Between 1903 and 1905, Sisley continued to be Morozov's favorite artist. In 1905, a visit to the aging Durand led to the purchase of another canvas by Sisley, *Windy Evening at Veneux*, which cost him 20,000 francs. In the space of a few years the prices of Sisley's works had risen dramatically; Morozov, however, was not driven by a desire to speculate, but bought only what he liked. One year later he acquired his first Monet, *Waterloo Bridge*, a choice that reflects his artistic sensibility rather than his audacity. He was attracted by the lively colors of Impressionism, but generally chose paintings that were more subdued in color and in mood. Of Monet's forty-two representations of Waterloo Bridge, Morozov undoubtedly chose one of the most delicate (seeing that it was possible to choose at the time). His *Waterloo Bridge* shows that Monet's painting was increasingly pervaded by pantheistic tensions, although the initial impulse for the creation of the entire series was the purely impressionistic attempt to capture the varying conditions of weather and light.
From the beginning Morozov's choices proved to be successful. This was true, for example, of the purchase in 1904 of *Portrait of Jeanne Samary* (1877; Pushkin Museum). Morozov often pointed out that he was continuing the work of his brother, in whose collection the full-length portrait of the actress held place of honor. Was this acquisition recommended by Mikhail? The circle of Russian and French artists acquired by Ivan had, in

fact, largely been traced in advance by his elder brother. On the other hand he showed with every new purchase that he was not merely a blind imitator, and not simply because of his love of Sisley, who was not among Mikhail's favorites. Turning to the works of Monet, Degas and Renoir, which dominated in the house on Boulevard Smolensky, Ivan Morozov showed that he had his own ideas. Quite soon his acquisitions were marked, though not always clearly, by an element of rivalry. Later this competition in artistic taste would continue with Sergei Shchukin.

In 1906, the first paintings by Bonnard, *Landscape in the Dauphiné* and *A Corner of Paris* appeared in the house on Prechistenka Street, together with Denis's *Sacred Spring in Guidel*. The three paintings are characterized by a refined use of color, particularly rare in Denis who was not always able to master color. 1906 was also marked for Morozov by his active participation in the Salon d'Automne: as part of the Salon Diaghilev had organized the exhibition "Two Centuries of Russian Art", for which Morozov loaned a series of paintings. At the end of the exhibition he was made an official member of the Salon d'Automne, and awarded the Légion d'honneur.

1907 marked a turning point for the collector. The extensive renovation work on his home was completed, and the Russian canvases which had previously dominated were now to have far less space. Morozov planned to build up a gallery in which modern French painting would be represented no less worthily than in that of Sergei Shchukin. The acquisitions made in 1907 pointed to his plans for the future. Morozov did not concentrate on a single artist or group of artists; his sight was set on the whole range of French painting in the last three decades. From now on he would act on such a scale that he sometimes surpassed Shchukin himself. "A Russian who does not bargain," as Vollard defined him. This, however, does not mean that he acted hastily. "No sooner had he descended from the train," wrote Felix Fénéon, an illustrious critic and art director of the Bernheim-Jeune Gallery, "than he was already in the studio where paintings were sold, sunk in an armchair that was deliberately low so that the collector could not get up until the canvases were passing before him, like episodes in a film. In the evening Monsieur Morozov, who observed the paintings with remarkable attention, was too exhausted even to go to the theater. After a few days spent in this way he returned to Moscow, having seen nothing but paintings; he took a few away with him, and they were carefully chosen."[65]

His success was largely tied to the name of Monet: four canvases, all of them of unquestioned importance: *Boulevard des Capucines, Pond at Montgeron, Corner of a Garden in Montgeron*, and *Haystack in Giverny* (Pushkin Museum). *Boulevard* and *Haystack* had previously belonged to the Faure collection: during the first exhibition of the Impressionists in 1874, one critic had written that Monsieur Faure was the only patron of these artists, since he desired to be original. At their second exhibition Faure owned half Monet's works. The Montgeron canvases were part of another prestigious collection, that of Ernest Hoschedé, who like Faure had been one of the few people to back Monet and his fellow Impressionists at the critical stage of their struggle. Morozov found *Corner of a Garden in Montgeron* in the Durand-Ruel Gallery. At the same time, in Vollard's backrooms he saw a rolled-up canvas of the same dimensions, signed by Monet, for which Vollard was asking a quarter of the price. Morozov realized that the two works were related; they did, in fact, belong to the same series executed for Hoschedé. This was the beginning of a special section in Morozov's collection, formed of remarkable decorative series by French artists.

As a *pendant* to the canvases by Monet on display in Prechistenka Street, Morozov purchased several masterpieces by Renoir: *Bathers in the Seine* (1869), *In the Garden. Under the Trees at the Moulin de la Galette* (1875), both at the Pushkin Museum, and *Young Woman with a Fan*.

In *Young Woman with a Fan*, which depicts one of the artist's favorite models, Angèle, the background is not as complex as *Portrait of the Actress Jeanne Samary*, but it contributes no less to revealing the character of the figure. Here, as always happens in the Impressionists, the use of light shades depends on the inner meaning of the painting. The bright, sunny background is closely linked to youth, to the pure adolescent oval of the girl's face. The melodic rhythm of repetition resounds throughout: in the regular oval, in

Angèle's sloping shoulders, in the outline of the armchair, and finally in the fan that sets the tone of the whole composition. The entire pictorial structure perfectly matches the physiognomy and the character of the dreamy-eyed girl. The painting played an important role in the Impressionist movement, and attracted attention during their seventh exhibition in 1882. Huysmans even preferred it to *Déjeuner des canotiers*, stating that "his *Young Woman with a Fan*, from this year, is delightful, with her bright black eyes".[66]

1907 brought Ivan Morozov his first canvases by Gauguin and Cézanne. Without for the moment showing any preference for one rather than the other, he sought and found their best works. At that time Sergei Shchukin was far ahead, and it seemed impossible to compete with him, especially where Gauguin was concerned. And yet one year later Morozov already owned eight remarkable works by the artist (and in all had collected eleven). He could match Shchukin's "iconostasis" with a group that was equally fine, though less homogeneous.[67] For Morozov's Gauguins are not simply beautiful, but are also marked by an unusual, distinct musicality. After beginning with the magnificent *Matamoe. Landscape with Peacocks* (1892; Pushkin Museum) and the more measured, though no less brilliant *Parau Parau. Conversation*, just a few months later the collector seemed already to have defined the outlines of his group of Gauguins, purchasing *Cafe in Arles* (1888; Pushkin Museum) from the Vollard Gallery, the only work in Russia belonging to the Arles period, and *The Great Buddha* (1899; Pushkin Museum). The following year he brought back *Fatata te Mouà. At the Foot of the Mountain*, one of the most expressive landscapes from the first trip to Tahiti, and *Nave Nave Moe. Delicious Water (Sweet Dreams)*.

Nave Nave Moe, the legend incarnate of the earthly paradise, was in some ways a synthesis of Gauguin's first trip to Tahiti. Painted when he was back in Paris, in terms of symbology the painting is one of the artist's most complex works. The spring is a symbol that belongs to all religions; in the Christian religion it is linked to salvation and to the spiritual life. Lilies, as we know, are the incarnation of purity and of moral integrity, while the apple in the hand of the Tahitian Eve is a symbol of original sin. The Christian ideas, represented by the figures in the foreground, are interpreted in an unusual manner. Situated next to the miraculous spring, Mary and Eve are portrayed in a rather Oriental manner, deep in meditation. At the same time they represent the youth of mankind, in contrast with the women in the background, for whom the time of dreams has already passed: they are chatting to each other, thus indicating the worldly, everyday aspect of life, which accompanies the more elevated, spiritual side. After concentrating, like Shchukin, on Gauguin's Tahitian painting, Morozov endeavored to extend his collection with other sides of the artist's output, such as landscape and genre painting, symbolic compositions and still lifes.

Immediately after Gauguin came the turn of Van Gogh. Their names were already often cited together, and not only because in autumn 1888 they had worked side by side in Arles. This unusual relation was nowhere seen more clearly than in Morozov's collection, where two canvases with the same subject were hung next to each other: Gauguin's *Cafe in Arles* and Van Gogh's *The Night Cafe in the Place Lamartine in Arles* (1888, Yale University Art Gallery, New Haven). Even more important was the fact that both, in going beyond Impressionism, placed the highest value on color. From an emotional point of view, the two artists are poles apart, but they are extremely similar in their desire to take the expressive power of color to its furthest limits. The Van Goghs in the collections of both Morozov and Shchukin are among the artist's greatest masterpieces: those of Morozov, however, are more tightly structured. It is unlikely that he would have bought a painting like Shchukin's *Spectators in the Arena at Arles*.

It is probably significant that the first work by Van Gogh bought by Ivan Morozov, in 1908, was *Thatched Cottages*, which despite the emotional tension typical of Van Gogh, was marked by great structural rigor. Morozov was profoundly struck by the dramatic luminosity of both *Thatched Cottages* and another masterpiece from Auvers, *Landscape with Carriage and Train in the Background* (1890; Pushkin Museum). He was even more moved by *The Night Cafe in the Place Lamartine in Arles*, which was rightly the most famous Van Gogh in his collection. The exhibition organized at the Salon d'Automne in 1907, immediately after the death of Cézanne, is noted for its important effect on the future of French art, and subsequently of European art in general. One of the most attentive visitors was Morozov himself,[68] who purchased his first four Cézannes: *Road in Pontoise* (1875-1877; Pushkin Museum), *Plain at the Foot of Mont Sainte-Victoire* (1878-1879; Pushkin Museum), *Mont Sainte-Victoire* and *Still Life with Drapery*. Less than one year later, on the advice of Maurice Denis, *Girl at the Piano* was also added to the Morozov collection.

Cézanne had originally developed a sort of immunity towards Impressionism, if we understand this artistic method as the capacity to reproduce ephemeral impressions. His youthful work *Girl at the Piano*, with its classically rigorous structure, already shows the qualities that prevented the artist from adhering unconditionally to Impressionism. The accentuated physical quality of the dark, thickly-laid tones and the static character of the whole composition contrast with the style of Monet's *Lady in the Garden*, painted at around the same time. Its "construction" is accompanied by Baroque and Romantic overtones, reflecting both his fondness for Rubens and the fact that the painting has a second title, *The "Tannhäuser" Overture*, which calls Wager to mind.

Road in Pontoise dates to the Impressionist period. The same subject had been painted by Pissarro (*Les Mathurins. Pontoise*, 1875): it is highly likely that Morozov knew the painting, and had thus been able to observe how, in comparison with Pissarro, the artist from Aix-en-Provence depicted nature: he altered the position of the patches of trees, moved the plane of the ground forward, and daringly created a dynamic construction that could not have been expected from Pissarro, despite the fact that Cézanne considered him to be his master. Cézanne's *Road in Pontoise* said more about its maker than about nature, and it was precisely this characteristic that struck Morozov.

Although he never rejected the discoveries of Impressionism with regard to the use of color, Cézanne subsequently entered into conflict with the movement. The purified tones and cold range of *The Banks of the Marne* would have been unthinkable without the revolution brought about by Monet and Pissarro. But the ephemeral, fluctuating, changing qualities of nature that they underlined began to irritate Cézanne, who sought the unchanging, the eternal. In *The Banks of the Marne* he tackles a subject which was particularly suited to the method of the Impressionists: for them, in fact, water with its fleeting reflections had become a true symbol of the general mutability of nature. Cézanne's river, however, cannot be covered in gleaming reflections. It is a mirror. The foliage of his trees does not rustle. Everything becomes still, obeying a supernatural crystalline structure. And this structure, in which the law of the construction of nature is expressed, is propitious to prolonged contemplation. The construction of his mature art derives from nature. One of the artist's main aims is to render the stability of the landscape, despite the changes that affect it.

Cézanne also painted the human figure in the same way. The pose of *The Smoker* is characterized by great stability. The figure is constructed in a solid, durable manner, thus creating the impression that the whole of eternity is contained in his pose. He is similar to a rock that never moves from its place. Nothing could be further from the aim to amuse the viewer than Cézanne's depiction of the man with the pipe. His face cannot be changed by any expression or grimace. Psychologism, as it was understood by Cézanne's contemporaries, had no place in his painting. He does not even define the eyes; only dark eye sockets can be seen. Yet he understands the character of the peasants, the powerful bond between his figures and the land from which they were born. The artist said himself that more than anything else he loved the faces of people who have aged without breaking with their own traditions, but obeying the laws of time. While Renoir had to succumb to the charm of his models in order to portray them successfully (most of them were beautiful young woman), in Cézanne we sense a certain harshness, or rather a fear of being deceived by the senses. This reflects not only the artist's character and his singular religious spirit, but also a deeper, more philosophical approach.

"Cézanne's soul," wrote S. Makovsky, the author of the first essay on the Morozov collection, in which he expressed not only his own views but also those of the collector, "was probably best expressed in the paintings without any content, in the still lifes. By depicting the same fruit and crockery innumerable times, by creating infinite variations on the same theme (apples, pears, or peaches, which form a bright patch of color on the pale blue of the crumpled tablecloth), free of compositional aims, inebriated by the inextinguishable thirst 'to imitate nature', he adhered to it completely; by capturing his simplest forms, he was attempting to capture not so much the concrete, physical reality of nature, but the very structure of its charm."[69] Makovsky was referring in particular to *Still Life with Peaches and Pears* (circa 1890; Pushkin Museum), Ivan Morozov's favorite still life.

The collector's other favorite Cézanne, *Blue Landscape*, was an example of his continuous, persistent obsession. "I remember that during one of my first visits to the gallery," wrote Makovsky, "I was amazed to notice an empty space among the Cézannes hung frame to frame. 'I have left it free for the blue Cézanne (the landscapes of the artist's last period)', Morozov explained, 'I've had my eyes on them for a while now, but I can't make up my mind which to buy.' The space remained empty for over a year, and it is only recently that a new, magnificent 'blue' landscape, chosen from among dozens of others, has taken its place next to the previous acquisitions."[70]

In 1911-1912 Morozov purchased a further six paintings from the Vollard Gallery, making his collection as complete as any in the world. The early masterpieces acquired three or four years earlier (*Girl at the Piano* and *Self-Portrait*) and the subsequent *Mont Sainte-Victoire* were now joined by still life with *Peaches and Pears*, *Bridge on the Marne at Créteil* (circa 1894; Pushkin Museum) and *Portrait of Madame Cézanne in the Conservatory* (1891-1892; The Metropolitan Museum of Art, New York).

Morozov would sometimes take a long time to make up his mind when it came to choosing the works of great artists. His eye had become practiced, but he still felt a certain hesitancy. He needed the advice of an artist friend or a dealer he could trust. This does not mean that he always followed their advice, which he used as a starting point for his dialogue with painting. "When Morozov came to visit Ambroise Vollard," observed Matisse, "he would say: 'I want to see a wonderful Cézanne'. Shchukin, on the other hand, asked to see all the Cézannes on sale, and made his own choice."[71] Both methods were valid, in that they matched the characters of the collectors. For Cézanne, who required particular shrewdness, Shchukin's method may have brought better results. In this case Morozov could trust Vollard: however crafty he was, he would never have risked offering the Russian collector a Cézanne that was anything less than remarkable. At the beginning of the twentieth century, Morozov's group of Cézannes, consisting of eighteen masterpieces, was the finest in the world, although in terms of quantity it was surpassed, for example, by the Parisian collection of Auguste Pellerin. Morozov was rightly proud of this, and when asked which painter he loved most would always answer Cézanne.[72]

While Shchukin's maturity as a collector was marked by the passage from Cézanne, Van Gogh and Gauguin to Matisse, Derain and Picasso, Morozov never lost sight of the Nabis artists, who had remained extraneous to the aspirations of the avant-garde. Contemporaries of the Fauves and the Cubists, for a long time they lacked courage and were marked by a spirit of compromise. Shchukin had been attracted for a while by Maurice Denis, but this was before he had met Matisse. Morozov, on the other hand, remained faithful to the pleiad of the Nabis, and was farsighted enough to realize that the best among them was Pierre Bonnard, whom Shchukin had never really noticed (he had once bought *The Crew*, but had sold it almost immediately). Each of the thirty paintings by Bonnard in Morozov's collection can be counted among his best work.

Morozov, like Bonnard, was convinced that Impressionism was not a closed chapter in the history of art. He instinctively sensed the profound, original manner in which Bonnard used the techniques of Monet, Renoir and Degas. This is especially clear in Bonnard's themes and constructions, which his predecessors had already explored.

When he commissioned two landscapes from Bonnard without imposing a specific subject, Morozov felt great satisfaction at the artist's decision to paint two views of Paris subtly linked one to the other. Here, more than in any other work, the central problem of Bonnard's art emerges: his relationship with Impressionism. In their attention to color and their surprising chromatic refinement, *Morning in Paris* and *Evening in Paris* closely resemble the masterpieces of Monet, Pissarro and Renoir. Like them, Bonnard presents the Parisian streets with all the impartiality of a spectacle that suddenly appears before one's eyes. However, although choosing subjects that lay outside his front door, he does not aim to render his immediate impressions, and did not usually paint them straight away, but only after they had settled in his consciousness and passed through the filter of memory (which was, after all, the memory of a painter). He did not set out to obtain a literal reproduction, so he left only those details of the subject that were dictated by the exigencies of painting: thus each fragment of the work was splendid in both technique and use of color. In the two pieces of Morozov's *pendant* the careful attention to composition is particularly striking: in this Bonnard was closer to Degas than to Monet and Pissarro. He also shunned precision of detail in the depiction of the figures and avoided excessively sharp focus in order to obtain delicate color effects, which we perceive even before we recognize the objects represented by each patch of color.

Bonnard's chromatic orchestrations are not arbitrary. In *Morning in Paris* the blue and pink tones of the sky, and the cold shades in the foreground are caught so exactly that they alone are enough for the viewer to realize what time of day it is, even before seeing the morning bustle of the passers-by and the rag-and-bone cart. However, the functional clarity of these tones does not deprive them of charm: on the contrary, their charm is increased by it. The patches of color do no more than "outline" the objects, they do not belong to them in an indissoluble way. They are quite autonomous, and the beauty of their arrangement is a powerful justification for the autonomy of their existence.

And yet Bonnard's brushstrokes and patches of color are characterized by great expressive precision. Conciseness does not harm, but helps. Take, for example, the dog in *Morning in Paris*: the patch of color outlines only the torso and the tail, yet the movement of the dog is captured with surprising efficacy. Similarly, in the same painting observe the outline of the donkey, which moves its legs heavily yet hurriedly over the slippery road. None of his contemporaries understood the character of animals better than Bonnard. The movements and the gestures of the human figures are rendered with equal precision. The old flower-seller in *Evening in Paris* moves as only an old woman counting every step can move. The children walk in their own special way, with their characteristic mischievous gait.

The details are linked in such a way as to make us feel the rhythm of Parisian life. In *Morning in Paris*, the foreground is occupied by people who have to get up early: the old rag-and-bone man, the girls rushing on their way to work, and the schoolboy who is in no hurry. In *Evening in Paris*, on the other hand, the rhythm of the movement is that of a stroll. *Morning* is set in a square, the crossroads of all kinds of activity, while *Evening* is set in a boulevard. In the former an open space is required, in the latter an enclosed space. For the morning it is important to show the sky getting lighter and the walls of the houses struck by the first rays of the sun, while different details are required when twilight descends.

Bonnard loved the balance between a conventional, abstract and decorative world, and reality in all its absoluteness. To extrapolate details arbitrarily from *The Train and its Trailers (Freight Train)* might lead us to a dead-end. The tree in the bottom right-hand corner is not immediately recognizable as a tree, nor the vineyard in the bottom left as a vineyard. They can only be recognized after we have looked at the painting carefully. All the details are determined by the pictorial tones of the whole; so that conciseness is an indispensable element for Bonnard. Sometimes, of course, though only sometimes, this conciseness can be explained as sensations captured in passing, walking along the country path. We do not immediately notice the curious little girl in the foreground, and this feature is extremely typical of Bonnard's painting: even when he bumps into his characters face to face, he avoids looking straight at them. The whole picture draws us involuntarily into a system of analogies. Either through pictorial meaning, or through some inner meaning, the head of the girl, the patches of the trees, the smoke of the engine and the carriages, the clouds, everything is linked in a single chain. Despite all the conventional rapidity with which the scene is captured, or perhaps as a result of this, the artist makes us feel we are part of what is happening. He does not observe from the outside, but seems to be inside the scene. For this reason, too, the foreground is focused less distinctly than the rest of the painting. Even here, in the panoramic landscape, Bonnard does not abandon his characteristic *intimisme*. In both the Paris scenes and *The Train and its Trailers (Freight Train)*, the characters are depicted in a rather blurred manner. The artist realized that he could not allow himself to plunge fully into reality. His painting never becomes the illusion of a real landscape or a real scene. There is never a metamorphosis similar to that which can be seen in the paintings of the Impressionists, in which a precise point of view, generally far-off, gives a sense of rapidity and almost of nonchalance to the brushstrokes that render the foliage rustling in the wind or the luminous complexion of a woman. However far we distance ourselves from Bonnard's paintings, the sensation of the physical nature of the colors remains. The conventional element is maintained, for it is precisely here that the artist's self is conveyed, his intellect and his sad and joyful smile.

The vagueness of the outlines, the sense of instability given by the material quality of the colors and by the brushstrokes, which cannot be explained either by the vibration of the air or as an attempt to depict the appearance of the object in a reliable manner, are all elements that find meaning within the overall structure of the painting, an autonomous world, full of color. For Bonnard color is more important than light. He has a wonderful ability to render the unique light of the Parisian dusk and the equally unique light of the early morning, and is deeply convinced that color as such is so noble and precious that it cannot be used simply as a support, a means, even in the attempt to reproduce effects of light.

As a result of the crucial role given to color, the problems of the construction of the painting assume even greater importance. Monet and Pissarro could paint the same subject *ad infinitum*, without even changing the point of observation. This method was no longer suitable for Bonnard. No two works, of the two thousand he painted, are entirely similar. The structural foundations of his painting are more hidden than those of his friend Vuillard, but no less firm. From this point of view, we need only observe the two Paris scenes, first separately and then together.

The Train and its Trailers (Freight Train), *Early Spring (Little Fauns)*, *Morning in Paris* and *Evening in Paris* make the artist's faint voice resound, together with the special lyricism and the enchanting mischief that make him unique. With his usual naturalness, in *Early Spring* he includes two little fauns, characters that would be unthinkable in the Impressionists. Notice the curious way the cheeks of the faun playing the pipes puff out! We do not notice the little horned creatures in the corner immediately, but after we have seen them we can no longer remove them from the very real corner of the Ile-de-France, and the delicate landscape itself, devoid of bright tones, is evocative of a musical accompaniment of hushed, silvery notes. By including the fauns in the composition, Bonnard gives them a dual function. A friend and fellow disciple of the Symbolists, he uses their techniques but at the same time makes fun of them. It is impossible to say whether in this case there is more humor or joy at the reawakening of nature. Precisely because the poetic joy is combined with an ironic, though not malevolent smile, the painting of the Parisian environs also becomes a personification of the legendary golden age.

While Sergei Shchukin built up his collection almost in a series of waves, in a crescendo in which each wave surpassed the previous one, Ivan Morozov developed his collection in a more solid, gradual manner, sometimes letting a masterpiece slip through his hands but always ultimately achieving his goal: the creation of an ideal gallery of contemporary painting capable of illustrating the new conceptions of color in European painting.

True, Morozov's caution might now be mocked, but it was part of his character. Building his gallery stone by stone, he not only left an empty space for the "blue Cézanne", but also for Manet, whom he counted among the exponents of modern painting. However, he did not simply want any Manet, and he would not be satisfied even with a Manet of exceptional quality: he wanted one of the artist's best landscapes, in which his links with the Impressionists were clearly visible. For this reason Morozov did not follow Igor Grabar's advice to buy *Portrait of Monsieur Pertuset, Lion-Hunter* (1880-1881, Museu de Arte, São Paulo) from Durand-Ruel. He did not "sit up and take notice" even when faced with *A Bar at the Folies-Bergère*, now at the Courtauld Institute, London. He could have bought the work at the exhibition "One Hundred Years of French Painting" organized in 1912 in St. Petersburg (for which Morozov was a member of the Committee of Honor). However strange it may seem, even the best Russian experts at the time reacted rather coolly to *A Bar*,[73] and this might have influenced Morozov, perhaps the only Russian collector of the time who might have bought the magnificent painting.

Many people knew about Morozov's interests. Maurice Denis and Valentin Serov were involved in the search. Manet's fine landscape *Rue Mosnier Decked with Flags* (1878, formerly in the Mellon collection) was owned by Pellerin, who had decided to sell his paintings by Manet and the Impressionists in order to buy works by Cézanne. Vollard was called to look after the sale, and he immediately wrote to Morozov in Moscow to offer him the landscape. Morozov asked Serov, who was in Paris, to help him. Serov judged the work to be "not of interest". Ivan, who placed too much trust in the opinions of Serov, with whom he had visited several Parisian exhibitions, turned down Vollard's proposal. For the sake of justice, we should point out that not all Serov's advice was so bad. It was on his recommendation that Morozov bought the celebrated *Red Vineyard at Arles* and *Prisoners at Exercise* (now both at the Pushkin Museum) at the Van Gogh exhibition in the Druet Gallery.

To tell the truth, Morozov acted with greater decision when he was faced with the works of young painters rather than the founding fathers of modern art. In 1907 he bought *Bunch of Flowers*, fresh from Matisse's easel, and shortly afterwards *Blue Pitcher and Lemon*, which marked the beginning of Morozov's remarkable collection of still lifes by Matisse. At around the same time he also acquired Vlaminck's *View of the Seine* and Derain's *Nets Hung Out to Dry* (1905; Pushkin Museum). He often bought works of this sort, which did not usually cost very much, at the exhibitions. For example, he acquired Derain's *Road Through the Mountains* at the 1907 Salon des Indépendants for 250 francs. As for Vlaminck's *View of the Seine*, one of his best *fauviste* landscapes, Vollard gave it to him free together with a group of paintings he had bought. Vollard was not famous for his disregard for money, but he had established a special relationship with Morozov, as he had with Sergei Shchukin. For Vollard and Kahnweiler, the collaboration with these collectors was a guarantee of success in their struggle to back the new art. Since the collections in Moscow were turning into fully-fledged museums with a growing reputation, the dealers wanted to make sure that truly great works would become part of them.

Morozov had not been able to attend the 1905 Salon d'Automne, in which one of the works that had caused a particular stir was *Nets Hung Out to Dry*, marking the birth of *fauvisme*. In the next eighteen months, however, he made up for this, turning in particular to Vollard. Puy, Marquet and Valtat, as well as Matisse, Derain and Vlaminck, were excellent representatives of this new movement in French art, whose main feature was a revolutionary freedom in the use of color and brushstroke.

Morozov gathered together a remarkable collection of works by Valtat, who was appreciated by very few people at the time. In both the themes and the colors of his paintings it is easy to see similarities with the Nabis, with whom he was also linked by friendship. Valtat's *A Gathering of Young Women* can be compared to Vuillard's "public gardens", as well as to the "walks in the park" by Denis, Bonnard and Roussel, from the first half of the 1890s. Valtat treated this subject, first explored by the Impressionists, in a markedly decorative manner, boldly neglecting the details that in some way went counter to the flatness of the colors. In a concise manner worthy of Vuillard, he was able to create a decorative complex out of the autumn leaves or the silhouettes of the ladies, whose gentle outlines, repeated several times, gave the composition a solid unity. In the early work *The Boat*, it is already apparent that the problems of color are more important than the recognizability of the details. The figures almost form a single whole with the background. Whatever Valtat depicted, a hill covered in grass and bushes in the background or a boat in the foreground, with every brushstroke he sought to maintain the extreme liveliness of handling and was tempted to use bright, unmixed colors.

His interest in pure color, which emerged very early in his career, helped him to find a style that anticipated *fauvisme*. He had begun to study the expressive possibilities of pure color long before the famous Salon d'Automne of 1905, where the term *fauvisme* was heard for the first time, although in actual fact he never became a member of the movement, but remained rather its prophet. *The Purple Cliffs*, a landscape painted five years earlier, shows this very clearly. The painting was soon acquired by Mikhail Morozov, and had a powerful effect on his brother Ivan. It is executed in large, energetic brushstrokes that convey not only the pulsating force of nature but also the feelings of the artist, who breathes with the same rhythm. Unlike Matisse, Valtat would later cease to push color to its limit, fearing that this would disrupt the integrity of the overall pictorial structure. In works such as *The Gulf of Anthéor* there is less impetus, and more naturalness. Valtat arrived at a sort of *fauviste* neo-Baroque, making all the elements of the composition subordinate to the firm, rather elegant movements of the brush.

Like Sergei Shchukin, Ivan Morozov was a great admirer of Marquet, who exhibited at the original Fauve show but did not share the style of the other participants. It is no surprise that many of his best works were to be found in their collections. Something of a latterday Impressionist, he would paint the same view time and time again, although always altering the composition. He particularly loved the Seine, and usually chose to live in houses close to the banks. In 1908 he moved to Matisse's former atelier in quai Saint-Michel, close to Notre-Dame. He had already painted the celebrated Cathedral, setting up his easel near the parapet. Now, constantly faced with a fine view of the church in the distance, he painted a whole series of landscapes, the best of which was probably *Notre-Dame in the Rain*. Here the cathedral appears as a compact outline whose architectural forms can only just be made out. The most important thing for Marquet, as with Monet and Pissarro, was the colorful, picturesque quality of the Parisian view. However, while Pissarro expressed a wide range of nuances in his city streets, Marquet sought determinacy and conciseness. His depiction of people moving are reduced to a minimum. The human figure is animated by means of two or three brushstrokes, acquiring a gait and almost even an individual character. Marquet, however, did not allow his facility of observation to run away with him. There are far fewer figures in his landscapes than in Pissarro's boulevards and squares. His Paris is no longer the incarnation of perpetual movement, but rather a conglomerate of static rocks that convey both clear certainty and a slight feeling of nostalgia.

A follower of the Impressionists, he filled his paintings with a luminous atmosphere, achieving this, however, in an incomparably simpler manner by means of very few patches of a limited range of tones. In *The Gulf of Naples* the white, the blue and the black are enough to ensure that the painting "breathes" the fresh sea air, surprisingly transparent and luminous. Here it is not a case of atmospheric vibrations. Marquet's nature is clear and calm, and devoid of all prolixity. Only the boats on the expanse of water allow us to perceive how the sequence of planes is constructed, fading into each other in a remarkably tranquil manner. *The Gulf of Naples*, undoubtedly the artist's masterpiece, stands out among his many fine representations of European ports. From the time of his childhood, which he spent in Bordeaux, Marquet visited the port every time he could to admire the play of light on the water and to watch the lighters and the tugs: when he was a painter, he would never miss the chance to visit the ports in the various countries he traveled through, to the point that he was even playfully nicknamed "the port superintendent".

Marquet was equally represented in the collections of both Shchukin and Morozov, but the situation with regard to other twentieth-century artists was different. Shchukin felt superior in this respect, though not always rightly so. It was he who took his younger colleague to the atelier of Matisse, and then to that of Picasso. Although he did not always understand Morozov's hesitancy, he could not fail to respect him. In Paris they would sometimes visit exhibitions together. There was still a certain element of rivalry, but it now played a secondary role: both of them realized that they were serving the same cause. It would be impossible to deny that Morozov was a daring man. How, otherwise, would he have taken an interest at such an early stage in the paintings of the Fauves? It was simply that he was less resolute than Shchukin. Without considerable courage, he would not have been able to collect modern painting. But this daring was backed up by a greater shrewdness, which gave him a certain advantage. Shchukin had no sooner taken one step than he was planning the next. At a certain point he stopped buying Monet, then Gauguin, attracted by the latest trend. Morozov, too, did not mark time. But if he had the chance to fill a gap in his collection of modern "classics", he would not let it slip. For Shchukin, on the other hand, with the passage of time the classics became a page that had been turned forever.

They were very different men,[74] even though they shared the same interest. Lacking Shchukin's passionate nature, Morozov always introduced an element of circumspection and rigor into his choice; he was afraid of excesses and of any kind of vagueness, and preferred searching calmly through Vollard's 'gold-mines' to the wandering temperament of Shchukin, who drove him towards unknown shores. Morozov's method of collecting was based on a precise project, an objective plan that allowed him calmly to string together one masterpiece after another, like pearls on a thread.[75] "Shchukin, who was more expansive, loved to discover an artist and launch him; he was attracted by the element of risk, and satisfied by the astonishment of his innumerable visitors; cautious and moderate, I.A. Morozov did not rush in pursuit of the latest innovative experiments, but tried to offer a clear, complete idea of the age that had just gone by."[76]

"We might put it this way," wrote Abram Efros, one of the most perceptive Russian critics of the first thirty years of the century. "In Shchukin's collection the famous Parisian artists always appeared as if on a stage, in costume and ready to act; in Morozov's collection, on the other hand, they appeared gradually, with greater intimacy and immediacy. As soon as word spread in Paris that a new star was born, Shchukin got hold of everything he could and took it back to Moscow, rejoicing when the neophyte in Paris turned swiftly into a maestro, and his works were already 'at Shchukin's house, in Znamensky Street'. Morozov, on the contrary, looked long and carefully for something of the new artist that only he knew, and eventually made his choice, always introducing a precious 'adjustment'. 'Shchukin is a master with the adjustment of Morozov': this, in my opinion, is the classic formula of Russian collections of modern Western art.

Morozov acted with reserve, just as Shchukin acted with great clamor. The 'representative of fashion' portrayed by Serov, so elegant and refined in the portrait, invisibly surrounded by advisors and counselors, had his own way of appearing at exhibitions with his large, rather clumsy figure, unexpectedly, never at inaugurations or peak times, when all Moscow was there. He went on week-days, alone, unhurried, and began to wander around the empty rooms. People would go and greet him, then leave him alone. And he would look, 'zig-zag fashion', without any visible order or logical system: he did not follow the walls, nor the order of the rooms, but went back and forth in different directions, then retraced his steps, set off towards a different corner. This is how I saw him at the 'Jack of Diamonds' exhibition in 1916…

And then when he bought a painting artists and art lovers would crowd around it, and there was no question: it was clear that Morozov had concluded another good deal."[77]

Shchukin aimed to follow the main path of French painting, which in his view ran from the Impressionists to Cézanne, Van Gogh and Gauguin, and then to Matisse and Picasso. The artists of the Nabis group, who did not belong to the main path, were of little interest to him. Morozov, on the other hand, believed that even the "side roads" could lead to great treasures, and he was consequently able to admire the works of Denis, Bonnard and Roussel. He established particularly close contacts with the first two of these painters.

After his mansion on Prechistenka Street had been renovated, Morozov realized that the new layout of the rooms held new possibilities for unexpected decorative solutions, and believed Denis to be the artist most suited to carry out his plans. After first meeting the painter in the spring of 1906, Morozov went to visit him in the summer of the same year in Saint-Germain-en-Laye, near Paris. On this occasion he reserved the still unfinished *Bacchus and Arianna* and commissioned the *pendant Polyphemus* (1907; Pushkin Museum). One year later he also asked Denis to paint *The Story of Psyche*. Moscow had never seen such a bold, ambitious commission for a private residence. In his old age, when listing his most significant works from memory in his diary, Denis cited the Moscow group and spoke of that period as one "of levity and of formula".[78] The *Story of Psyche* series is not, in fact, devoid of naturalness, although it was the well educated and well practiced naturalness of the Art Nouveau formula, skillfully adapted and accessible to everyone. In the fine architectural setting of Morozov's gallery, where works of applied art, sculpture and painting lay side by side, it was the latter which set the tone, being the prevalent genre. It was not the painting, however, but the two large bronze statues added to his collection some time later that would assume a salient role in the history of Western art.

When Denis introduced Morozov to Aristide Maillol, the collector commissioned four figures for the Psyche room. Maillol worked on the project with great commitment and energy. The first two statues, *Pomona* and *Flora*, ready in plaster in the summer of 1910, were an immediate success. Valentin Serov wrote to the collector from Paris: "Yesterday I saw the two statues that Maillol has executed for you. They are very beautiful, and the one with the fruit is particularly fine, a genuine sculpture, original and perfect."[79]

Maillol became Morozov's favorite sculptor. As well as the four large statues, he possessed seven small bronzes. His collection also included works by Rodin (*Eternal Spring* and *The Kiss*), Guino, Bouchard, Camille Claudel, and Albert Marque, as well as by sculptors from countries other than France. As a whole, however, the sculpture section did not match the painting section. Only the four statues by Maillol could rival the best of the paintings: originally planned by Morozov to be a "complement" to Denis's decorations, they turned out to be the most significant part of the whole *ensemble*.

The success obtained by *The Story of Psyche* among Morozov's guests convinced him to embellish the main staircase of his residence with a decorative panel. This time he turned to Pierre Bonnard. Bonnard did not seem to possess the characteristics of a painter of monumental works, but his great triptych *On the Mediterranean Sea* is one of the high points of monumental decorative painting. The artist had never been to Moscow, and although Morozov showed him a photograph of the staircase, this was not enough to form a good idea of the architectonic context he had been called on to decorate with his gigantic "painting", divided into three parts by two half-columns. It is thus all the more astonishing that the triptych is so successful. The secret of this success, however, is not some special intuitive quality on the part of the artist, but the fact that he had no intention of reducing his painting to the role of a "handmaid" to architecture. The work is so full of natural *bonheur de vivre* that it would be at home in any architectonic setting.

When the enthusiastic Morozov commissioned another two panels in 1912, Bonnard chose his favorite themes of early spring and late autumn: *Early Spring in the Village* and *Autumn. Fruit Harvest* (both now at the Pushkin Museum).[80] These two works thus formed the "brackets" that enclosed the main part, that is the triptych, which is dominated by the summer, and the whole group became a cycle of the seasons. The triptych, resplendent on the main staircase, required a certain depth and illumination. The two new panels, destined for the side walls on the landing of the staircase, were flatter and less bright. The trees, in their decorative richness, recall ancient tapestries.

Morozov had always appreciated painting with markedly decorative qualities. But not every type of decorative painting. He continued to view Matisse's *The Dance* and *Music* as an "excess", although he much admired the artist's work and even intended to commission some decorative canvases. At the beginning of 1913 Sergei Shchukin, probably with a degree of irritation, wrote to Matisse: "Mr. Morozov is still under the strong influence of other artists, who do not understand the latest evolution of your art. He wanted to give you the commission for the decoration of a room, but now under the influence of these gentlemen he has purchased instead a large panel by Bonnard."[81] In this case Shchukin was wrong to attribute the decision to external influence alone. Another factor may well have been Matisse's slowness, for the artist had made Morozov wait too long for a work commissioned previously.

The work in question was *Moroccan Triptych* (1912, Pushkin Museum), which occupied the place of honor among the eleven works by Matisse in Morozov's collection. Morozov had commissioned two landscapes in the spring of 1911. As the end of summer approached, the following letter reached Moscow: "I have been thinking about your landscapes ever since I arrived in Collioure, but I fear I will not be able to paint them this summer. I will most probably work on them in Sicily, where I am planning to spend the winter."[82] One year later another letter arrived: "I am extremely embarrassed to have to tell you that I have not been able to do the two landscapes I promised you, and therefore they will not be at the Salon as I wrote. But tomorrow I am setting off for Morocco, where I hope to paint them."[83] Morozov's commission was evidently one of the reasons that led Matisse to hurry to the parks of Tangiers to paint in the open air. The project gradually changed, eventually leading to the triptych *View from the Window. Tangiers*, *Zora on the Terrace* and *Entrance to the Kasbah*. In the spring of 1913, Matisse wrote to inform Morozov with great satisfaction that the triptych had met with great success at the exhibition of his Moroccan works.

The repeated delays in keeping his promise would be inexplicable if we did not take into account the fact that Matisse had visited the house in Prechistenka Street, and was well aware of the remarkable quality of the collection. He wanted his own painting to be represented in the collection in a worthy manner.

While Matisse and Picasso had very quickly left all the others behind in Shchukin's collection, Morozov consciously avoided such "imbalances". He owned only three works by

Picasso, but each was a masterpiece. The first was *Family of Acrobats*, which Vollard sold to him for the modest sum of 300 francs. At that time Picasso was not among the collector's main interests, but five years later he was to buy two extraordinary works: *The Young Acrobat on a Ball* (1905; Pushkin Museum), the best work from the Rose period, which had previously belonged to Gertrude Stein, and *Portrait of Ambroise Vollard* (1910; Pushkin Museum), a supreme example of Cubism in the art of portrait-painting. In 1913, the final year of his activity as a collector, Morozov managed to fill a few more gaps in his collection. He bought two large decorative compositions by Roussel, Renoir's *Boy with a Riding Whip*, a work from his "countryside" period, which up to that time was not represented in Moscow, Cézanne's first painting, the romantic *In the Rooms* (circa 1870; Pushkin Museum), and canvases by Marquet and Derain. He planned to extend his collection with works by Daumier, Guys, Seurat and Toulouse-Lautrec, but in 1914 he was unable to make his customary autumn trip to Paris, for the First World War had broken out.

The beginning of the war put a stop to the art-collecting activities of Morozov and Shchukin. Both of them were to face hard trials in the future. From February 1917 onwards, the situation in Moscow became increasingly alarming. There was already talk during the summer of anarchic groups forming and of "revolutionary" theft or expropriation. Shchukin joined the Moscow Soviet for problems of art, and then the Board of the Tretyakov Gallery. Unlike the other collectors, he not only had no intention of hiding, but also very much wanted to work. On 3 December the newspaper *Novaya zhin* (New Life) wrote that the famous art collector Sergei Ivanovich Shchukin had put forward a proposal to set up a national gallery, composed mainly of five private collections in Moscow, in one of the Kremlin buildings. It is very likely that this idea had already been developing in his mind before the October Revolution. After the political revolt, the threat of a terrifying general crisis became dramatically clear. The collections had to be saved. But the new Soviet power did not want "bourgeois recommendations", and already had its own plans for the Kremlin. On the other hand, with the slogan "steal what has been stolen" (or, in Lenin's "scientific" formula, "expropriate the expropriators") the authorities gave their blessing to abuses of all kinds. It was soon apparent, in fact, that the "initiative of the popular masses" encouraged from above could quite easily turn into criminal conduct. Having realized their error, the new political rulers soon began to take measures. On 15 February 1918, the Presidium of the Moscow Soviet assigned the recently-established Committee for the Safeguard of Works of Art and Antiquity with the task of drafting urgent inventories of villas and palaces of particular value.

A group of the most famous collectors immediately came to the assistance of the Committee by suggesting that it should acquire their collections, together with the buildings that housed them, as a donation to the Soviet Republic, and appoint the former owners as curators for life. This group was formed of Sergei Shchukin, Dmitry Shchukin, Ivan Morozov, Alexei Morozov, Ilya Ostrouchov, A.A. Bachrushin, and the heirs of L.K. Zubalov. The Committee accepted the donation, and established with the resolution dated 5 March that the collections and the buildings in which they were housed "are under safeguard like all other state deposits of works of art and antiquity".[84]

As we know, however, it is easier to make decisions than to put them into practice. The anarchists occupied the house of Alexei Morozov, formally protected by the resolution together with his remarkable collection. The threat of theft hung over the other houses. During this period acts of theft could take place with the blessing of some arbitrarily established representative of the government, or by "revolutionary" initiatives from below. Ivan Morozov used to tell the story of the visit he received one day from the envoy of a certain territory who had come to "confiscate" a series of paintings, for the sole reason that there were no works by Cézanne or by Derain in that area. It was only with the help of Grabar, who at the time was the director of the Tretyakov Gallery, and above all the right-hand man of comrade Trotskaya, the wife of the celebrated political leader, that he managed to get rid of the unwanted "art lover".[85]

For Shchukin, too, there was some cause for hope. A man appeared in Moscow who might be able to protect him. The historian Mikhail Povrosky, the husband of his cousin Lydia Shchukina and once a persecuted student and then a political emigrant helped financially by Shchukin himself, was appointed deputy to the People's Commissar for Culture Lunacharsky. According to the Bolshevik division of power, museums and collections were the responsibility of this office, but the support of the former member of the social-democratic workers' party did not go so far as to ignore the "principles of social justice". Obeying the general "reorganization", Shchukin was forced to move out of the rooms he occupied together with his family. Yuri Annenkov, who at the time was painting the portraits of all the revolutionary leaders, told of the time when he visited the house of Sergei Shchukin together with Trotsky, a great admirer of Picasso: "Once we popped into the Shchukin Museum, which was a stone's throw from the Revolutionary Military Soviet."[86] The museum had been nationalized, and "Shchukin, who had discovered Picasso and Matisse, Shchukin, who had created a museum of contemporary European painting of inestimable value here in Moscow, this munificent Shchukin had been assigned the servants' quarters, next to the kitchen, in his own house."[87]

Much worse than the discomfort of everyday life, however, was the danger of arrest that loomed over Sergei's head from one moment to the next as an exponent of the bourgeoisie. In 1915 he had got married for the second time, to the pianist N.A. Konjus. Shortly afterwards his last child, Irina, was born. Becoming a father again at such a late age was a cause of great joy, but also of considerable concern.

The nationalization of the various spheres of industry undertaken by the Soviet powers in the summer of 1918 convinced Shchukin that the former factory owners would not be left in peace, and that to stay in Russia was dangerous, all the more so when he himself was arrested for a few days. Later that summer he sent his wife and daughter secretly to Germany. The family jewels hidden inside the little girl's doll would turn out to be very useful in the future, when Shchukin, having heard the news that they had crossed the border safely, followed them illegally with his son. This was the most dangerous journey of the many he had taken. The family left with only what they were wearing: any luggage would have aroused suspicion.[88]

At around this time a new phase in the organization of museums began. In October 1918, Lenin signed the "decree on the registration, inventorying, and protection of works of art and antiquity currently in the possession of private individuals, associations and bodies." It is highly likely that the main target of the decree was Shchukin's gallery: in fact the registration of the gallery began even before the decree, with its "stick and carrot" policy, was published. The fourth comma of the decree read as follows: The possessors of the objects or collections inventoried will be protected in their personal safety and provided with safe-conduct." The eleventh comma, on the other hand, was rather sinister: "Those guilty of failure to comply with this decree will be prosecuted with all the rigor of the revolutionary laws, by means of the confiscation of all their property and of imprisonment."[89]

After the decisions of the People's Commissariat with regard to the nationalization of imperial palaces and monasteries, it was now the turn of private collections. The first to "pass to the people" was Shchukin's gallery. On 5 November 1918, a decree signed by the President of the Board of People's Commissars Vladimir Ulyanov (Lenin) was published in *Izvestiya*: "In consideration of the fact that the Shchukin gallery of art is an extraordinary collection of great European artists, prevalently French, from the end of the nineteenth and the beginning of the twentieth century, and that due to its great artistic value it is of state importance in the education of the people, the Board of People's Commissars decrees that: 1. The art collection of Sergei Ivanovich Shchukin is declared the state property of the Russian Soviet Socialist Federative Republic and is placed under the jurisdiction of the People's Commissariat for Culture under the same conditions as other state museums; 2. The building in which the gallery is situated (8, B. Znamensky Street), with the attached plot of land that constitutes the former property of S.I. Shchukin, with all the inventory, is placed under the jurisdiction and at the disposal of the People's Commissariat for Culture."[90]

A month and a half later, the decree providing for the nationalization in one fell swoop of three remarkable galleries (Ivan Morozov, Alexei Morozov, and Ilya Ostrouchov) already omitted the rhetorical reference to their utility for the education of the people, and read simply: "They are declared the property of the state."[91]

The Shchukin gallery began operation as a state museum (the First Museum of Modern Western Painting) right from November 1918. The transfer, in fact, did not involve any particular difficulties. The pictures stayed where they were, in their original places.

Things were more complicated for the gallery of Ivan Morozov, called the Second Museum, which was only opened to the public at the beginning of May 1919. On 11 April, the College for the problems of museums and the safeguard of monuments notified Morozov that: "B.N. Ternovez is appointed curator of the museum, and you are appointed as his deputy. V.V. Denisov is appointed political commissar."[92] The presence of a new director and a political commissar put Morozov in a clearly unenviable position.

Before the Revolution, the collection occupied both floors of his mansion. After October 1917, the first floor was requisitioned as accommodation for the functionaries of the military district of Moscow, and then gradually occupied by a whole range of bodies: the library fund of the University of Yaroslavl, the literary section of the Main Archive, the A.P. Chekhov Museum, and the nationalized collection of Dmitry Shchukin. The upper floor was also much coveted, of course, in this state of confusion that saw the birth and multiplication of the most improbable institutions, which naturally always required more space. Morozov was drained by this battle and by the general folly. In the summer of 1919 he managed to obtain permission to go abroad for treatment, which he really did need. He settled in Germany, then went on to Paris, and from there to Karlsbad, where he died soon after.

Sergei Shchukin settled in France, but he was not the man he was before, and no longer devoted himself to searching out works of art. When Matisse heard that Shchukin was in Nice, he tried to re-establish their relationship. Having deliberately withdrawn from public life, Shchukin gave way only once, when together with Matisse he went to Cannes to visit Renoir shortly before the artist's death. The artists he had supported in the past had now achieved universal recognition, but however much they tried to keep up friendly relations, he no longer felt on an equal footing with them. Without the wealth he had once enjoyed, he could no longer afford to devote himself to collecting. Some of the gallery-owners would have liked to use his name, and offered him money so that he could buy paintings and thus advertise the artists they were promoting, but he considered this role to be degrading. "S.I. did not agree to this proposal, but said that if he could still afford it he would have collected the works of Raoul Dufy."[93]

Dufy, whom Shchukin had "missed" before the war, managed with remarkable sensibility to capture the atmosphere of post-war European society, the chaotic spirit of the *folle époque*. Shchukin, with his sharp sense of the times, could not remain indifferent, and eventually gave in, buying three canvases by the artist. Having got to know Le Fauconnier, he asked him to paint several works. He also possessed a portrait in pencil of his mother-in-law, drawn by Picasso. This was the extent of his new collection, if it can be defined as such.[94]

Meanwhile in Russia, after the first phase of the reorganization of the museums, further changes took place. In 1923, the collections of Shchukin and Morozov were united. The new museum also included canvases taken from other nationalized collections, which had belonged in the past to M.P. and N.P. Ryabushinsky, S.A. Sherbatov, M.O. Cetlin, etc. In 1925, the paintings by European artists donated to the Tretyakov Gallery by Margarita Kirillovna Morozova were transferred to the State Museum of Modern Western Art in Moscow, while in turn the Russian works in the Morozov collection were housed in the Tretyakov Gallery.

However, the modern Western painting only remained for a short time in Morozov's mansion: shortly afterwards the Museum of Modern Western Art was forced to hand over some of its works to the Hermitage following a number of exchanges between Moscow and St. Petersburg. These exchanges coincided with a tragic period in the history of the museums of the two cities, marked by the secret sale of some of the best works to buyers in the West (kept secret only from the Soviet people, of course),[95] deals which took place mainly in Berlin. In relation to these sales, a number of incidents took place involving the former owners of the nationalized collections. "…It was said that S.I. Shchukin wanted to take legal action to reclaim his collections. I recall that when I asked him whether this was true, he looked very upset. He always suffered from a stutter, but now he tripped over his words even more, saying: 'You know, I did not collect so much for myself, but for my country and my people. Whatever happens in our land, my collections must stay there'."[96]

For a time the emissaries of the "Antiquities Department" who worked for the People's

Commissariat for Foreign Trade and the GPU, the secret police, were no longer interested in the Museum of Modern Western Art. Their attention now turned to the Hermitage, with its celebrated collection of paintings, which was robbed shamelessly of masterpieces by Van Eyck, Raphael, Titian, Perugino, Rubens, Van Dyck, Rembrandt, Hals, Poussin and other great artists. In 1932, however, the turn of the Museum of Modern Western Art came round. The activities of the "Antiquities Department" on the American market had to be cautious and secret. Potential buyers would shun deals that might bring about legal action from the former owners of the nationalized collections and their heirs. At the beginning of 1933, when it became clear that the new President of the United States, Franklin Roosevelt, was in favor of the recognition of the Soviet Union and that America would consequently cease, due to the threat of legal action, to be a convenient place for secret deals, the "Antiquities Department" and the Knoedler Gallery of New York, to which it was secretly linked (in the wings of the gallery was the famous "friend" of Soviet leaders Armand Hammer, who would later become the sole owner), began to act quickly. In April the Director of the Gallery sent a telegram: "Have customer extremely interested Madame Cézanne Cafe Van Gogh Waitress Renoir Green Singer Degas. You can indicate interesting price..."[97] The customer was Stephen Clark. The paintings were sent immediately.[98]

Fortunately for the paintings acquired in different periods by the Russian collectors, the political changes taking place on the world stage led the Soviet government to refrain from further sales. The rise of Hitler deprived the People's Commissariat for Foreign Trade of the possibility of using Germany as a base for the sale of Russia's national patrimony. Stalin and his entourage also finally began to realize that this kind of activity was undermining the country's prestige, and did not in any case bring much profit.

During the 1930s, ever-darkening clouds began to hang over the Museum of Modern Western Art. The official flirtation with avant-garde art, which happened in the period just after the Revolution, was long a thing of the past. There was now a growing tendency to argue that it was harmful to allow the workers to see the paintings in the Museum of Modern Western Art. In an attempt to save the museum, the directors gradually began to make concessions to the dominant ideology, trying to prove that the museum actively propagated the so-called revolutionary art of the West. This art was generally of amateurish level, and its dissemination was nothing but a purely ideological action. It was, however, the very existence of the museum that bothered the comrades at the helm of the nation. If the war had not broken out in 1941, the museum would probably have been closed even before that. As a result of the war, the paintings were evacuated to Siberia. The largest canvases had to be rolled up in great haste (and remained in this state for several years). The museum, meanwhile, was damaged by enemy bombs.

After returning to Moscow, the paintings were housed temporarily in the basement of the Museum of Oriental Arts. The Morozov palace was restored, but the re-opening of the museum was continually postponed. In 1948, when the climate in the country was characterized by ideological campaigns against the formalism, the cosmopolitanism and the servilism of the corrupt West, V.S. Kemenov (former student of the Museum of Modern Western Art and future *éminence grise* of the Academy of Fine Arts of the USSR, highly decorated as a member of the state security forces) wrote articles in which he railed against Picasso with pseudo-scientific arguments. And Alexander Gerasimov, the first president of the brand-new Academy and the author of the endlessly-reproduced painting *Lenin on the Rostrum*, knew no restraint: "If anyone dares to show Picasso, I will hang him." It would certainly have been no problem for him to have someone locked away.

The opening of the Museum of Modern Western Art now depended on Stalin himself, whose wishes were carefully observed by his entourage. At that time the Superintendent for Culture in the Politburo was Marshal Kliment Voroshilov. It was later rumored that he had earned himself a name among the party leaders as a man of great learning due to the enormous library he had built up with confiscated books. It was precisely this inept graduate, who before the war had been involved in the murder of almost the entire corps of generals of the USSR, and had botched several highly important operations during the war, who was awaited expectantly by the museum staff in 1948. They were ordered to reopen the exhibition in the space of a night. N.V. Yavorskaya, the director of the museum's research activity at the time, recalled forty years later: "One of the bosses had guessed we were being cunning and not putting works 'at risk' on display (it seems strange to write these things now, when these works are exhibited in the Hermitage). A phone call… By eleven the next morning Matisse's *Music* and *The Dance* had to be unrolled and hung. I tried with various reasons to convince them that it was impossible to carry out this request: to unroll the panels we needed restorers, and we didn't have any. They sent us some and Matisse's panels were unrolled on the floor. To tell the truth, next to them we placed a large 'realist' canvas by Jean-Paul Laurens, *The Execution of Maximilian*."[99] When the Marshal arrived, Alexander Gerasimov, who accompanied him, "managed to get Voroshilov to visit the exhibition not from the start, as we had planned, but from the end, leading him straight to Matisse's works. Voroshilov looked at them and uttered the sound 'Ah, ah', and everyone joined him, 'ah, ah, ah'. Thirty years have gone by, but that chorus of sneers still resounds in my ears."[100]

The fate of the museum was sealed, although in fact it had already been decided before the visit of the illustrious figure. Morozov's mansion became the seat of the Academy of Fine Arts of the USSR, which celebrated its triumph over the art it hated and from this moment on was to declare war with renewed force against "bourgeois influences". The very fact that it had occupied "the enemy's den" was seen as a symbolic act. "The museums section of the Committee for the problems of art planned to disperse the works in various provincial museums, and even to destroy some of them. Only the best things would be given to the Museum of Fine Arts and to the Hermitage."[101]

The words of the former curator of the museum might have seemed to be the echo of rather unreliable rumors, until a secret government decree signed by Stalin was recently made public. "The Council of Ministers of the Union of Soviet Socialist Republics believes that the collections of the State Museum of Modern Western Art of the city of Moscow consists prevalently of works devoid of ideological content, anti-popular and formalist, from the bourgeois art of Western Europe, which have no progressive educational value for Soviet viewers. The formalist collections belonging to the State Museum of Modern Western Art, acquired in the countries of Western Europe in the late nineteenth and early twentieth centuries have been a breeding-ground of formalist conceptions and of servilism towards the decadent bourgeois culture of the era of imperialism, and have inflicted serious harm on the evolution of Russian and Soviet art. To exhibit the collections of the museum to vast numbers of people is a politically harmful action that contributes to disseminate alien, bourgeois and formalist conceptions in Soviet art.

Moreover, in the art museums of the capitalist countries of Western Europe and America the collections on display include no works not only of contemporary progressive Soviet art, but also by progressive artists of the great Russian Realist school, whose great educational significance is indisputable."[102]

On the basis of this preamble, the Council of Ministers of the USSR decreed that the Museum of Modern Western Art should be closed, after ceding the works of greatest value within fifteen days to the Pushkin Museum and to other museums.

The selection of the "works of greatest value" could have become a catastrophe for many works, declared to be formalist and "anti-popular", in that the Pushkin Museum to which they were destined did not have the premises necessary to house them.

In the meantime the Director of the Hermitage, I.A. Orbeli, and the Director of the Pushkin Museum, Sergei Merkurov, reached an agreement regarding the dividing-up of the Museum of Modern Western Art. The speed with which it was shut down, without any consultation with museum officials, is reflected in the imbalances inherent in the selection, in which even works belonging to the same groups were sometimes split up. It is not difficult to work out the principle that lay behind the carve-up: the Pushkin Museum, on whose territory the process took place, had a much stronger bargaining hand, and used this superior strength to make sure that the oldest works stayed in Moscow. The capital retained not only the paintings of Courbet and Manet, but also the compositions close to the realism of the Salons by Bastien-Lepage and Dagnan-Bouveret. Most of the works of the Impressionists and the Post-Impressionists were assigned to the Pushkin Museum. The division was as follows: Monet, 11 and 4 (the first figure refers to the number of paintings assigned to the Pushkin, the second to the Hermitage); Renoir, 5 and 3; Degas, 4 and 2; Pissarro, 3 and 1; Cézanne, 14 and 7; Van Gogh, 5 and 2; Gauguin, 14 and 8. In some cases, taking account of the works transferred previously from the Museum of Modern Western Art to the Hermitage, the collections in Moscow and

Leningrad were almost equal: for example, both possessed 3 paintings by Sisley, and almost the same number of Gauguins (15 at the Hermitage compared to 14 at the Pushkin Museum, although all the artist's main works went to the latter). Often the Leningrad Museum ended up with fewer works, even when the transfers of the 1930s are taken into account: Monet, 11 to 8; Cézanne, 14 to 11; Signac, 3 to 1; Henri Rousseau, 4 to 3. Things went very differently with regard to the work of Matisse, Derain and Picasso, in which the Pushkin Museum was not particularly interested. The Shchukin collection of Picasso's Cubist paintings was ceded, without the slightest regret, to the Hermitage. The Pushkin Museum had serious problems of capacity, not only in terms of exhibition space but also in terms of storage space.[103] The most difficult thing was obviously to find room for the large-scale canvases, which also involved the risk of being accused of "ideological levity". Orbeli, however, listened to the experts and didn't think twice about accepting for his museum works considered as harmful to socialist realism, which had played a fundamental role in the history of twentieth-century art: Matisse's *The Red Room, The Dance, Music, Family Portrait*, and *Portrait of the Artist's Wife*, Picasso's *Two Sisters, Dance with Shawls, Three Women*, and *Woman with a Fan*, Derain's *Portrait of a Man Reading a Newspaper*, and Bonnard's *On the Mediterranean Sea*.

The 93 paintings moved to the Hermitage in the first half of the 1930s had now been joined by a further 150. Among them were canvases that were already considered classics of twentieth-century painting, perhaps not by the Soviet leaders but certainly by art experts: Monet's *Corner of a Garden in Montgeron* and Renoir's *Portrait of the Actress Jeanne Samary*, Van Gogh's *Memory of the Garden in Etten* and Gauguin's *Women by the Sea (Maternity)*, Cézanne's *Girl at the Piano* and *Fruit*. At this point the Hermitage's collection of French painting from the second half of the nineteenth century and the early twentieth century was such as to allow an evaluation of the main phenomena of the period, in the same way as the museum's collection of ancient masters. In addition to the paintings from the Shchukin and Morozov collections, in 1948 the Hermitage also acquired the works from the 1920s gathered together by the Museum of Modern Western Art: Léger, Lhote, Ozenfant, Survage, Favori, and Alix. In terms of quality these paintings are, of course, far inferior to the best works from the previous periods, but their presence allows us to observe the single line of development of French painting.

Although it had acquired a patrimony of inestimable value, the Hermitage was not able to exhibit any of the works it had received from the Museum of Modern Western Art. For a long time they remained in storage, where a handful of artists and the occasional foreign expert were given special permission to view them. After Zhdanov's cultural pogroms, to exhibit "modern Western" art in public would almost have been the equivalent of suicide. Only after the death of Stalin, in the mid-1950s, did the collection gradually become open to the public. First the Impressionists, then Cézanne, Van Gogh and Gauguin. At the end of the 1950s, many works by Matisse and Picasso were still in storage. At the beginning of the following decade most of the works of "modern painting", now rather aged, were on exhibit in the museum's rooms.[104] From this moment onwards, the great paintings from the collections of Shchukin and Morozov were loaned increasingly frequently to exhibitions abroad. Their life in the Hermitage assumed new significance. In the museum of universal art, side by side with the masterpieces of the past, these works became a link in the uninterrupted chain of world culture.

It would not be true to say that the collection was not expanded after 1948, although it would obviously be unrealistic to expect later additions to be able to rival the group of 150 paintings. The resources of the domestic art market were, and still are terribly limited, especially with regard to contemporary Western art. And where, after all, could we expect such resources to come from in a country of poor people, segregated for decades from the rest of the world by the Iron Curtain? The passion for collecting did not disappear entirely, of course, but it turned mainly towards postage stamps, postcards and badges. The Western paintings that found their way by chance into the hands of collectors could hardly lay the foundations for a reasoned collection, and were either sold or offered to museums. Among the acquisitions of the Hermitage from the 1960s to the 1980s, it is worth mentioning Redon's *Woman with Field Flowers*, the rare early work by Dufy *Portrait of Suzanne, the Artist's Sister*, Vlaminck's *Landscape with a House on a Hill*, and the watercolor-book by Blaise Cendrars and Sonia Delaunay Terk *The Prose of the Trans-Siberian and of Little Jeanne of France.*

Some works were consigned to the Hermitage on the orders of the Ministry of Culture. Thus Léger's *The Postcard* arrived from Moscow: the artist's followers, of Communist faith, had offered it with the best of intentions to Stalin, little knowing that the Soviet leader could not bear expressions of "formalism" of this kind. The painting was diplomatically placed in the Museum of Gifts to Comrade Stalin, which was closed after the death of the "genius of all times and of all peoples".

Perhaps the most important part of the new acquisitions is made up of donations. Marquet's drawing was given by his wife, while the family of Maurice Denis donated the studies for *The Sacred Wood* and the fine preparatory drawing for *The Story of Psyche*. Picasso's extraordinary drawing *Scenes from the Ballet "La Boutique fantasque"* was offered to St. Petersburg by Mikhail Barishnikov.

Of inestimable significance are the donations made by Lydia Delektorskaya, Matisse's secretary and assistant for many years. After the death of the maestro, to whom she was unconditionally devoted, her life was anything but easy. She could have been well-off, instead of earning a living with the occasional translation, if she had agreed to sell the works the artist had given her. She believed, however, that this would have been sacrilege, and preferred to donate the works in her possession to the Hermitage and the Pushkin Museum. Thanks to the two portraits of Lydia Delektoskaya, the museum now has examples from the artist's last phase. The same is true of the sculptures she donated to the museum, the unrivaled collection of book illustrations and the drawings, of remarkable perfection, in which the museum was previously lacking. The 24 drawings by the artist are undoubtedly among the finest in the twentieth century. Thanks to the addition of these works, the Matisse collection is now exceptionally exhaustive.

Other important steps towards the completion of the collection of contemporary art in the Hermitage have been taken in very recent times. Shchukin and Morozov were both remarkably farsighted, but they would not have been able and did not aim to cover the entire artistic panorama. The passing of time underlines the importance of certain works already acquired, but also helps us to understand what is lacking. Where the classics of contemporary art are concerned, filling the gaps is an extremely complex task. The high level of the Hermitage's collections makes it even more demanding with respect to new acquisitions. Unfortunately, works worthy of the Hermitage, which cost relatively little at the time of Shchukin and Morozov, now fetch astronomical prices. Considerable funds are needed. In this sense we should applaud the decision by Boris Yeltsin in 1998 to earmark funds specifically for the completion of the museum's collections. Most of these funds have been used to extend the collection of modern French art, in the attempt to fill a number of unfortunate lacunae.

The first acquisition was Boudin's *Trouville Beach*,[105] a painting that places the artist on a level footing with his disciple Claude Monet. The landscape shows that the painting of the founders of Impressionism had not lost any of its vitality at the end of the century. During his life Boudin painted hundreds of studies of the Normandy coast and of bathers. After studying all the nuances of the seaside landscape over the course of four decades working *en plein air*, he was able to paint the same composition without leaving his studio, all the more so in that his work already had many admirers. However, even if Boudin worked in his studio rather than on the beach, as is clearly the case with *Trouville Beach*, he always created a completely new composition. The range of motifs was rather limited, and he would have risked appearing repetitive if it were not for his characteristic restlessness. Walking along the beaches in Trouville and Deauville that he had studied from one end to the other, he managed even in old age to capture new impressions, and for this reason always found new points of observation and new conditions of the sea and the sky.

Another landscape, Utrillo's *Rue Custine a Montmartre*, is the first example in the museum's collection of the work of this great bard of Paris. The Hermitage is a particularly appropriate home for this view of Paris, as it allows comparison with Pissarro's *Boulevard Montmartre in Paris* – a comparison that highlights the painful fixedness of sad forebodings after the animation that Impressionist spontaneity combined with the ephemeral dazzle of the *belle époque*. After those of Boudin and Utrillo, the museum has acquired canvases by Soutine, Rouault and Dufy. Soutine's *Self-Portrait*, the first work of European Expressionism present in the museum, is also his only work in Russia, which is ironic when we remember that this exponent of the Paris school originated from the Russian empire. Rouault's *Head of Christ*, which joins his youthful watercolors from the collections of Ivan Morozov and N.P. Ryabushinsky, is a fine example of the creative processes of the 1930s, filling at least partially a gap in the collection of French painting. Another important acquisition, Dufy's *Sailing-Boats in the Port of Deauville*, has finally allowed the fulfillment of the "spiritual testimony" of Sergei Shchukin.

The collection of works from later periods is unlikely ever to surpass the exuberance of the art of the late nineteenth and early twentieth centuries, but for the moment this does not sadden us excessively, for the latter was undoubtedly the most flourishing period in the history of French art.

[1] *Enciklopedichesky slovar'. Izd. "Brogkauz i Efron"* (Encyclopedic Dictionary, ed. Brogkauz-Efron), vol. LXXXI, St. Petersburg, 1904, pp. 38-39.

[2] The pre-Revolution Hermitage, comprising the Picture Gallery, the Archaeological Section and the Numismatic Collection, could not be considered a real museum of universal culture. This only became true in the Soviet era, with the addition of new sections and the expansion of the existing ones, when the idea developed to exhibit contemporary works as part of the overall evolution of the various strands of world culture.

[3] P.A. Buryshkin, *Moskva kupecheskaya* (Mercantile Moscow), Moscow 1991, p. 145.

[4] Over the years many objects from his collection have ended up in the Hermitage.

[5] The paintings were subsequently sold by his children, and the collection ceased to exist.

[6] P.B. [P.D. Boborykin], 'Pisma o Moskve', in *Vestnik Evropy*, no. 3, 1881, p. 378.

[7] In 1878 the eldest sons of Ivan Vasilevich, Nikolai, Pyotr and Sergei, became partners of the "I.V. Shchukin & Sons" firm. As a result they now had sufficient funds to buy works of art.

[8] *Shchukinsky muzey za 18 let svoego sushchestvovanya (1892-1910)* (The Shchukin Museum in the eighteen years of its existence, 1892-1910), Moscow, 1910, p. 1.

[9] Perhaps the most valuable objects were the numerous historical documents, above all 46 archives of Russian statesmen (Demidov, Voronzov, Shachovskoy, A.P. Ermolaev, etc.).

[10] With the advent of Soviet rule the Shchukin Museum was closed. The buildings specially designed by Pyotr Ivanovich for the collections, in which the spirit of Ancient Russia prevailed, were given over to the K.A. Timiryazev Museum of Biology, an absurd decision but one which enjoyed influential protection: the museum had, in fact, been created by the Faculty of Biology of the Y.M. Sverdlov Communist University. The objects were deposited in the basement of the Historical Museum, where they are still to be found.

[11] Letter from A.P. Chekhov to O.L. Knipper, 23 January 1902. In *Polnoe sobranie sochneny i pisem* (Complete Works and Letters), Moscow, 1950, p. 230.

[12] *Katalog der Sammlung Iwan Stchoukin*, Paris. *Gemälde alter Meister. Auktion bei Keller und Reiner*, Berlin, 9 April 1907.

[13] Ivan Shchukin possessed several paintings by El Greco, now definitely attributed to the artist by modern critics, in particular the canvas *Repentance of St. Peter* (now in the Phillips Collection, Washington), which undoubtedly belongs among the maestro's best works. Even though in some cases the works were not by the artist himself, but by his circle, this did not justify the use of the term fakes. It would have been difficult to find a well-executed fake at the beginning of the twentieth century, when El Greco had only just been rediscovered after a long period of neglect. Both Ivan Shchukin and Zuloaga would easily have recognized a recent fake.

[14] Y. Tugendhold, *Pervy muzey novoy zapadnoy zhivopisi* (The First Museum of Modern Western Painting), Moscow, 1923, p. 12.

[15] Tugendhold's statement is repeated several times in the bibliography: according to him the first Impressionist painting bought by Shchukin was Monet's *Lilacs at Argenteuil* (1873; Pushkin Museum). "In 1897 F. Botkin, who had been living in Paris for years, drew his attention to the works of Claude Monet in the private Durand-Ruel Gallery. Shchukin immediately bought *Lilacs at Argenteuil*, which was the first work by Monet to set foot in Russia." (Y. Tugendhold, *op. cit.*, p. 13). It is more probable, however, that this painting arrived one year later. Sergei's son, Ivan, mentioned *The Cliffs at Belles-Isles* as the first painting by Monet to have appeared in their house (letter from Ivan Shchukin to A.A. Demskaya, 3 December 1972, Archive of the Pushkin Museum): this corresponds to the information in Wildenstein's catalog, which gives 1898 as the year it was sold (Wildenstein, *Claude Monet*, 1084).

[16] V.V. Perepletchikov, *Dnevnikovye zapisi* (Diary Notes), Moscow, CGALI, 824, inv. 1, doc. 14, f. 170.

[17] Monthly literary supplement of the journal *Niva* (The Crops), January-February 1897.

[18] A.N. Benois, *Moi vospominanya* (My Memories), vol. I, Moscow, 1990, pp. 490-491.

[19] Y. Tugendhold, 'Francuzskoe sobranie S.I. Shchukina' (The French collection of S.I. Shchukin), in *Apollon*, nos. 1-2, 1914, p. 6.

[20] P.P. Muratov, 'Shchukinskaya galereya' (The Shchukin Gallery), in *Russkaya mysl*, no. 8, 1908, p. 129.

[21] 'Matisse parle a Teriade', in *Art News Annual*, no. 21, 1952. Cited in *Henri Matisse. Ecrits et propos sur l'art*, Paris 1972, p. 118.

[22] Y. Tugendhold, *op. cit.*, p. 18.

[23] P.P. Muratov, *op. cit.*, p. 116.

[24] J. Freeman, *The Fauve Landscape*, Los Angeles, 1990, p. 83.

[25] Ibid., p. 92.

[26] G. Charbonnier, *Entretien avec Henri Matisse. Le Monologue du peintre*, vol. II, Paris, 1960, p. 7.

[27] Letter from Matisse to A. Romm, 19 January 1934. Archive of the Pushkin Museum, Dep. 13, coll. 6, no. 127/7.

[28] The gigantic canvases are now displayed much better, in one of the rooms of the Winter Palace, which they were not actually destined for.

[29] B.W. Kean, *French Painters, Russian Collectors. The Merchant Patrons of Modern Art in Pre-Revolutionary Russia*, London, 1994, p. 161.

[30] He kept it in his house in New York, in full view.

[31] A. Barr, 'Russian Diary', in *Defining Modern Art. Selected Writings of Alfred H. Barr, Jr.*, New York, 1986, p. 147.

[32] Letter of 20 December 1910. A. Kostenevich, 'La correspondance de Matisse avec les collectionneurs russes', in A. Kostenevich, N. Semionova, *Matisse et la Russie*, Moscow-Paris, 1993, p. 168.

[33] K.S. Petrov-Vodkin, *Chlynovsk. Prostranstvo Evklida. Samarkandya* (Tardonia. The Space of Euclid. Samarkand), Leningrad, 1970, p. 361.

[34] For example, Pyotr Perzov thought that there were too many paintings by Henri Rousseau and André Derain in the gallery. P. Perzov, *Shchukinskoe sobranie francuzskoy zhivopisi. Muzey novoy zapadnoy zhivopisi* (Shchukin's Collection of French Painting. The Museum of Modern Western Art), Moscow, 1922, p. 86.

[35] F. Olivier, *Picasso et ses amis*, Paris, 1933, p. 118.

[36] Ibid., pp. 118-119.

[37] John Richardson, the author of the latest and most detailed biography of Picasso, claims that the tone of the caricature was due to Picasso's disappointed hopes that the Russian collector would buy his paintings. J. Richardson, *A Life of Picasso, vol. I: 1881-1906*, New York, 1991.

[38] According to Richardson, Shchukin might have met Picasso for the first time in the spring of 1906, at the exhibition by Matisse at the Druel Gallery or at the Salon des Indépendants. His claim that Shchukin, well-informed about the Paris art scene, acquired several paintings from the Rose period or the Blue period in 1906-1907 is, however, unfounded and not based on any known facts. J. Richardson, *op. cit.*, vol. I, p. 392.

[39] W. Rubin, *Picasso and Braque. Pioneering Cubism*, New York, Museum of Modern Art, 1989, p. 363.

[40] N. Preobrazhensky, 'V galeree S.I. Shchukina v Moskve. Mecenaty i kollekcionery' (In the gallery of S.I. Shchukin. Merchants and collectors), in *Almanach Vserossyskogo obshchestva ochrany pamyatnikov istorii i kultury* (Almanac of the Russian Association for the Safeguard of Historical and Cultural Monuments), Moscow, 1995, p. 49.

[41] Y. Tugendhold, *op. cit.*, p. 30.

[42] Y. Tugendhold, *Pervyy muzey novoy zapadnoy zhivopisi* (The First Museum of Western Painting), Moscow-St. Petersburg, 1923, p. 112.

[43] P. Perzov, *op. cit.*, 1922, pp. 92-93. Perzov's reference to Sergei Bulgakov is very characteristic. The paintings by Picasso in Sergei Shchukin's collection were a powerful stimulus for Russian poetic and philosophical thought before and during the First World War. Cf. N. Berdjaev, 'Picasso', in *Sofya*, 1914; G. Chulkov, 'Demony i sovremennost' (Demons and the present-day), in *Apollon*, nos. 1-2, 1914; S.N. Bulgakov, 'Trup krasoty' (The corpse of beauty), in *Russkaya mysl*, no. 8, 1915.

⁴⁴ *Katalog kartin sobraniya S.I. Shchukina* (Catalog of the paintings in the collection of S.I. Shchukin), Moscow, 1913. The catalog was published in two languages and included 225 inventory numbers. In Shchukin's personal copy, conserved in the Archive of the Pushkin Museum, some handwritten notes have been added at the end.
⁴⁵ P. Perzov, *op. cit.*, p. 92.
⁴⁶ B.N. Ternovez, 'Novye postuplenya vo II Muzey novoy zapadnoy zhivopisi v Moskve' (New acquisitions of the II Museum of Modern Western Painting in Moscow), in *Sredi kollekcionerov*, nos. 5-6, 1922, p. 27.
⁴⁷ Archive of the State Historical Museum of Moscow, Dep. 265, doc. 9.
⁴⁸ Ibid.
⁴⁹ There is no precise information on when exactly Mikhail Morozov began to collect paintings.
⁵⁰ P.A. Buryshkin, *op. cit.*, p. 130.
⁵¹ Ibid., p. 97.
⁵² *Dzhentlmen. Polnoe sobranie sochneny kn. A.I. Sumbatova* (The Gentleman. Complete Works of Prince A.I. Sumbatov), vol. III, Moscow, 1901, p. 398.
⁵³ *Konstantin Korovin vspominaet...* (Konstantin Korovin remembers...), Moscow, 1971, p. 604.
⁵⁴ S. Diaghilev, 'M.A. Morozov', in *Mir iskusstva*, no. 9, 1903, p. 141.
⁵⁵ B.N. Ternovez, 'Muzey novogo zapadnogo iskusstva (Morozovskoe otdelenie)' (The Museum of Modern Western Art, Morozov section), in B.N. Ternovez, *Pisma. Dnevniki. Stati* (Letters. Diaries. Articles), Moscow, 1977, p. 107.
⁵⁶ S. Diaghilev, *op. cit.*, p. 141.
⁵⁷ *Konstantin Korovin vspominaet...*, cit., p. 606.
⁵⁸ Letter to Durand-Ruel, March 1881. *Les Archives de l'impressionisme*, ed. Venturi, vol. I, Paris, 1939, p. 115.
⁵⁹ J.-K. Huysmans, *L'Art moderne*, Paris, 1911, pp. 69-70.
⁶⁰ A. Belyj, *Nachalo veka* (Beginning of the Century), Moscow-Leningrad, 1933, pp. 460-462.
⁶¹ The official publications of the Tretyakov Gallery do not usually use the term donation, but testament, which is not correct. Cf. *Gosudarstvennaja Tretyakovskaya galereya. Ocherki istorii. 1856-1917* (The Tretyakov State Gallery. Essay on the History. 1856-1917), Leningrad, 1981, p. 212; *Gosudarstvennaya Tretyakovskaya galereya. Katalog zhvopisi XVIII-nachla XX veka (do 1917 goda)* (The Tretyakov State Gallery. Catalog of painting from the eighteenth to the beginning of the twentieth century, up to 1917), Moscow, 1984.
⁶² After the Revolution he was forced to hand it over to the Tretyakov Gallery.
⁶³ M.K. Morozova, 'Moi vospominanya' (My memories), in *Nashe nasledie*, 1991, p. 97.
⁶⁴ These figures are cited by Ternovez, who was in charge of the nationalization of the Morozov Collection (B.N. Ternovez, *op. cit.*, p. 108). Ivan Morozov mentioned a much higher number of works of Russian art: 430 (F. Fénéon, 'Les Grands collectionneurs. Ivan Morosoff', in *Bulletin de la vie artistique*, 1920, p. 355), but he may also have been counting drawings.
⁶⁵ F. Fénéon, ibid.
⁶⁶ J.-K. Huysmans, *op. cit.*, p. 290.
⁶⁷ Alfred Barr, founder of the Museum of Modern Art of New York, would later visit Moscow to study the collections of both Shchukin and Morozov, even expressing his preference for Morozov's Gauguins. A. Barr, *op. cit.*, p. 116.
⁶⁸ In the Archive of the Pushkin Museum there is a copy of the catalog of this exhibition with handwritten notes added by Ivan Morozov.
⁶⁹ S. Makovsky, 'Francuzskie chudozhniki iz sobranya I.A. Morozova' (French artists in the I.A. Morozov collection), in *Apollon*, nos. 3-4, 1912, p. 11.
⁷⁰ Ibid., pp. 5-6.
⁷¹ 'Matisse parle à Teriade', in *H. Matisse, Ecrits et propos sur l'art*, Paris, 1972, p. 119.
⁷² F. Fénéon, *op. cit.*, p. 356.
⁷³ Even before this exhibition, in an essay on Manet, Tugendhold stated that *A Bar at the Folies Bergère* "was certainly not his most successful painting". Y. Tugendhold, *Francuzskoe iskusstvo i ego predstaviteli* (French art and its exponents), St. Petersburg, 1911, p. 29.
⁷⁴ Marguerite Dutuit, the daughter of Matisse, recalled that Ivan Morozov was a "good man with a rough exterior, sociable and kind", while according to her Shchukin was defined by Matisse as a sharp, refined and very serious man. B.W. Kean, *op. cit.*, p. 102.
⁷⁵ B. Ternovez, *op. cit.*, p. 119.
⁷⁶ B. Ternovez, 'Sobirateli i antikvary proshogo. I.A. Morozov' (Collectors and antique dealers of the past. I.A. Morozov), in *Sredi kollekcionerov*, no. 10, 1921, p. 41.
⁷⁷ A. Efros, 'Chelovek s popravkoy. Pamyati I.A. Morozov' (The man of adjustment. In memory of I.A. Morozov), in *Sredi kollekcionerov*, no. 10, 1921, pp. 3-4.
⁷⁸ M. Denis, *Journal*, vol. III, Paris, 1959, p. 214.
⁷⁹ Letter from Valentin Serov, 12 July 1910. Cited in B. Ternovez, *Pisma. Dnevniki. Staty*, cit., pp. 106-107.
⁸⁰ The commission of new panels from Bonnard took place through Fénéon, who brought Ivan Morozov a letter from the artist expressing his pleasure at the fact that the collector had liked the triptych. He also asked for a photo, even a small photo, showing how the work was displayed so that he could work on the next two parts. There was a slight delay due to the fact that Bonnard did not want to give in and had asked for 25,000 francs for the two panels, as for the triptych *On the Mediterranean Sea*. Morozov finally agreed to the artist's demands. Bonnard's letters to Fénéon and Morozov are conserved in the Archive of the Pushkin Museum.
⁸¹ Letter from Sergei Shchukin to Matisse, 10 January 1913. A. Kostenevich, *op. cit.*, p. 173. The panel to which Shchukin was referring was *Summer. Dance* (1912; Pushkin Museum).
⁸² Letter from Matisse to Ivan Morozov, 19 September 1911. A. Kostenevich, *op. cit.*, p. 181.
⁸³ Letter from Matisse to Ivan Morozov, 29 September 1912. A. Kostenevich, *op. cit.*, p. 182.
⁸⁴ Ju. N. Zhukov, *Sochranennye revoljuciey. Ochrana pamyatnikov istorii i kultury v Moskve v 1917-1921* (Conserved by the revolution. The conservation of historical and cultural monuments in Moscow from 1917 to1921), Moscow, 1985, p. 67.
⁸⁵ F. Fénéon, *op. cit.*, p. 357.
⁸⁶ Its location close to the Revolutionary Military Soviet turned out to be fatal for Shchukin's mansion. The Revolutionary Military Soviet was replaced by the People's Commissariat and then by the Ministry of Defense, which took over the surrounding area, constructing ugly buildings for the high command and the Military Academy. Fortunately, Shchukin's mansion was not demolished, but renovated according to the requirements of the Ministry. Entrance is still strictly prohibited..
⁸⁷ Ju. Annenkov, *Dnevnik moich vstrecû* (Diary of my meetings), vol. II, Leningrad, 1991, p. 275.
⁸⁸ Before leaving Sergei Shchukin probably entrusted a friend with all his papers, in particular his correspondence with dealers and artists. Judging by his letters, conserved in the Matisse archives in Paris, he must have had many letters from the artist. The innumerable attempts to find Shchukin's archives have been unsuccessful. We can only suppose that the person to whom he entrusted his papers destroyed them during the years of mass repression. To keep correspondence belonging to a "White emigrant", especially since much of it was written in foreign languages, would have meant risking death.
⁸⁹ *Dekrety Sovetskoy vlasti* (Decrees of the Soviet Government), vol. III, Moscow, 1964, pp. 399-400.
⁹⁰ Ibid., vol. III, p. 460.
⁹¹ *Dekrety Sovetskoy vlasti* (Decrees of the Soviet Government), vol. IV, Moscow, 1968, p. 240.
⁹² Central State Archive of the USSR, Dep. 2306, inv. 28, un. cons. 84, f. 2. It is not clear who this Denisov, charged with supervising Ternovez and Morozov, was. He probably belonged to the Cheka, the secret police of the Bolshevik regime.
⁹³ P.A. Buryshkin, *op. cit.*, p. 148. Shchukin's opinion probably ensured that the Bernheim-Jeune Gallery, which had asked Shchukin to collaborate with it, stipulated a contract with Dufy in 1920.
⁹⁴ Dufy's paintings and Picasso's drawing were later sold by Shchukin's daughter, while the paintings by Le Fauconnier are still owned by the grandson of the collector, André-Marc Deloque-Fourcaud. These four solitary portraits of women

[94] had a profound significance in the eyes of Sergei Shchukin, who saw in them the personification of members of his own family.

[95] The sales of works of art began in 1928, two years after the appointment as People's Commissar for Foreign Trade of A.I. Mikojan, who played a particularly damaging role in the selling-off of Russia's art treasures. The so-called "Antiquities Department" was created, an organization assigned with the task of selling works from state museums abroad. It soon became clear that the most convenient base for these operations was Germany, which had recognized the Soviet government, and therefore its nationalization of private collections, on the basis of the Rapallo treaty. While the first auctions in 1928 involved works of varying quality, their artistic value subsequently grew constantly. The Hermitage and the noble residences in Leningrad and its environs suffered particularly badly from these sales.

[96] P.A. Buryshkin, *op. cit.*, p. 148.

[97] R.C. Williams, *Russian Art and American Money. 1900-1940*, Cambridge, Mass.-London, 1980, p. 34.

[98] The group of paintings in the Museum of Modern Western Art acquired by Clark included *Madame Cézanne in a Red Dress*, which had belonged to Ivan Morozov, Renoir's *A Waitress at Duval's Restaurant* from the collection of S.A. Shcherbatov, *Singer in Green* from the collection of M.P. Ryabushinsky (all now at the Metropolitan Museum of New York), and Van Gogh's *The Night Cafe in the Place Lamartine in Arles* from the collection of Ivan Morozov (now at the Art Gallery, Yale University).

[99] N.V. Javorskaya, Rasskaz ochevidca o tom, kak byl zakryt Muzey novogo zapadnogo iskusstva (Eye-witness account of how the Museum of Modern Western Art was closed), in *Dekorativnoe iskusstvo SSSR*, no. 7, 1988, p. 13.

[100] Ibid.

[101] Ibid. From the zealous officials of the Committee even the destruction of works of art could be expected, as the Nazis had done with the works of "degenerate art" that remained unsold at the auction in Lucerne in 1939.

[102] Decree of the Council of Ministers of the USSR no. 672, of 6 March 1948. State Archive of the Russian Federation, R-5446, inv. 1, doc. 327. Published in the article by M. Aksenenko, 'Kak zakryvali Sezanna i Matissa' (How Cézanne and Matisse were put under lock and key), in *Mir muzeya*, nos. 6-7 (November-December), 1998, pp. 47-48.

[103] The deposits of the museum were overflowing. For the dictator's seventieth birthday an absurdly pompous exhibition of gifts to Stalin was organized. For years the museum remained cluttered with these pieces, which meant that the works of the old masters that were part of the permanent exhibition had to be stored in the deposits. The deposits of the Pushkin Museum also housed the entire Dresden Picture Gallery, brought from Germany in 1945. The problem of its return had still not been addressed.

[104] At the end of 1962, however, the Hermitage came under renewed pressure from the Presidium of the Academy of Fine Arts, directed by Vladimir Serov, who tried once again to "cut" the exhibition by excluding the boldest works by Matisse and Picasso. During the discussion about the exhibition, conducted in the usual bitter spirit, Serov only gave way in the face of the calm resistance put up by the curator of nineteenth- and twentieth-century European painting, A.N. Izergina, who read out the decree for the nationalization of the Shchukin collection, at that time forgotten and now rediscovered in the archive ("due to its high artistic value it is of state importance for the education of the people"). Serov shouted: "Who wrote this nonsense?", and when he heard the reply: "Signed by Ulyanov (Lenin)", he was forced to give in, though without hiding his great annoyance.

[105] The need to acquire the landscape by Boudin was also dictated by the fact that the authenticity of the only painting by Boudin at the Hermitage, *On the Beach*, purchased from the collection of the artist Natan Altman in 1968, is now seriously in doubt. The museum is trying to make sure that such mistakes are avoided, calling on the analysis of art critics and on technical examinations, and also ensuring that the provenance of works is reliably documented.

Illustrations

1
Claude Monet
Dame dans le jardin, 1867
Lady in the Garden

2
Claude Monet
L'étang à Montgeron, 1876
The Pond at Montgeron

3
Claude Monet
Waterloo bridge.
Effet de brouillard, 1903
Waterloo Bridge.
Sun Breaking Through the Fog

> Impressionism is Monet himself, isolated in his genius, glorious thaumaturge
>
> *Rémy de Gormont*

> Only one thing is true:
> doing immediately
> what is seen.
> I hate everything
> that is useless.
> The rules
> of painting
> have ruined us.
> How can we
> get rid of them?

M

Edouard Manet

4
Edouard Manet
*Portrait de M.me
Jules Guillemet*, circa 1880
*Portrait of M.me
Jules Guillemet*

5
Auguste Renoir
*Portrait de M.lle
Jeanne Samary,* 1878
*Portrait of the Actress
Jeanne Samary*

Auguste Renoir
Jeune femme à l'éventail,
1880
Young Woman with a Fan

What he has painted is still before our eyes: he has recorded existence in images that will certainly be remembered as being among the most alive and harmonious

R

Edmond Renoir

D They call me the painter of ballerinas, they don't understand that for me the ballerina has been a pretext for painting beautiful fabrics and rendering movement

Edgar Degas

7
Edgar Degas
Danseuse assise ajustant les souliers, 1875-1876
Seated Ballerina Adjusting Her Shoes

8
Camille Pissarro
Boulevard Montmartre.
Soleil après-midi, 1897
Boulevard Montmartre.
Afternoon Sun

9
Alfred Sisley
Villeneuve-la-Garenne, 1872
The Town of Villeneuve-la-Garenne on the Seine

10
Alfred Sisley
*La berge de la rivière
à Saint-Mammes*, 1884
*The River Bank
at Saint-Mammes*

11
Eugène Boudin
Plage de Trouville, 1893
Trouville Beach

12
Paul Cézanne
Jeune fille au piano.
L'ouverture de "Tannhäuser",
circa 1869
Girl at the Piano.
The "Tannhäuser" Ouverture

13
Paul Cézanne
Fruits, 1879-1880
Fruit

14
Paul Cézanne
Les bords de la Marne,
1888
The Banks of the Marne

R and realist. The nudity

Of all contemporary artists Cézanne is perhaps the most precise and realist. The intermittent romanticism of his style is a splendid garment in which he clothes the nudity of his impressions

Joseph Ravaison

15
Paul Cézanne
Le fumeur, circa 1890-1892
The Smoker

> When I talked with him about the Impressionists, I realized that, out of friendship, he didn't want to speak badly of them... but he considered that experience outmoded

Emile Bernard

16
Paul Gauguin
Fatata te Mouà.
Au pied de la montagne,
1892
Fatata te Mouà.
At the Foot of the Mountain

"In painting one must seek suggestion rather than description"

Paul Gauguin

17
Paul Gauguin
Nave Nave Moe.
Eau délicieuse
(Douces rêveries), 1894
Nave Nave Moe.
Delicious Water
(Sweet Dreams)

18
Paul Gauguin
*Femmes au bord de la mer
(Maternité)*, 1892
*Women by the Sea
(Maternity)*

19
Paul Gauguin
Te Avae No Maria.
Le mois de Marie, 1899
Te Avae No Maria.
The Month of Mary

20
Paul Gauguin
*Trois femmes tahitiennes
sur fond jaune*, 1899
*Three Tahitian Women
on a Yellow Ground*

21
Paul Gauguin
Les tournesols, 1901
Sunflowers

Odilon Redon

22
Odilon Redon
*Femme étendue
sous un arbre,* 1900-1901
Woman Lying Under a Tree

But it is always
the conflict
between the cold shade
and the sun,
the flashes and effects
of light,
which
wishes to
condense in a
syntheses of color

Maurice Denis

23
Henri Edmond Cross (Delacroix)
Eglise Santa Maria degli Angeli près d'Assise, 1909
The Church of Santa Maria degli Angeli near Assisi

24
Georges Manzana-Pissarro
Zèbres s'abreuvant,
circa 1906
Zebras at the Watering Hole

25
**Henri Rousseau
(Le Douanier)**
*Combat du tigre
et du taureau. Un bois
tropical*, circa 1908-1909
Fight Between Tiger and
Bull. In the Tropical Forest

26
Henri Rousseau
(Le Douanier)
*Vue des fortifications
à gauche de Vanves*, 1909
*View of the Fortifications
at Vanves*

27
Henri Rousseau
(Le Douanier)
*Jardin du Luxembourg.
Monument de Chopin,* 1909
*Luxembourg Gardens.
Monument to Chopin*

28
Maurice Denis
La visitation, 1894
Mary's Visit to Elizabeth

29a
Maurice Denis
Marthe et Marie
(première version, verso
du tableau suivant), 1896
Martha and Mary
(first version, back
of following painting)

29b
Maurice Denis
Marthe et Marie, 1896
(deuxième version)
Martha and Mary
(second version)

The depth of our emotion comes from lines and colors that are self-explanatory and simply beautiful, of a divine beauty.

Maurice Denis

30
Maurice Denis
Fontaine de pèlerinage en Guidel, circa 1905
Sacred Spring in Guidel

31
Edouard Vuillard
Intérieur, 1899
Interior

32
Edouard Vuillard
Enfants, 1909
Children

33
Pierre Bonnard
Premier printemps
(Les petits faunes), 1909
Early Spring (Little Fauns)

34
Pierre Bonnard
Le train et les chalands,
1909
*The Train and Its Trailers
(Freight Train)*

"Through seduction or the prime idea the painter attains the universal. Seduction determines the choice of subject and corresponds precisely to painting."

Pierre Bonnard

35
Pierre Bonnard
Le matin à Paris, 1911
Morning in Paris

36
Pierre Bonnard
Le soir à Paris, 1911
Evening in Paris

37
Ker Xavier Roussel
Sujet mythologique,
circa 1903
Mythological Scene

38
Félix Vallotton
Une dame au piano, 1904
A Lady at the Piano

39
Félix Vallotton
Jeune femme au chapeau noir, 1908
Young Woman with a Black Hat

40
Félix Vallotton
Portrait de Georges E. Haasen
Portrait of Georges E. Haasen

41
Louis Valtat
Une réunion de jeunes femmes, circa 1898
A Gathering of Young Women

42
Louis Valtat
La barque, 1899
The Boat

43
Louis Valtat
Les falaises violettes, 1900
The Purple Cliffs

44
Louis Valtat
Le golfe d'Anthéor,
circa 1906-1907
The Gulf of Anthéor

45
Albert Marquet
*Vue de la Seine
et le monument de Henri IV,
circa 1906
View of the Seine and
the Monument to Henri IV*

Albert Marquet
Le port de Hambourg, 1909
The Port of Hamburg

47
Albert Marquet
Naples, 1909
The Gulf of Naples

48
Albert Marquet
Notre-Dame sous la pluie,
1910
Notre-Dame in the Rain

A skilled painter possessed by a somewhat literary sensibility and in love moves in sure, measured-but-fast descending vulgarity

Guillaume Apollinaire

49
Albert Marquet
Vue aux environs de Rouen, 1927
View in the Environs of Rouen

50
Henri Manguin
Paysage à Saint-Tropez,
1905
Landscape at Saint-Tropez

51
Henri Manguin
Matin (Au bord du golfe de Cavalière), 1906
Morning (On the Shore of the Gulf of Cavalière)

52
Maurice de Vlaminck
Une vue de la Seine,
circa 1906
A View of the Seine

53
Maurice de Vlaminck
Bourg, circa 1908-1909
Market Town

C The street with its gray houses, the stalls, the gleaming sidewalks and everyday things always the same; a wandering, roving heart since his bohemian days

Francis Carco

54
Maurice Utrillo
Rue Custine à Montmartre,
1909-1910
Rue Custine in Montmartre

55
Kees Van Dongen
Printemps, 1908
Spring

> He soaked up the life of Montmartre. He has maintained his realistic, somewhat coarse aspect, which is still found in some of his portraits
>
> — Fernande Olivier

56
Kees Van Dongen
Lucie et son danseur, 1911
Lucie and Her Dancer

57
Georges Rouault
Filles, 1907
Girls

R

I am not addressing those who claim painting has nothing more to say: everything remains to be said in the field of form and color through the infinite nuances of sensibility

Georges Rouault

58a
Georges Rouault
Le printemps, 1911
Spring

58b
Georges Rouault
Esquisse de vase
(verso de *Le printemps*),
circa 1910-1911
Sketch of Vase
(back of *Spring*)

59
André Derain
Le bois, 1912
The Wood

D

Unlike the generations who have preceded us, we must tend toward calm. Calm is certainty. Thus beauty will be an aspiration to calm.

André Derain

60
André Derain
Table et chaises, 1912
Table and Chairs

61
André Derain
Nature morte, circa 1913
*Still Life. Basket with
Bread, Jug and a Glass
of Red Wine*

62
André Derain
Portrait d'une jeune fille en noir, 1913-1914
Portrait of a Young Girl in Black

63
Henri Matisse
Jeu de boules, 1908
Game of Bowls

64
Henri Matisse
*La chambre rouge
(Harmonie rouge)*, 1908
The Red Room
(Harmony in Red)

65
Henri Matisse
La nymphe et le satyre,
1908-1909
The Nymph and the Satyr

66
Henri Matisse
*Fruits, fleurs, panneau
"La Danse"*, 1909
*Fruit, Flowers, Panel
"The Dance"*

67
Henri Matisse
Statuette rose et pot d'étain sur commode rouge, 1908
Pink Statuette and Pewter Tankard on Red Chest of Drawers

68
Henri Matisse
Jeune fille aux tulipes, 1910
Girl with Tulips

69
Henri Matisse
La Danse, 1910
The Dance

I love dance. Dance is an extraordinary thing: it is life and rhythm. It is easy to live with dance

Henri Matisse

193

70
Henri Matisse
Nature morte d'Espagne,
1910
Spanish Still Life

71
Henri Matisse
Nature morte de Séville,
1910
Sevillian Still Life

The work is the emanation, the projection of ourselves. My drawings and canvases are a part of me. The whole is Henri Matisse

Henri Matisse

72
Henri Matisse
Portrait de la femme de l'artiste, 1913
Portrait of the Artist's Wife

73
Henri Matisse
Etude de modèle, 1934
Study of a Model

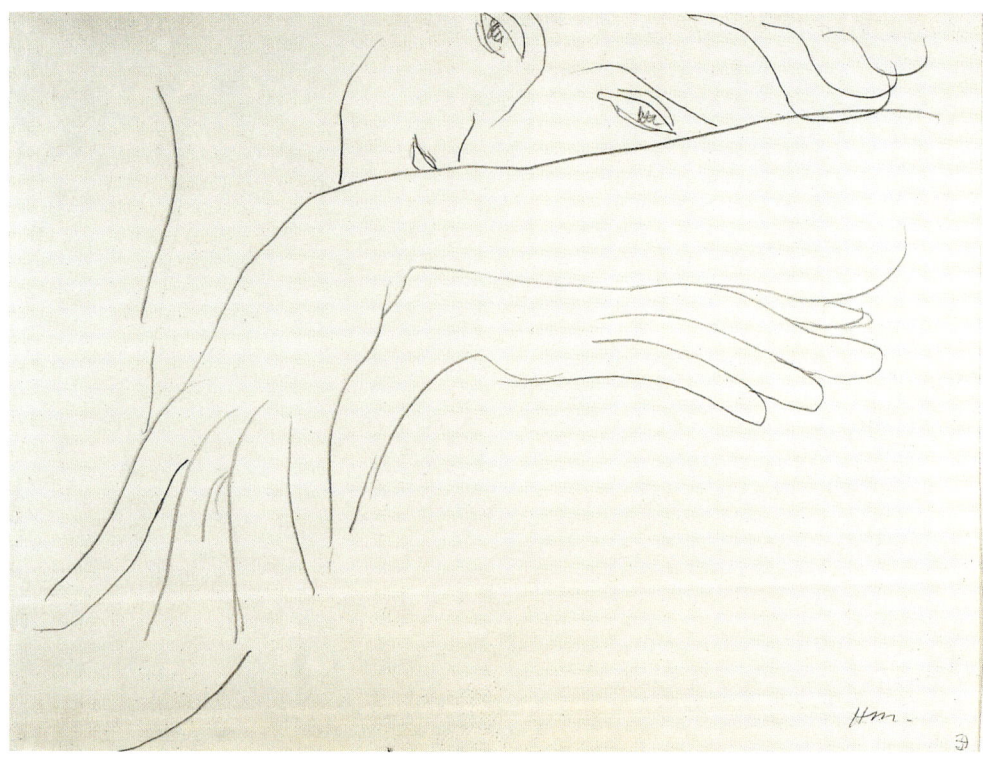

74
Henri Matisse
Nu couché, 1935
Reclining Nude
(The Artist and the Model)

75
Henri Matisse
Portrait de jeune femme,
1935
Portrait of a Young Woman

76
Henri Matisse
Portrait de femme en capuchon, 1939
Portrait of a Woman with a Hood

77
Henri Matisse
Nature morte. La cruche et les pommes, 1940
Still Life. Pitcher and Apples

78
Henri Matisse
*Profil de femme
(Portrait de Lydia
Delektorskaya)*, 1942
*Profile of a Woman
(Portrait of Lydia
Delektorskaya)*

79
Henri Matisse
Jeune femme aux seins nus,
1948
*Young Woman
with Bare Breasts*

80
Henri Matisse
Tête de femme, 1948
Head of a Woman

81
Henri Matisse
Face de femme, 1935
Woman's Face

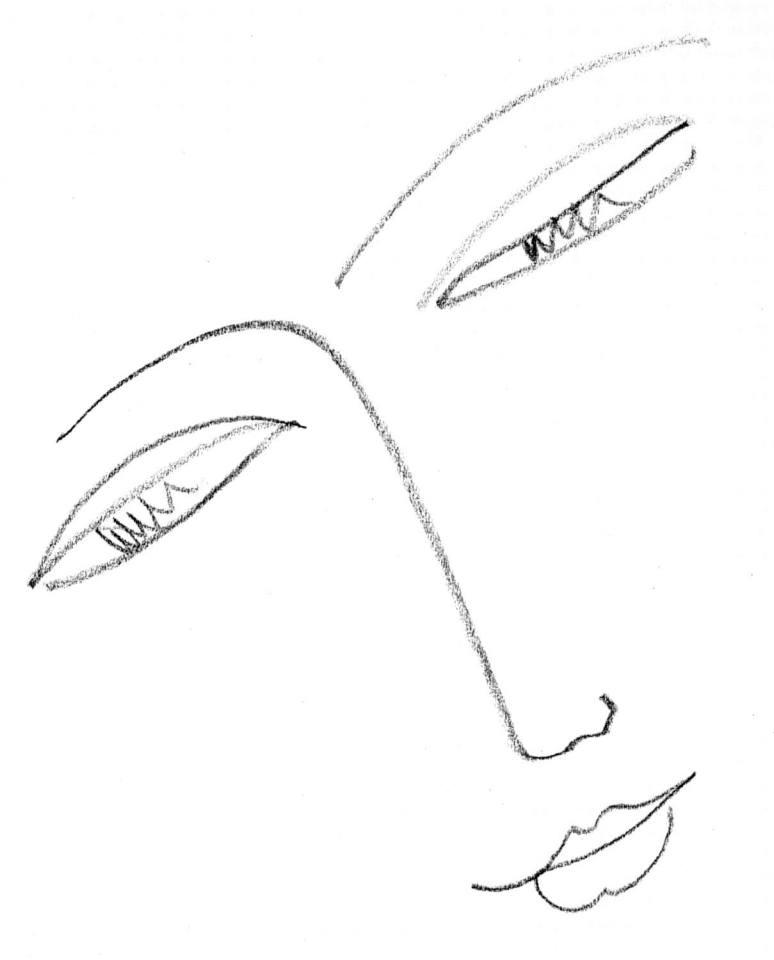

82
Henri Matisse
Tête de femme, 1935
Head of a Woman

83a
Pablo Picasso
La buveuse d'absinthe, 1901
The Absinthe Drinker

83b
Pablo Picasso
Verso de *La buveuse d'absinthe*
Back of *The Absinthe Drinker*

The blue period was not a problem of light or color. It was an inner need that drove me to paint in that way

Pablo Picasso

84
Pablo Picasso
Portrait de Benet Soler,
1903
Portrait of Benet Soler

85a
Pablo Picasso
Garçon au chien, 1905
Boy with a Dog

85b
Pablo Picasso
Deux figures et tête d'homme en profil
(verso de *Garçon au chien*),
1904-1905
Study of Two Figures and Man's Head in Profile
(back of *Boy with a Dog*)

86a
Pablo Picasso
Garçon nu, 1906
Nude Boy

86b
Pablo Picasso
Femme couchée et garçon nu
(verso de *Garçon nu*),
1904-1905
Reclining Woman and Nude Boy (back of *Nude Boy*)

87
Pablo Picasso
Composition avec tête de mort, 1908
Composition with a Skull

> We had to make a break to create a revolution and start again from scratch. I forced myself to approach the new movement. Now the problem is to go beyond the object and give plastic expression to the result.

Pablo Picasso

88
Pablo Picasso
Femme assise, 1908
Seated Woman

89
Pablo Picasso
Femme à l'éventail,
1907-1908
Woman with a Fan

90
Pablo Picasso
Maisonnette dans un jardin,
1908
Cottage in a Garden

91
Pablo Picasso
Vase avec fruits, 1909
Vase with Fruit

92
Pablo Picasso
L'homme aux bras croisés,
1909
Man with Arms Folded

Cubism is neither seed nor fetus, but an art concerned mainly with forms, and when a form is created, it lives its own life.

Pablo Picasso

93
Pablo Picasso
La briqueterie à Tortosa,
1909
The Brick Factory at Tortosa

94
Pablo Picasso
Violon et guitare,
circa 1912-1913
Violin and Guitar

> Painting is stronger than me, it makes me do everything it wants
>
> Pablo Picasso

95
Pablo Picasso
Composition. Compotier et poire coupée, 1914
Composition.
Fruit Dish and Cut Pear

96
Pablo Picasso
Vase à fruits et grappe de raisin, 1914
Vase with Fruit and Grapes

97
Pablo Picasso
Scènes du ballet
"La Boutique fantasque",
1919
Scenes from the Ballet
"La Boutique fantasque"

From my early works on, I sought to achieve the maximum intensity of color. My spiritual masters were Van Gogh for intensity and Gauguin for his research into colored surfaces

Sonia Delaunay

98
Sonia Delaunay Terk,
Blaise Cendrars
*La prose du transsibérien
et de la petite Jehanne
de France*, 1913
*The Prose of the
Trans-Siberian and
of Little Jeanne of France*

99
Fernand Léger
Violon et guitare, 1924
Violin and Guitar

Plastic creation, the painting, consists in harmonious relations between volumes, lines, colors. These three forces must support the painting

Fernand Léger

100
Fernand Léger
La Carte postale,
1932-1948
The Postcard

Descriptions of the Works

by
Albert Kostenevich
Asya Kantor-Gukovskaya

Note
Albert Kostenevich wrote the descriptive texts on the paintings, Asya Kantor-Gukovskaya wrote the descriptive texts on the graphic works

Abbreviazioni
GMII: *Gosudarstvennyj muzej izobrazitel'nych iskusstv umeni A.S. Puškina* (State Pushkin Museum of Fine Arts, Moscow)
GMNZI: *Gosudarstvennyj muzej novogo zapadnogo iskusstva* (State Museum of Modern Western Art, Moscow)

Claude Monet
1840-1926

1. *Dame dans le jardin*, 1867
Lady in the Garden
Oil on canvas, 32½ × 40 in.
Signed bottom left:
"Claude Monet"
Inv. no. 6505

Provenance: acquired from the GMNZI in 1930.
Formerly: Lecadre Collection, Sainte-Adresse; from 1880 Mennier Collection, Sainte-Adresse; Lebas Collection, Paris; from 1893 Galerie Durand-Ruel, Paris; from 1899 P.I. Shchukin Collection; from 1918 GMNZI

This picture was painted in the garden of the artist's aunt at Sainte-Adresse near Le Havre. This is confirmed by the Galerie Durand-Ruel card on the back of the canvas (bearing the title *Paysage de Sainte-Adresse*) and by the owner of the garden's great grandson and the grandson of the "lady", Jeanne-Marguerite Lecadre, wife of Monet's cousin.
On 25 June 1867 the artist wrote to Bazille: "I have been staying with my family for two weeks, I am happy and could not be better. They are all very good to me and go into ecstasy over every brushstroke. I am up to my eyes in work, I am working on about twenty canvases, marvelous seascapes, figures and gardens, everything in other words. (D. Wildenstein, *Claude Monet*, vol. I, Lausanne-Paris, 1974, p. 424, letter 33). One of these twenty paintings was definitely *Lady in the Garden*, another *Garden in Flower* (*Jardin en fleur*; Musée d'Orsay, Paris), which shows part of the same garden adjacent to the house. The most important work in the group is *Terrace at Sainte-Adresse* (Metropolitan Museum of Art, New York). Here too the "lady" in the Hermitage composition appears in a white dress holding a parasol. The artist dated *Terrace at Sainte-Adresse* "1867", hence the date given by Wildenstein, author of the Monet *catalogue raisonné*, cannot be accepted, since he attributes *Lady in the Garden* to 1866.
The title he gave to the canvas in the Hermitage, *Jeanne-Marguerite Lecadre in the Garden*, is also arbitrary, since Monet did not intend to paint a portrait, but was simply attracted by the woman's white dress.
An X-ray examination of the picture has revealed the figure of a man a little to the woman's right, which was subsequently erased. Perhaps the artist originally planned the composition around a theme.
This painting was shown at the fourth Impressionist exhibition in 1879 when it was entitled *A Garden* (*Un jardin*, 1867; owned by M. Lecadre, no. 155).

2. *L'étang à Montgeron*, 1876
The Pond at Montgeron
Oil on canvas, 68½ × 76½ in.
Signed bottom right with the initials
"Cl. M.t"
Inv. no. 6562

Provenance: acquired from the GMNZI in 1931.
Formerly:
Hoschedé Collection, Montgeron-Paris;
Galerie Vollard;
from 1907 I.A. Morozov Collection;
from 1918 GMNZI

Financier and entrepreneur Ernest Hoschedé and his wife Alice (who was to become Monet's second wife) were among the few supporters of the Impressionists when they were struggling to win recognition.
In the autumn of 1876, the painter was their guest on the Rottenbourg estate at Montgeron (a small village on the River Yerres, on the outskirts of Paris).
Together with *Un coin de jardin à Montgeron*, in the Hermitage, this picture was part of a decorative series that embellished the Hoschedé home. It is still not clear how this group of works was arranged, but it also included *The Turkeys* (*Les dindons*; Musée d'Orsay, Paris) and *The Hunt* (*La chasse*; Durand-Ruel Collection, Paris), painted during the same period. These works are the same height as the pictures in the Hermitage, but their width differs.
Unlike the artistic method he usually adopted at the time, Monet did not paint this picture *en plein air*, but in his studio from a preliminary study (in a private collection). The woman holding the fishing rod may be perceived to bear some resemblance to Alice Hoschedé, though the figure is somewhat stylized to harmonize with the overall atmosphere of the picture. An argument in favor of this hypothesis is the fact that in *The Hunt* Monet depicted Ernest Hoschedé.
Though he devoted himself to the genre of decorative painting, Monet sought to reproduce his impressions of nature with great accuracy.

3. *Waterloo bridge. Effet de brouillard*, 1903
Waterloo Bridge. Sun Breaking Through the Fog
Signed and dated bottom right: "Claude Monet 1903"
Inv. no. 6545

Provenance: acquired from the GMNZI in 1930.
Formerly:
from March 1906 Galerie Durand-Ruel, Paris (acquired from the artist);
from November 1906 I.A. Morozov Collection;
from 1918 GMNZI

In 1899, 1900 and 1901, Monet spent some weeks in London, staying at the Savoy Hotel on the Victoria Embankment, which had a wonderful view of the Thames with Charing Cross Bridge and Waterloo Bridge. The series of paintings of Waterloo

Bridge dates from his visits in 1900 and 1901 and comprises forty-one works. Very few of them were completed in London (only three are dated 1900). Most or perhaps all of the canvases were begun at the Savoy, which is confirmed by the memoirs of the painter Sargent, who had visited Monet and seen about ninety canvases stacked in his hotel room. This figure comes very close to the whole number of pictures in the London series, which includes views of the Houses of Parliament, Charing Cross Bridge and Waterloo Bridge.
Probably begun in 1900, the Hermitage canvas was com-

pleted at Giverny.
In March 1900, Monet wrote to Durand-Ruel that he was painting non-stop, but because of the constantly changing atmospheric conditions he was forced to work on several pictures at the same time, without managing to finish them. The problem, of course, was not only the variable weather. The task took several years because Monet was attempting to express something more profound than the impression of a real scene or a fleeting atmospheric effect. Though the initial creative impulse for the London series had been the purely impressionistic attempt to capture the differing temporal and atmospheric conditions, in the best paintings (and the Hermitage canvas is definitely one of these) the focus becomes the expression of pantheistic moods and feelings.

Edouard Manet
1832-1883

4. *Portrait de M.me Jules Guillemet*, circa 1880
Portrait of Mme. Jules Guillemet
Italian pencil on paper, 12½ × 8¾ in.
Signed bottom right: "E.M."
Inv. no. 43094

Provenance: acquired in 1938.
Formerly:
private collection, Leningrad

Close friends of Manet, Madame Guillemet (the leading-spirit of her fashionable salon in Paris), her husband, and younger sister, Marguerite, often posed for the artist. The Guillemets are depicted in the painting *In the Conservatory* (1879; Neue National Galerie, Berlin), and both sisters appear in many drawings and sketches between the end of the 1870s and 1882. The two women

regularly corresponded with the artist and were often his guests at Bellevue, where, probably in the summer of 1880, he drew three female heads with fashionable hats, on a sheet of notepaper (Musée des Beaux-Arts, Dijon). One of these, at the top of the piece of paper, bears a great resemblance to the portrait in the Hermitage, the only difference being that the head is turned to the right. Judging from the style, the portrait was painted from life in a single sitting, and, probably on the same occasion, it was repeated in the pastel *M.me Jules Guillemet with a Hat* (City Art Museum, Saint Louis).
Madame Guillemet was a young American famous for her beauty and elegance. In his portraits Manet not only captured the features of the sitter, but also created the image of the typical Parisienne. In fact, the pastel *M.me Jules Guillemet Bare-Headed* (Ordrupgaardsamlingen, Charlottenlung) was entitled *Parisienne* at the posthumous exhibition of Manet's works held at the Ecole des Beaux-Arts in 1884; another of his portraits was also entitled *Parisienne* (1882; Henri T. Madd Collection, Los Angeles).

Auguste Renoir
1841-1919

5. *Portrait de M.lle Jeanne Samary*, 1878
Portrait of the Actress Jeanne Samary
Oil on canvas, 68½ × 40 in.
Signed and dated bottom left: "Renoir 78"
Inv. no. 9003

Provenance: acquired from the GMNZI in 1948.
Formerly:
from 1881 Galerie Durand-Ruel;
from 1886 Prince Edmond de Polignac Collection, Paris;
from 1897 La Salle Collection, Paris;
from 1898 Galerie Bernheim-Jeune;
M.A. Morozov Collection;
from 1903 M.K. Morozova Collection;
from 1910 Tretyakov Gallery (gift of M.K. Morozova);
from 1925 GMNZI

Jeanne Samary (1857-1890) was born into a family of artists and made her debut at the Comédie-Française at the age of eighteen. Two years later she played all the maid-servant roles in Molière's comedies. During this period, in 1877, Renoir began to use her as a model and he painted twelve portraits of her in the space of three years.
The twenty-year-old girl had rapidly become a celebrity in Paris, as is evident from the fact that two portraits of her were exhibited at the 1877 Salon; a painting by Georges de Dramard (whereabouts unknown) and a marble bust by David d'Anger, now lost.
At the same time, the third Impressionist exhibition, organized in opposition to the Salon, showed yet another portrait of her by Renoir (GMII).
This *Portrait of Mademoiselle S...*, as the artist entitled it in the catalog, was described by Zola as the "success of the exhibition".

Naturally the spectators easily guessed the girl's name from the initial, and according to a friend of Renoir's, Rivière, in this "pink portrait" she shone like a "ray of sunshine".
Two years later, struggling to win the recognition that would finally put an end to his straitened circumstances, Renoir fought the masters of official art on their own ground.
The large full-length portrait, the most monumental of the pictures depicting Jeanne Samary, and the portrait of *Madame Georges Charpentier and Her Children* (1878; Metropolitan Museum of Art, New York), were exhibited at the 1879 Salon.
Here, however, success smiled only on *Madame Georges Charpentier and Her*

Children. This influential owner of the gallery "the whole of Paris" visited, had "her picture" hung in the best position, while the portrait of the actress was placed virtually just below the ceiling. Moreover, unbeknown to the artist, before the vernissage of the Salon this portrait was covered with a thick layer of varnish, which was not removed until ninety years later

in the 1960s, when it was already in the Hermitage.
It was only then that the stunning beauty of the painting was finally revealed.
The fact that Renoir did not portray Jeanne Samary in the guise of a theatrical character can be easily explained.
The artist admitted that he had rarely seen her on stage: "I don't like the way they act at the Théâtre Français" (A. Vollard, *Auguste Renoir*, Paris, 1920, p. 169).
On the other hand, the portrait in the Hermitage does not have any elements of everyday life, it does not give the impression that the model is posing, as was the case in the realist art of that period. Essentially this picture too has become a kind of fantasy. It is not surprising that after seeing it Marguerite Charpentier described the actress as follows: "She is very beautiful but what protruding collar bones!" (G. Rivière, *Renoir et ses amis*, Paris, 1921, p. 77). In effect, all Renoir's paintings of Jeanne Samary are far more flattering than the photographs taken at the time.
In this painting she is wearing an evening gown, a *toilette* she might have appeared in at the Charpentiers' house, where it is thought Renoir first made her acquaintance and where many literary and artistic celebrities regularly gathered.
However, it cannot be stated with absolute certainty that the Charpentiers' salon was the setting for the portrait of this charming woman, though it may have been, since the Japanese screen on the lefthand side of the canvas can also be seen in the painting of Madame Charpentier and her children in the Metropolitan Museum.
The artist told Vollard that he painted all his "Samarys" in the garden in rue Cortot. However, Renoir's son, Jean, claimed that this full-length portrait had been painted in the atelier in rue Saint-Georges.

6. *Jeune femme à l'éventail*, 1880
Young Woman with a Fan
Oil on canvas, 25½ × 19¾ in.
Signed top right: "Renoir"
Inv. no. 6507

Provenance: acquired from the GMNZI in 1930.
Formerly:
from 1881 Galerie Durand-Ruel, Paris;
from 1908 I.A. Morozov Collection;
from 1918 GMNZI

This picture, which became very famous after the seventh Impressionist exhibition in 1882, was often dated to 1880-1881 or 1881, whereas now after learning the date in which it was purchased by Durand-Ruel (6 January 1881), we can state with certainty that it was painted in 1880. Despite the mocking caricature by Jules Dranet, who had depicted the *Young Woman with a Fan* among the other major works in this exhibition (*Chiarivari*, 9 March 1882), Renoir's work was received favorably and even enthusiastically by some critics: "delightful in its topicality and femininity" (S. Silvestre, 'Septième exposition des artistes indépendants', in *La vie moderne*, 11 March

1882); "the vibrancy of his palette is extraordinary especially in *Young Woman with a Fan*" (A. Sallanche, 'L'Exposition des artistes indépendants', in *Journal des arts*, 3 March 1882).
It is generally thought that Alphonsine Fournaise posed for *Young Woman with a Fan*, she was the daughter of the owners of the restaurant at Chatou, where the scene of *Luncheon of the Boating Party* (*Le déjeuner des canotiers* (1880-1881; Phillips Collection, Washington) is set, the most important work of this period. There are other paintings that critics attempt to identify as portraits of this woman, but when they are compared it can be seen that different models were used. A further problem is the fact that Renoir tended to make his subjects more beautiful than they actually were, as his favorite eighteenth-century masters were in the habit of doing, thus reducing the figures to a "common denominator" and eliminating individual traits.
Attempts have been made to recognize Alphonsine Fournaise in the central figure of *Luncheon of the Boating Party*. However, contemporary scholars of Renoir's work (J. Isaacson, John House and others), in referring to Meier Graefe's identification of the figures in the Washington composition, consider it impossible to identify this woman with a real person. Despite the resemblance, it is unlikely that the central figure of *Luncheon of the Boating Party* and *Young Woman with a Fan* were one and the same person, especially since the former is a dark blonde and the latter has raven black hair. The case of the woman next to the "unknown woman" (the one drinking from the goblet) is quite different. We learn from Rivière, who knew how *Luncheon of the Boating Party* was painted, that Angèle posed for the picture. She was a vivacious model from Montmartre who frequented Renoir's friends. Today it is thought that the woman with the goblet is a portrait of her. Rivière also pointed out that Angèle posed for *Young Woman with a Cat* (1880; Sterling and Francine Clark Art Institute, Williamstown). The resemblance between the model in this picture and the one in *Young Woman with a Fan* suggests that Angèle posed for both these works, all the more so since the red armchair appears in both paintings. They were executed in the same period and were both shown at the 1882 exhibition.

Edgar Degas
1834-1917

7. *Danseuse assise ajustant les souliers*, 1875-1876
Seated Ballerina Adjusting Her Shoes
Charcoal and chalk on blue-white paper,
18¾ × 12 in.
Signed bottom right: "Degas"
Inv. no. 42160

Provenance: acquired from the GMNZI.
Formerly:
from 1898 Galerie Durand-Ruel;
from 1903 I.S. Ostrouchov Collection, Moscow (purchased from Durand-Ruel in 1903 for 1,200 francs);
from 1918 Museum of Icons and Painting, Moscow;
from 1923 GMNZI

From the early 1870s on Degas repeatedly returned to this theme. As regards execution and compositional technique this study in the Hermitage is very similar to the drawing *Ballerina Adjusting the Laces of her Left Shoe*

(1881-1883; Musée Bonnat, Bayonne). It is also reminiscent of the sketches of the young dancer Méline Darde (formerly in the Baroness A. De Ginsbourg Collection)

and can presumably be dated to 1875-1876. Later this study was duplicated by monotype (Statens Museum for Kunst, Copenhagen). The pastels of 1878-1879 (Lemoisne, 530, 531) are also similar to the Hermitage drawing. One of the two ballerinas sitting on a bench in the pastel of 1879 (Lemoisne, 559) is depicted in virtually the same pose; a similar theme is repeated in the pastels featuring a single ballerina (1881-1883; Lemoisne, 600, 658, 699). The pastel of the ballerina bending down towards the left, her head almost touching her right ankle, (National Gallery of Victoria, Melbourne) is also one of the variations on this theme. Edgar Degas returns to the same motif in one of his later compositions, *Two Ballerinas Seated on a Bench* (circa 1900-1905; Lemoisne, 1256). It has also been suggested that there is a link between the drawing in the Hermitage and the study for *The Orchestra of 'Robert le Diable'* (The Metropolitan Museum of Art, New York).

Camille Pissarro
1830-1903

8. *Boulevard Montmartre. Soleil après-midi*, 1897
Boulevard Montmartre. Afternoon Sun
Oil on canvas, 29 × 36½ in.
Signed and dated bottom right:
"C. Pissarro 97"
Inv. no. 9002

Provenance: acquired from the GMNZI in 1948.
Formerly:
François Depeaux Collection, Rouen;
from 1901 M.P. Ryabushinsky Collection, Moscow;
from 1917 Tretyakov Gallery;
from 1925 GMNZI

On 8 February 1897 the artist wrote to his son Georges: "I am returning to Paris on the 10th, the day after tomorrow, to begin a series on Paris. I have booked a room at the Grand Hôtel de

Russie, 1 rue Drouot, from the 10th. I hope to paint about ten canvases. Durand liked my small pictures very much and advised me to paint the boulevards in the same style, though big, of course." (J. Bailly-Herzberg, *Correspondance de Camille Pissarro*, vol. IV: *1895-1898*, Paris, 1989, p. 323).
As soon as he arrived in his hotel room, Pissarro wrote to his other son Lucien: "...From the window I can see the whole array of boulevards almost as far as Porte Saint-Denis, in any case as far as boulevard Bonne-Nouvelle." (J. Bailly-Herzberg, *op. cit.*, p. 324). In a letter to Georges of 13 February he wrote: "...I've started the Boulevard series, an incredible subject that has to be depicted by any means possible; on the left there is another terribly difficult scene to be rendered as a bird's eye view of carriages, omnibuses, people among tall trees, near tall houses, a balance must be found for the whole, it's crazy!...It goes without saying, a solution must be found." (J. Bailly-Herzberg, *op. cit.*, p. 325).
In the space of two months he painted a series of thirteen pictures featuring the same composition, in which the street lamp in the foreground constitutes a kind of reference point both for the perspective and the overall tonal values. On 28 March, Pissarro wrote that the pictures "are very well studied", but that "the lack of sun is slowing me down". The series is painted on canvases of three standard formats. The largest was chosen for two pictures: the one in the Hermitage and the one in the National Gallery of Victoria, Melbourne (in which the boulevard is depicted on an overcast morning).

Alfred Sisley
1839-1899

9. *Villeneuve-la-Garenne*, 1872
The Town of Villeneuve-la-Garenne on the Seine
Oil on canvas, 23¼ × 31½ in.
Signed and dated bottom left:
"Sisley 1872"
Inv. no. 9005

Provenance: acquired from the GMNZI in 1948.
Formerly:
from 1872 Galerie Durand-Ruel, Paris;
from 1898 I.P. Shchukin Collection;
from 1912 S.I. Shchukin Collection;
from 1918 GMNZI

Until recently this painting was known as *Village on the Banks of the Seine* (*Village au bord de la Seine*), as it was entitled in the S.I. Shchukin Collection. In the summer of 1872 Sisley regularly visited the village of Villeneuve-la-Garenne, depicted here, now part of the suburbs of Paris and separated from Saint-Denis by the river.
The bank in shadow in this picture from the Hermitage is

the island of Saint-Denis, from where the artist had a good view of Villeneuve-la-Garenne. The village could be reached by crossing a bridge from the island. Soon after it was built in 1844, Parisians began to make Sunday excursions to this quiet spot.
Sisley began painting at Villeneuve in the spring of 1872. In this period, having set his easel not far from the bridge, facing Saint-Denis, he painted the picture *Pêcheurs étendant leur filets* (1872; Kimbell Art Museum, Fort Worth) and another three landscapes.
In the height of summer Sisley went back to the bridge of Villeneuve and painted three pictures, choosing the island of Saint-Dennis as his "vantage point".
While the artist focuses on the opposite bank in the landscape held by the Hermitage, in the other two he is more interested in the bridge. The section of the village depicted in *Village on the Banks of the Seine* is in the vicinity of the bridge. Two houses on the lefthand side of the picture also appear on the right in the landscape *Bridge of Villeneuve-la-Garenne* (1872; The Metropolitan Museum of Art, New York), which is almost an extension of the view of the village.
It is thought that the painting had already been exhibited in 1872 under the title *On the Seine* (*Sur la Seine*), at the "Fourth Exhibition of the Society of French Artists" organized at the German Gallery in London by Durand-Ruel (no. 124).

10. *La berge de la rivière à Saint-Mammes*, 1884
The River Bank at Saint-Mammes
Oil on canvas, 19¾ × 25½ in.
Signed and dated bottom left: "Sisley. 84"
Inv. no. 9167

Provenance: acquired from the GMNZI in 1948.
Formerly:
from 1884 Galerie

Durand-Ruel, Paris;
from 1907 I.A. Morozov Collection;
from 1918 GMNZI

This picture was painted in early spring 1884, when Sisley was living in the village of Les Sablons, near Moret-sur-Loing, and he often painted in the surrounding countryside, for instance near the village of Saint-Mammes on the River Loing. On 7 March he wrote to Durand-Ruel that he had returned to work, he had started on various canvases depicting the banks of the river, he wanted to take full advantage of the good weather, and not leave his easel. On 24 March the painting *The River Bank at Saint-Mammes* was delivered to Durand-Ruel. At the same time the artist was also producing a portfolio of sketches (Musée du Louvre, Cabinet des Dessins, Paris). The subject of this picture in the Hermitage is to be found in drawing no. 22 in this portfolio. Sisley executed a large number of paintings of the river at Saint-Mammes and they can be divided into various groups. The Hermitage canvas is one of the series of landscapes with the bridge over the Loing in the background (F. Daulte, *Alfred Sisley*, Lausanne, 1959, pp. 511-516).

Eugène Boudin
1824-1898

11. *Plage de Trouville*, 1893
Trouville Beach
Oil on canvas, 22 × 36 in.
Inscribed, dated and signed bottom left:
"Trouville 93 / E. Boudin"
Inv. no. 10597

Provenance: acquired in 1997.
Formerly:
from 1894 Galerie Durand-Ruel, Paris;
from 1909 Carnegie Art Gallery, New York;
Durand-Ruel Gallery, New York;
D.M. Look Collection, New York;
Nivian Gallery, New York;
Galerie Alex Maguy, Paris;
Wildenstein and Co. Gallery, New York;
private collection, Switzerland

At the end of the nineteenth century Trouville, a small port on the Channel coast, was a famous seaside resort. Boudin loved the place and painted it very often. The first pictures of Trouville date from 1860, the last ones are dated 1897. In the early 1860s, he established the compositional scheme for his

paintings of Trouville. The wide beach was depicted in the foreground, usually at low tide, and enlivened by some figures, the line of the horizon was usually quite low in order to give the landscape greater spatial depth; in addition, the frequently very cloudy sky played an important role in the general composition of the picture.

Trouville Beach (*Plage de Trouville*, 1863; private collection; R. Schmidt, *Eugène Boudin*, vol. III, Paris, 1973, p. 273) can be considered the model for many subsequent compositions, including the one in the Hermitage.
Though he constantly tackled a subject that he seems to have studied in minute detail, Boudin, in actual fact, never repeated himself and successfully avoided monotony, as the canvas we are concerned with here excellently demonstrates. It is one of his most masterly and lively paintings of Trouville.
At the posthumous exhibition of Boudin's works in New York this picture was entitled *La Plage de Trouville. Vue prise de la Jetée-Promenade, Mare-montante, en octobre* ("Exposition of Painting by the Late Louis Eugène Boudin", Durand-Ruel Gallery, New York, 1989, no. 46)

Paul Cézanne
1839-1906

12. *Jeune fille au piano. L'ouverture de "Tannhäuser"*, circa 1869
Girl at the Piano.
The "Tannhäuser" Ouverture
Oil on canvas,
22¾ × 36½ in.
Inv. no. 9166

Provenance: acquired from the GMNZI in 1948.
Formerly:
Maxime Conil Collection, Monbriant;
from 1899 Galerie Vollard;
from 1908 I.A. Morozov Collection;
from 1918 GMNZI

This picture was painted at Jas de Bouffan. The same patterned wallpaper is reproduced as the backdrop of *Portrait de l'artiste au chapeau de paille* (1878-1879;

Museum of Modern Art, New York), also executed at Jas de Bouffan, while the armchair appears in the portrait of the artist's father engrossed in reading *L'Evénement* (*Louis-August Cèzanne, père de l'artiste, lisant "L'Evénement"*, 1866; National Gallery of Art, Washington). It has been suggested that the figures in this picture are Cézanne's mother and elder sister Marie. In his *catalogue raisonné* Rewald doubted that the woman intent on knitting was the artist's mother; he agreed, however, that the figure on the right must be Marie, while the girl at the piano was his younger sister Rose.
The picture's second title refers to the music of Wagner, whom Cézanne greatly admired and who was one of the symbols of avant-garde art at that time. In a letter to Heinrich Morstatt, the musician who had increased the painter's love for Wagner, Cézanne wrote in May 1868: "I have recently had the good fortune to listen to the 'Tannhäuser', 'Lohengrin' and 'Flying Dutchman' ouvertures." (P. Cézanne, *Correspondance*, Paris, 1978, p. 130). His interest in Wagner had evidently been awakened earlier. The composer's opera had been staged in Paris in Spring 1861. Baudelaire had immediately published an article on him and probably Zola had shown it to Cézanne when he first arrived in the capital.
Work on *The "Tannhäuser" Ouverture* began in 1866. In August of the same year the artist's friend, Antoine Marion, wrote to Morstatt that Cézanne "in the space of a morning painted an extraordinary canvas... It will be called *Tannhäuser Ouverture* [*sic*]. This painting belongs to the future, like Wagner's music...This is the subject. A girl at the piano; white on blue; all in close-up. The piano is rendered with broad brushstrokes, the old father, seen in profile, is sitting in an armchair; at the back of the room there is a small boy listening to the music with a rapt expression. All in all one has the impression of irresistible, overwhelming power." (P. Cézanne, *op. cit.*, p.149).
In the summer of 1867, Marion wrote to Morstatt, who had returned to Germany, that Cézanne had begun some large canvases, one of which was *The "Tannhäuser Ouverture*, but in lighter tones. In another letter, of 6 September 1867, Marion described this second version in greater detail. He wrote that Cézanne had returned to the subject of the *Tannhäuser* ou-

verture, but in completely different, extremely light shades, and that all the figures were very carefully studied. In his opinion the blonde head of the girl was very beautiful and painted with extraordinary power, and Marion's own profile was a very good likeness. In addition, the whole picture had been painted without the harsh colors of the earlier one and the violent elements that had aroused aversion. He thought the piano had been executed as splendidly as in the other canvas, and the drapery, as usual was magnificently true to life. (J. Rewald, *The Painting of Paul Cézanne*, vol. I, New York, 1996, pp. 124-125).
All in all, work on the composition was moving in the direction of greater precision. The first versions had been painted over other canvases, whereas an X-ray examination of the Hermitage picture has revealed no trace of other compositions. The first two versions have been lost: evidently Cézanne was dissatisfied with them and destroyed them.
Dating this painting has been rather problematic. The artist's son proposed the somewhat vague date, 1865-1870; Venturi initially suggested before 1869-1871, then 1867; Rewald stated it was executed in 1869-1870; and finally Henri Loyrette, in the catalogue of the artist's latest retrospective (*Cézanne*, Paris-London-Philadelphia, 1995-1996, no. 17), established the period of its execution more precisely at about 1869.

13. *Fruits*, 1879-1880
Fruit
Oil on canvas, 18½ × 21¾ in.
Inv. no. 9026

Provenance: acquired from the GMNZI in 1948.
Formerly:
circa 1891 Julien Tanguy Collection, Paris;
from 1891 Sarah Hallowell Collection, Chicago;
from 1894 Durand-Ruel Gallery, New York;
from 1895 Galerie Durand-Ruel, Paris;
from 1903 S.I. Shchukin Collection;
from 1918 GMNZI

Venturi included this canvas in the series of still lifes with objects against a backdrop of leaf-patterned wallpaper, dating the whole group to between 1879 and 1882. He added that this kind of wallpaper must have been at Melun, where Cézanne lived from 1879 to 1888, or in rue Ouest in Paris, where the artist lived in 1881-1882. Subsequently experts have sought to change this kind of

grouping by suggesting that the wallpaper with geometric or leaf motifs painted by Cézanne in this period, may also have been elsewhere and not only in rue Ouest. Sterling, Gowing, Rivière, Rewald and other experts have sought to establish the chronology of the still lifes with wallpaper more precisely. It is very likely that the picture in question was painted around 1879-1880.
A similar still life is *Milk Can and Apples* (*Boîte à lait et pommes*; Museum of Modern Art, New York); the same crumpled napkin appears in the center, the milk can is on the left, and the backdrop is leaf-patterned wallpaper.
The Galerie Durand-Ruel archive contains documentation according to which its New York gallery purchased the picture from Sarah Hallowell, a friend of Mary Casatt, who promoted Impressionist works in America by buying pictures for her first collectors.
She often went to Paris, and it is very likely that she purchased two still lifes from Tanguy around 1891 (*Fruit* and *Milk Can and Apples*).
Tanguy (who died in 1893) was the only art dealer at the time who sold Cézanne's paintings (Vollard only began selling them in 1895). Sarah Hallowell must have been taking a big risk, since no American collector was interested in Cézanne's still lifes in those years.
She was therefore obliged to offer the pictures to the Durand-Ruel Gallery in New York, which had till then refused to have anything to do with Cézanne's works.
In 1945, Henri Matisse mentioned these two works that had gone to the United States: "At the Galerie Durand-Ruel I saw two splendid still lifes by Cézanne, biscuits, a milk can and fruit against a dull blue backdrop. Durand pointed them out to me when I took him the still lifes I had painted. 'You see these Cézannes, I can't sell them – he said – You'd better paint interiors with figures, like this one or that one.'" (H. Matisse, 'De la couleur', in *Verve*, vol IV, no. 13, November 1945).
Matisse did not say when he had this conversation with Durand-Ruel, but it is reasonable to suppose that it was around 1899-1902.

14. *Les bords de la Marne*, 1888
The Banks of the Marne
Oil on canvas, 25¾ × 32 in.
Inv. no. 6513

Provenance: acquired from the GMNZI in 1930.
Formerly:
Galerie Vollard;
from 1906 Havemeyer Collection, New York;
from 1909 Galerie Durand-Ruel, Paris;
from 1909 I.A. Morozov Collection;
from 1918 GMNZI

The photo of this picture in the Vollard archive bears a note by the artist's son: "Marne 1888". This means that the painting must have initially been held by the Galerie Vollard.
While living in Paris during the summer of 1888, Paul Cézanne painted some landscapes of the banks of the Marne near Creteil, not far from the spot where the river flows into the Seine.
The same section of the bank with a villa is depicted, from a similar angle, in a landsca-

pe that bears the same title (*Bords de la Marne II*; private collection).
In another landscape, *House on the Banks of the Marne* (*Maison au bord de la Marne*; The White House, Washington), Cézanne chose a vantage point a little further away.
The villa, which in the Galerie Vollard record of acquisitions is called *Petit château dans l'eau* (the former title of *The Banks of the Marne II* which at the time was owned by this art dealer), is far more visible in the Hermitage picture.
In his catalogue Rewald gives the same date to all three landscapes, 1888-1890.
There also exists a watercolor on the same subject (L. Venturi, *Paul Cézanne. Son art, son oeuvre*, Paris, 1936, no. 935).

15. *Le fumeur*,
circa 1890-1892
The Smoker
Oil on canvas, 36½ × 29 in.
Inv. no. 6561

Provenance: acquired from the GMNZI in 1931 (I.A. Morozov Collection).
Formerly:
Galerie Vollard;
from 1910 I.A. Morozov Collection;
from 1918 GMNZI

The pose of this figure leaning on his elbow, the image of stability and peace, is already to be found in Cézanne's early work *Garçon accoudé* (1867-1868; private collection, Switzerland). In this case the artist was inspired by the *Boy* by Bachiacca (Musée du Louvre, Paris), thought at the time to be by Raphael, and may have based his painting on a lithograph of this work that was probably in his possession. Much later another "leaning" figure was to appear, *Boy with a Red Waistcoat* (*Garçon au gilet rouge*, 1888-1890; Bührle Collection, Zürich). The compositional scheme of this picture with all the details (the table, the drapes in the corner, the fragment of another picture in the background) was used by Cézanne for *The Smoker* in the Hermitage, in which the pose itself

has become more convincing. Of all Cézanne's works depicting smokers, those bearing the closest resemblance to the Hermitage picture are *Le fumeur accoudé* (circa 1891; Kunsthalle, Mannheim) and the watercolor sketch of this variant (Barnes Foundation, Merion). The Mannheim smoker is portrayed in the same pose and on a canvas of the same size, but with a smooth wall in the background. He has a less absent-minded expression since his pupils are more accentuated. Canvases by Cézanne himself can be seen on the wall behind the Hermitage smoker. These pictures within a picture are important elements, both with respect to content and color, that reflect the artist's ideals. The early still-life with the bottle and the apples, that remained at Jas de Bouffan for quite a time (1867-1869; now in the Neue National Galerie, Berlin), and the canvas higher up depicting the bathers (*Baigneurs en plein air*, 1890-1891; formerly in the Krebs Collection, now in the Hermitage, R. 748) are reminiscent of the temptations of the outside world and are by no means chance additions to the background of this scene, which is pervaded by the artist's aspiration towards attaining inner equilibrium.

Another *Smoker* in the same pose, but depicted almost full-length, is held by the GMII. In the past it was thought that the three pictures had been painted around the same time. Venturi dates them to between 1895 and 1900. Not finding any stylistic similarity between these and the works dated between 1896 and 1900, Douglas Cooper considers them to date from 1893-1894, and Reff dates them even earlier. Rewald is of the opinion that the Moscow picture was painted in 1893-1896, whereas the Mannheim and St. Petersburg variations must be dated to around 1891. The artist's son had written "1890" on the photo of the picture (Vollard archive). He also stated that the model for the Mannheim painting, and hence for the one in the Hermitage, was the peasant (or gardener) Alexandre Paulin.

Paul Gauguin
1848-1903

16. *Fatata te Mouà. Au pied de la montagne*, 1892
Fatata te Mouà.
At the Foot of the Mountain
Oil on canvas, 26¾ × 36¼ in.
Inscribed, signed and dated bottom left:
"Fatata Te Mouà.
P. Gauguin 92"
Inv. no. 8977

Provenance: acquired by the GMNZI in 1948.
Formerly:
Galerie Vollard;
from 1908 I.A. Morozov Collection; from 1918 GMNZI

The ex-governor of Tahiti, Bengt Danielsson, stated that this landscape had been painted on the south coast of the island. Gauguin lived there, in the village of Mataiea, from the end of 1891 to the middle of 1893. The large tree, the main element in this landscape, features in another two pictures of 1892, *Women at the River* and *Matama* (*Past Times*) (G. Wildenstein, *Gauguin: Catalogue*, vol. I, Paris, 1964, pp. 482, 467), and later in *Hina Maruru* (*The Feast of Hina*) (1893; G. Wildenstein, *op. cit.*, p. 500) and *Nave Nave Moe* (Hermitage; cf. no. 17 in the present catalog). At the beginning of this series we find the small studies *Women at the River* and *At the Foot of the Mountain* that are not yet imbued with the religious symbolism that distinguishes *Matamua* and the later compositions, when the motif of the large tree became associated in the artist's mind with the figure of Hina, the lunar divinity of Tahiti. This picture was exhibited at the exhibition of Gauguin's works held at the Galerie Durand-Ruel in 1893 ("Exposition d'oeuvres récentes de Paul Gauguin. Galerie Durand-Ruel", Paris, no. 26), and is mentioned in a letter by Gauguin regarding the 1895 exhibition-sale of his paintings: "I shall make an exception for the friends who have supported me recently and not raise the prices in the catalog for a few more days: *Fatata te Mouà*...400."
(*Gauguin: Catalogue de l'exposition de l'Orangerie*, Paris, 1949, appendix III).

17. *Nave Nave Moe. Eau délicieuse (Douces rêveries)*, 1894
Nave Nave Moe. Delicious Water (Sweet Dreams)
Oil on canvas, 29 × 39½ in.
Inscribed, signed and dated bottom left: "NAVE NAVE MOE P. Gauguin 94"
Inv. no. 6510

Provenance: acquired from the GMNZI in 1931.
Formerly:
Gauguin exhibition-sale at the Hôtel Drouot, Paris, 18 February 1895, no. 23;
from 1895 E. Schuffenecker Collection;
Dosbourg exhibition-sale, Paris, 10 November 1897, no. 16;
Prince Wagram Collection;
Galerie Vollard;
from 1908 I.A. Morozov Collection;
from 1918 GMNZI

The second title of this picture, *Delicious Water*, generally used in Russia, comes from the catalog of the 1895 Gauguin exhibition-sale, probably organized by the artist himself (where in fact it was entitled *Eau délicieuse*). In actual fact the title written on the canvas in Tahitian is different. Georges Wildenstein translates it as "Joy of Repose" ("Joie de se reposer"). Bouge and Danielsson have suggested more precise alternatives: "Sweet Dreams" or "Golden Chimeras".
This picture dates from the period between Gauguin's two stays on Tahiti. It was painted at the beginning of 1894 after the two windows executed at the end of the previous year for the artist's studio in Paris, *Nave Nave* and *Woman of Tahiti with Landscape* (Musée d'Orsay, Paris), which feature the lily that was later also to appear in *Delicious Water*. The picture was painted in Paris from his recollections of Oceania and is based on images from his early Tahitian period. Gauguin's studio in Paris was full of canvases brought back from the tropics. The figures in the foreground appear in *Te Fare Maorie* (*House of Maorie*) (1891; G. Wildenstein, *Gauguin: Catalogue*, vol. I, Paris, 1964, p. 436); the nude woman seated in the center appears in *Aha oe feii* (*Are You Jealous?*) (1892; GMII); the Tahitian woman standing nearby can be seen in three paintings of 1892 (G. Wildenstein, *op. cit.*, pp. 472-474); and the two Tahitian divinities are depicted in *Vairoumati tei oa* (*His Name is Vairaomati*) (1892; GMII). Richard Field suggests that this is a sculpture that represents the supreme god Taaroa and one of his wives (R.S. Field, *Paul Gauguin: The Painting of the First Voyage to Tahiti*, New York-London, 1977, p. 95). Further similar details can be found in other works.
The painting *Delicious Wa-*

ters is mainly based on his *Women on the River Bank* (*Femmes au bord de la rivière*; private collection, Paris; G. Wildenstein, *op. cit.*, p. 574). Wildenstein mistakenly attributed it to 1898, whereas it had evidently been brought to Paris from Tahiti. This canvas that reproduces the central and righthand portions of *Delicious Water* was executed from life, in the somewhat Impressionist style that the artist abandoned when he turned to stylized, synthetic compositions, imbued with religious feeling. The need to express these religious ideas led him to include the two divinities (which do not appear in *Women on the River Bank*) in the landscape and set the Virgin Mary and Eve holding the apple in the foreground, depicted as two Tahitians.

18. *Femmes au bord de la mer (Maternité)*, 1892
Women by the Sea (Maternity)
Oil on canvas, 37¾ × 29 in.
Signed and dated bottom right:
"Paul Gauguin 99"
Inv. no. 8979

Provenance: acquired from the GMNZI in 1948.
Formerly:
from 1900 Galerie Vollard;
from 1903 or 1904 S.I. Shchukin Collection;
from 1918 GMNZI

In March 1899 Pahura, the artist's Tahitian companion, gave birth to a boy, whom Gauguin christened Emile (like the son he had had by his first wife Mette, who had stayed in Copenhagen). Danielsson and other critics associate two paintings with this event. Like Wildenstein, they give them the general title *Maternity I* (Hermitage) and *Maternity II* (D. Rockefeller Collection, New York). The latter is painted in vibrant colors, is very decorative, and does not have the dog and figures in the background. It is very likely that the picture was executed in 1899, after *Women by the Sea*. The Hermitage canvas was one of a group of ten works that the artist sent to Vollard in January 1900 with the following description: "8. Three figures. In the foreground a seated woman is breast-feeding her baby. On the right a small black dog. On the left a woman in a red dress standing and a basket. Behind her, a woman in a green dress with flowers in her hand. A backdrop of blue lagoons and reddish-orange sand." (J. de Rotonchamp, *Paul Gauguin*, Paris, 1926, p. 221). In painting *Women by the Sea* Gauguin used his own observations, the iconography of scenes of the Adoration of the Christ Child by old masters, and the compositional techniques of Puvis de Chavannes. He also repeated the figures in *Three Tahitians* (1897; National Gallery of Scotland, Edinburgh). The central figure of the woman holding flowers is one of the most recurrent images in Gauguin's painting of this period and it also appears in the canvases painted in 1899, *Two Tahitians (Breasts with Red Flowers – Les seins aux fleurs rouges*; The Metropolitan Museum of Art, New York), *Rupe Rupe* (GMII), *The Month of Mary* (cf. no. 19 in the present catalog) and in several other works. This picture was shown at the Gauguin exhibition at the Galerie Vollard in 1903 (no. 2)

19. *Te Avae No Maria*.
Le mois de Marie, 1899
Te Avae No Maria.
The Month of Mary
Oil on canvas, 38 × 29½ in.
Inscribed, signed and dated bottom left: "TE AVAE NO MARIA. Paul Gauguin 1899"
Inv. no. 6515

Provenance: acquired from the GMNZI in 1930.
Formerly:
from 1903 Galerie Vollard (sent by Gauguin from Atuona);
from 1908 S.I Shchukin Collection (purchased before 1910);
from 1918 GMNZI

This picture is also known as *Woman with Flowers in Her*

Hand, a title found in the list of canvases that Gauguin sent to Vollard in 1903: "9. Te Avae No Maria. Woman with Flowers in Her Hand, on a golden yellow ground. On the left a fruit tree and an exotic plant." (J. de Rotonchamp, *Paul Gauguin*, Paris, 1925, p. 221). The Tahitian title means "the month of Mary", in other words, May the month the Catholic Church devotes to the worship of the Virgin Mary. At the beginning of May the originally pagan feast of the return of spring takes place, which has been celebrated in Western Europe since ancient times. The reflowering of nature is also the main subject of Gauguin's painting as can be seen from the yellow ground and the way in which the woman is depicted. Her gesture is taken from a bas-relief at Borobudur *The Washing of Bodhisattva* (circa 800). Gauguin had taken a photo of the bas-relief with him to Tahiti, and in 1898-1899 he repeated the pose of the stone figure in the Javanese temple several times. The prototype for the "exotic plant" is also to be found in the bas-relief at the temple of Borobudur.
The essential elements of this picture already appear in *Faa Iheihe* (*Tahitian Pastoral*) (1898; Tate Gallery, London, W.G. 569). The far lefthand portion of this composition also appears, with a few changes, in *Rupe Rupe* (1899; GMII) and becomes an independent motif in *The Month of Mary*. Moreover the gesture of the main figure in this picture is repeated in other canvases of 1899: *Three Tahitian Women on a Yellow Ground* (cf. no. 20 in the present catalog), the two versions of the *Maternity* (cf. no. 18 in the present catalog) and (*Te tiai na oa ite gata? (Are You Expecting a Letter?)* (G. Wildenstein, *Gauguin: Catalogue*, vol. I, Paris, 1964, p. 587).

20. *Trois femmes tahitiennes sur fond jaune*, 1899
Three Tahitian Women on a Yellow Ground
Oil on canvas, 26¾ × 29 in.
Signed and dated bottom right:
"Paul Gauguin 99"
Inv. no. 7708

Provenance: acquired from the GMNZI in 1934.
Formerly:
from 1903 Galerie Vollard (sent by Gauguin from Atuona);

around 1905 Gertrude Stein Collection, Paris;
Galerie Vollard again;
from 1910 I.A. Morozov Collection;
from 1918 GMNZI

Like *The Month of Mary* (cf. no. 19 in the present catalog), this picture is also inspired by the bas-relief in the temple at Borobudur; here Gauguin reproduces not only the pose of the central figure, but also the same kind of foliage in the upper portion of the canvas. This picture is also a reworking of the motif on the left in the symbolic composition *Faa Iheihe* (*Tahitian Pastoral*) (1898; Tate Gallery, London), where three Tahitian women are rendered in similar poses. The same group is found again in *Rupe Rupe* (1899; GMII). All four canvases have a yellow ground. This picture cannot be considered a purely decorative work, since the symbolism of the other above-mentioned paintings is also partially echoed here. The poses seem to indicate symbolic overtones, since two women are depicted turning away from the central figure. However, the painting remains enigmatic.

21. *Les tournesols*, 1901
Sunflowers
Oil on canvas, 28¾ × 36½ in.
Signed and dated bottom right:
"Paul Gauguin 1901"
Inv. no. 6516

Provenance: acquired from the GMNZI in 1931.

Formerly:
S.I. Shchukin Collection
(purchased before 1908);
from 1918 GMNZI

This picture was painted on the island of Hiva-Oa. Here Gauguin uses the composition of his early work *To Make a Bouquet* (*Pour faire un bouquet*, 1880; Jaggli-Corti Collection, Winterthur). The subject of the sunflowers is taken from Van Gogh. When the two artists were living in Arles, Gauguin had painted the picture *Van Gogh Painting Sunflowers* (*Van Gogh peignant des tournesols*, 1888; Rijksmuseum Vincent van Gogh, Amsterdam). He returned to this theme in 1901 when he executed a series of four still lifes (G. Wildenstein, *Gauguin: Catalogue*, vol. I, Paris, 1964, pp. 602-604, 606). One of these, *Sunflowers on an Armchair* (E. Stiftung, G. Bührle, Zürich; G. Wildenstein, *op. cit.*, p. 602), is very similar to the picture in the Hermitage, and is virtually a variation of it, so much so that Wildenstein called them both the *Sunflowers on an Armchair* pictures, the Zürich picture being the first and the Hermitage painting the second. The Zürich canvas is smaller, the armchair is set in a frontal position, and there is no head at the window. A similar head to the one depicted here

is found in Gauguin's drawing for the manuscript of the book *Avant et après* (J. Rewald, *Gauguin Drawings*, New York, 1958, no. 119).

Odilon Redon
1840-1916

22. *Femme étendue sous un arbre*, 1900-1901
Woman Lying Under a Tree
Tempera on canvas,
10½ × 13¾ in.
Signed bottom left:
"Odilon Redon"
Inv. no. 43782

Provenance: acquired from the GMNZI in 1948.
Formerly:
S.I. Shchukin Collection;
from 1918 GMNZI

The composition of this small picture appears in Redon's early works, particularly in

Woman Sitting Under a Tree in the Wood (circa 1875; private collection, Paris), a study executed in the manner of Corot. The charcoal drawing *The Tree* (circa 1875; Art Institute of Chicago, Chicago), dating from the same period, is the model for the central element in this painting.
The tree, which plays an important role in the composition, is one of the most recurrent motifs in Redon's oeuvre. A tree with a massive trunk, like the one depicted here, is an indispensable feature of the landscape in his Symbolist works. (*The Centaur* 1883; [Museum of Fine Arts, Boston]; *The Sleep of Caliban* [*Le Sommmeil de Caliban*, circa 1900; private collection, Paris]; *Buddha* [*Le Bouddha*, 1904; Bonger Collection, Almen - France]; *Saint Sebastian* [1910; Kunstmuseum, Basel]. In all these pictures the tree has an important compositional and symbolic significance.
Redon deeply believed the ancient symbolism of the tree as the sign of the continual renewal of nature and the link between the sky and the earth, but in his oeuvre this motif acquires further meanings. In the lithograph *Day* (*Le jour*), from the portfolio *Dreams* (*Songes*, 1891), the young green tree symbolizes not only nature reawakening in spring, but also light and day, the opposite of the bare tree in the Hermitage canvas that represents night.

Henri Edmond Cross (Delacroix)
1856-1910

23. *Eglise Santa Maria degli Angeli près d'Assise*, 1909
The Church of Santa Maria degli Angeli near Assisi
Oil on canvas, 29 × 36¼ in.
Signed and dated bottom right:
"Henri Edmond Cross 09"
Inv. no. 8891

Provenance: acquired from the GMNZI in 1948.
Formerly:
Galerie Bernheim-Jeune;
S.I. Shchukin Collection;
from 1918 GMNZI

Cross spent two weeks in Assisi in the summer of 1908. The church of Santa Maria degli Angeli, to which the artist was attracted since it is one of the major Christian sanctuaries in Italy, was in a sad state of disrepair after the 1832 earthquake (the façade was to be restored in 1928). Built in 1569, it also included

the older chapels in which St. Francis of Assisi had preached. This painting was executed from drawings and sketches, which have been lost, after the artist's return to France. According to Isabel Compin, this landscape was painted between September 1908 and March 1909, but it would be more exact to date it to the beginning of 1909. It is therefore one of the last, or perhaps the very last, in the series of canvases depicting views of Assisi and Perugia.

Georges Manzana-Pissarro
1871-1961

24. *Zebres s'abreuvant*, circa 1906
Zebras at the Watering Hole
Gouache, watercolor and gold on paper, 26 × 21 in.
Signed bottom right:
"G. MANZANA"
Inv. no. 42161

Provenance: acquired from the GMNZI in 1931.
Formerly:
Galerie Vollard;
from 1907 I.A. Morozov Collection;
from 1918 GMNZI

Son of Camille Pissarro, from 1894 onwards Georges began to sign his works with the surname Manzana (which was his paternal grandmother's) or with the double-barreled name Manzana-Pissarro. *Zebras at the Watering Hole* is one of the most characteristic and harmonious compositions in his decorative cycle and was exhibited in Paris in 1906-1907.

**Henri Rousseau
(Le Douanier)
1844-1910**

25. *Combat du tigre et de taureau. Un bois tropical*, circa 1908-1909
Fight Between Tiger and Bull. In the Tropical Forest
Oil on canvas, 18 × 21¾ in.
Signed bottom left:
"Henri Rousseau";
on the back, a card with the artist's inscription and signature: "Combat du tigre et de taureau. Reproduction de mon tableau exposé au Salon des Indépendants 1908. Henri Rousseau"
Inv. no. 6536

Provenance: acquired by the GMNZI in 1930.
Formerly:
from 1909 Galerie Vollard;
from 1912 S.I. Shchukin Collection; from 1918 GMNZI

The picture referred to by the artist in the inscription on the back of the painting is now in the Cleveland Museum of Art. The Hermitage canvas is not an exact reproduction, despite Rousseau's statement. The landscape in the picture in the United States is more exotic, the vegetation is larger than the animals.
Most critics hold that the version in the Hermitage was painted in 1908, though a later date cannot be excluded, given that Vollard purchased it on 5 August 1909.
The iconography of *Fight Between Tiger and Bull* had already appeared in earlier works by Rousseau. He had handled the motif of the rampant tiger in the two large

canvases *Storm in the Jungle* (*Orage dans le jungle*, 1891; National Gallery, London) and *Tiger Attacking Explorers* (*Tigre attaquant des explorateurs*, 1904; Barnes Foundation, Merion).
In effect, the source of inspiration for the Cleveland picture and hence also for the Hermitage canvas is the etching by Eugène Pirodon that reproduced the picture by the Belgian artist Charles Verlat *Royal Tiger Attacking a Buffalo* (*Tigre royale attaquant un buffle*; H. Certugny, 'Une source inconnue de Douanier Rousseau', *l'Oeil*, October 1979, pp. 74-75. This etching was published for the first time in 1883 and a second time in 1906 in the magazine *L'Art*. Evidently the latter publication had also attracted 'le Douanier's' attention, because the following year he painted the Cleveland *Fight Between Tiger and Bull*. The etching reproduced Verlat's composition as a mirror image. Perhaps in order to avoid being accused of plagiary Rousseau turned it the right way round.
Verlat's picture and hence Pirodon's etching are in the animal genre and, in fact, the figures of the animals occupy most of the space, whereas Rousseau focuses on the depiction of an imaginary jungle.
For this reason, in Russia the picture was entitled *In the Tropical Forest*.

26. *Vue des fortifications à gauche de Vanves*, 1909
View of the Fortifications at Vanves
Oil on canvas, 12¼ × 16 in.
Signed bottom left:
"Henri Rousseau";
on the back, a card with inscription, date and artist's signature:
"Vue prise commune de Vanves à gauche de la porte de ce nom. Septembre 1909. Henri Rousseau"
Inv. no. 6535

Provenance: acquired by the GMNZI in 1930.
Formerly:
from 1909 Galerie Vollard;
from 1912 S.I. Shchukin;
from 1918 GMNZI

This small canvas could be described as a landscape and a memory. Rousseau had worked as a customs official at the tollgates at Vanves, where taxes on imported food and other goods were collected. Vanves was on the edges of Paris (now Place Porte de Vanves is a subway station).
The picture in the Hermitage, which depicts the road leading from Paris to Versailles and was painted at the beginning of September 1909, was preceded by another two paintings of the tollgates at Vanves, executed in the

spring of the same year: a sketch, perhaps from life, belonging to Robert Delaunay (present whereabouts unknown) and *View of the Fortifications* (Hiroshima Museum of Art, Hiroshima). The latter is larger than the picture in the Hermitage, possesses a greater refinement of detail and chromatic effect, and shows only one figure.

27. *Jardin du Luxembourg. Monument de Chopin*, 1909
Luxembourg Gardens. Monument to Chopin
Oil on canvas, 15 × 18½ in.
Signed and dated bottom left:
"Henri Rousseau 1909";
on the back a card with an inscription by the artist:
"Vue du Luxembourg. Monument de Chopin. Composition. Henri Rousseau"
Inv. no. 7716

Provenance: acquired from the GMNZI in 1934.
Formerly:
from 1909 Galerie Vollard;
from 1912 S.I. Shchukin Collection;
from 1918 GMNZI

The theme of the walk often recurs in Rousseau's oeuvre. The woman with the parasol occupies a key position in the early *Walk in the Wood* (1886-1890; Kunsthaus, Zürich). The later works more frequently show isolated figures walking gravely to one side of the painting, while the trees are handled in a more stylized and decorative manner. The series of paintings of Paris parks (particularly Montsouris) dates from between 1905 and 1910, and develops the motif of the avenue enlivened by ladies with the inevitable parasol and gentlemen with the unfailing walking stick. The Hermitage canvas differs from the other works in this genre because it includes the monument to Chopin, a sculpture executed by the artist Georges Dubois, who has now been forgotten, which was erected in 1900 and destroyed during the

German occupation. The word "Composition" in the inscription on the back of the picture indicates that the painting was executed in the artist's studio and not from life. A year earlier, based on his impressions of the Luxembourg Gardens, Rousseau had composed the background of the painting *The Poet and the Muse*, portraying Guillaume Apollinaire and Marie Laurencin (one variation on this theme is held by the Kunstmuseum, Basel, the other is in the GMII). On 31 August 1908 the artist wrote to Apollinaire that he intended to go to the Luxembourg Gardens, where he had found a delightful spot and needed "to capture the background". An undated drawing has been preserved, *Coin du Jardin du Luxembourg* (private collection, Japan; exhibition "Banquet in Honor of 'le Douanier' Rousseau", Tokyo, 1985, no. 18), but it has no connection with the picture in the Hermitage.

Maurice Denis
1870-1943

28. *La visitation*, 1894
Mary's Visit to Elizabeth
Oil on canvas,
40½ × 36¾ in.
Signed and dated at the
bottom towards the right
with the initials: "MAUD 94"
Inv. no. 6575

Provenance: acquired
from the GMNZI in 1934.
Formerly:
from 1899 S.I. Shchukin
Collection; from 1918 GMNZI.

Mary's visit to Elizabeth (Luke 1, 36-56) is one of the most recurrent themes in Denis's early work. In the *Notes on Painting*, written in 1893 during his honeymoon, he drew up a program of religious compositions that also included two Visitations. The *Visitation with Dovecote* (*Visitation au colombier*; private collection) where Elizabeth and Mary are depicted against the background of a trellis dates from the same year. In the lithograph *Mary's Visit to Elizabeth* (1894) the composition is simplified and the small house is replaced by a lattice work fence. In the picture in the Hermitage this motif is further elaborated so that the simple fence becomes a series of arched trellises covered in creepers with autumn foliage.
The *Visitation with Dovecote* shows a horse and carriage with a coachman in the foreground. This element seems to extend the limits of the subject by alluding to the journey Mary has made. In the Hermitage canvas the carriage is barely visible and this notably changes the relationship between the figures and the background.
Like the other works of the 1890s, the two main figures bear a marked resemblance to Marthe Denis.
This is definitely an autumnal scene, though the Catholic Church celebrates the Visitation on 31 May. This may be explained by the fact that the picture was painted shortly before the birth of the artist's son Jean-Paul. Denis usually expressed the main events of his life in traditional subjects.

29a. *Marthe et Marie*
(première version, verso
du tableau suivant), 1896
Martha and Mary
(first version, back
of following painting)
Oil on canvas, 30½ × 45¾ in.
Inv. no. 9124

This version represents the biblical episode narrated by Luke (10, 38-42). Denis approached this theme for the first time in the watercolor *Holy Conversation* (*La conversation sacrée*, 1890; private collection, Saint-Germain-en-Laye), where the scene of Christ's conversation with the women set against a rural landscape occupies a relatively small space. However, the conflict between the sisters is evident. Mary is listening intently to Christ's words, while Martha is giving her sister a disapproving look. A few years after his marriage Denis returned to the same subject. Since his wife's name was Marthe, the theme took on a special, personal significance for the artist. In fact, his wife is easily recognizable even in the stylized depiction of the female figures in the picture. Martha and Mary have the same facial features and confront each other like two aspects of the same figure, like light and shade that are always destined to coexist.

29b. *Marthe et Marie*, 1896
(deuxième version)
Martha and Mary
(second version)
Oil on canvas, 30½ × 45¾ in.
Signed and dated at
the bottom towards the right
with the initials: "MAUD 96"
Inv. no. 9124

Provenance: acquired
from the GMNZI in 1948.
Formerly:
from 1903 Galerie Vollard;
from 1903 S.I. Shchukin
Collection;
from 1918 GMNZI

Dissatisfied with the first version of *Martha and Mary*, which he had left unfinished, Denis turned the canvas over and changed the overall spatial effect of the composition, thus achieving greater lightness and airiness. In both versions he rejected the original idea of the vertical composition, which can be seen in the sketch of the painting formerly owned by Vollard (now in a private collection). The model for the figurative scheme of *Martha and Mary* can be found in *The Road to Emmaus* (1894; private collection), where Christ and the pious women are very similar from the iconographic viewpoint to the figures in the Hermitage painting.
The background of the painting depicts a real place. The landscape of Saint-Germain-en-Laye is virtually the same as that in *Mary's Visit to Elizabeth* (cf. no. 28 in the present catalog), except that

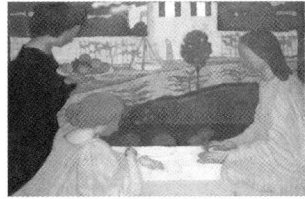

only the top portion of the arch is visible and does not stand out against the dark green grass; by contrast, the yellow house and the wall in the background are more accentuated.
It is very likely that even the individual elements of the composition are linked to actual events in the artist's life. Bouillon, a contemporary expert on the artist's work, explains Martha's black dress by the fact that their son Jean-Paul had died the year before, and he also points out that there is a veiled allusion to Maurice Denis's acceptance of death, "which is also a promise of resurrection" (J.P. Bouillon, *Maurice Denis*, Geneva, 1993, p. 76).
This picture contains a direct reference to Maeterlink's opera *Martha and Mary* staged by Denis's friend, Lugné-Poë, on 15 March 1895, and also expresses the artist's mood

triggered by the vicissitudes of his private life and the tragic loss of his first son, as well as the new hope springing in his heart.
This picture held a special significance for Denis and he exhibited it at the Salon of the Societé Nationale des Beaux-Arts in 1897.

30. *Fontaine de pèlerinage en Guidel*, circa 1905
Sacred Spring in Guidel
Oil on canvas, 15½ × 13½ in.
Signed bottom right
with the initials: "MAUD"
Inv. no. 7711

Provenance: acquired
from the GMNZI in 1934.
Formerly:
from 1906 I.A. Morozov
Collection
(purchased at the Salon des
Indépendants exhibition;
from 1918 GMNZI

Denis mentions Guidel in his diary notes written at Le

Pouldu in August 1905. As he and Marthe were in Bretagne they made a few excursions in the environs of Quimper in order to attend the religious feasts and processions that were taking place at Pont-Aven, Clohars and Guidel, "located on the always fresh and delightfully green plain." (M. Denis, *Journal, 1884-1943*, vol. I, Paris, 1967, p. 20).
The painting under consideration here was probably executed in August 1905, and it is distinguished from Denis's other works by its bright shades of green. It seems that shortly afterwards he painted *The Religious Procession in Guidel* (*La procession religieuse en Guidel*), which he gave to Sérisier's wife (private collection, Lausanne).

Edouard Vuillard
1868-1940

31. *Intérieur*, 1899
Interior
Oil on paper mounted on wood, 20½ × 31 in.
Signed and dated top right: "E. Vuillard 99"
Inv. no. 6538

Provenance: acquired from the GMNZI in 1930.
Formerly:
S.I. Shchukin Collection (purchased before 1908);
from 1918 GMNZI

Since the last figure of the date is illegible, this picture is sometimes attributed to 1893

and sometimes to 1899. It is difficult to date the work precisely because the artist's style did not undergo any substantial changes during this period. It is correct to read the date as "1899", however, since by the end of the 1890s, Vuillard preferred to use gray, ochre and neutral tones rather than bright colors, and these are dominant in this composition. Moreover, in the interiors painted in 1898-1899, particularly pictures like *Two Armchairs* (*Deux fauteuils*, 1898; private collection, Paris) and *Drawing Room with Three Lamps* (*Le salon aux trois lampes*, circa 1899; Zumsteg Collection, Zürich) there is a similar relationship between the figures and furniture on the one side and the spatial context on the other. A further argument in favor of dating the work in the Hermitage to 1899 is its similarity to Vuillard's series of colored lithographs *Landscapes and Interiors* (*Paysages et intériors*), published by Vollard that same year.

32. *Enfants*, 1909
Children
Tempera on paper mounted on wood, 33¼ × 30¾ in.
Signed bottom right: "E. Vuillard"
Inv. no. 42153

Provenance: acquired from the GMNZI in 1934.
Formerly:
Galerie Bernheim-Jeune;
M.O. Cetlin Collection, Moscow;
Rumyanchev Museum, Moscow;
from 1925 GMNZI

This picture was painted at Saint-Jacu-de-la-Mer, a village on the Normandy coast where Vuillard had been invited by Alfred Nathanson. A partial view of Saint-Jacu can be seen from the balcony. The three Nathanson brothers, sons of the wealthy banker who had founded the *Revue Blanche*, were friends of the artist. All three showed a very keen interest in Vuillard's painting. The youngest, Alfred, who owned some of his works, made his debut as a playwright by collaborating with Tristan Bernard. Alfred

Nathanson's daughter, Annette, recalled that Vuillard had painted a portrait of her and her sister Denise at Saint-Jacu in the summer of 1909, while her father and Tristan Bernard were working on a new play, *Les Costauds des Epinettes*, in the next room. There is a pencil sketch of the picture (private collection, Paris; B. Thompson, *Vuillard*, London, 1988, p. 96), evidently drawn from life. The essentials of the composition can already be seen, but a comparison between this study and the painting shows that this realistic impression was only a starting point and was later altered considerably. The sisters' positions were changed, the carpet was moved from right to left, and a Japanese screen with aquatic decoration was added, which introduced a typically Nabis note. The sketch clearly shows the children sitting on a couch, however in the painting this is barely visible. The initial desire to draw the little girls had driven Vuillard to take up his pencil, but in the painting they play a minor role. The faces cannot be seen and the figures become patches of color that have no more importance than the other background features, for instance, the carpet, screen and door.

Pierre Bonnard
1867-1947

33. *Premier printemps (Les petits faunes)*, 1909
Early Spring (Little Fauns)
Oil on canvas, 40½ × 49¼ in.
Signed bottom right: "Bonnard"
Inv. no. 9106

Provenance: acquired from the GMNZI in 1948.
Formerly:
1909 Galerie Bernheim-Jeune;
from 1909 Bernstein Collection, Paris;
from 1912 I.A. Morozov Collection;
from 1918 GMNZI

Bonnard first handled pastoral motifs in 1902 in the illustrations for *Daphnis and Chloe* by Longo, commissio-

ned by Vollard. In 1907 he painted a small canvas, known as *The Faun*, *Pan and the Nymph*, *Afternoon of a Faun* (*L'Après-midi d'un faune*; J. and H. Dauberville, *Bonnard. Catalogue raisonné de l'oeuvre peint*, vol. II: *1906-1919*, Paris, 1967, p. 471), and later (around 1910) *The Fauns* (*Les Faunes*; private collection, Switzerland). Mythological characters from the Dionysian world only appear in these two canvases and the picture in the Hermitage. Moreover, in *The Fauns*, a work in a more decorative style, the subject of the Hermitage composition is further developed in the bottom lefthand corner, where the creature with goat's hooves is playing music in exactly the same way.
Early Spring had also been preceded by *Early Spring or Thoughts* (*Premier Printemps ou les pensées*, 1908; Phillips Collection, Washington). This depicts, with slight modifications, the same landscape of Vernouillet (a small town on the Seine, not far from Paris) that partially appears in *Storm at Vernouillet* (1908; private collection, Switzerland) with two children running to escape from the storm. By replacing the children in the 1908 canvas with mythological characters set against the real landscape of Vernouillet with modern architectural elements, as opposed to an idealized natural setting, Bonnard creates a completely unexpected counterpoint.

34. *Le train et les chalands*, 1909
The Train and Its Trailers (Freight Train)
Oil on canvas, 30¼ × 42½ in.
Signed bottom right: "Bonnard";
dated on the frame: "1909"
Inv. no. 6537

Provenance: acquired from the GMNZI in 1930.
Formerly:
from 1909 Galerie Bernheim-Jeune;
from 1910 I.A. Morozov Collection;
from 1918 GMNZI

This picture, executed in the late spring of 1909, was first exhibited with the title *The Train and Its Trailers* in Bonnard's one-man show at the Galerie Bernheim-Jeune in 1910. In the handwritten catalog of I.A. Morozov, who purchased the painting at this exhibition, it was described as *Landscape with Freight Train*, the title that was subsequently used at the GMNZI and the Hermitage. The picture depicts the environs of Vernouillet. The local thirteenth-century church was a

celebrated Romanesque building, but Bonnard did not depict its architectural beauty. What really interested him at the time were the vast, distant horizons beyond the perimeter of the small town.

35. *Le matin à Paris*, 1911
Morning in Paris
Oil on canvas, 30 × 48 in.
Signed bottom right: "Bonnard"
Inv. no. 9107
(companion piece to inv. no. 9105)

Provenance: acquired from the GMNZI in 1948
Formerly:
from 1912 I.A. Morozov Collection;
from 1918 GMNZI

The pair of works *Morning in Paris* and *Evening in Paris* depict a neighborhood often painted by the artist between 1893 and 1912. His studio was located here in the vicinity of the boulevards Clichy and Batignolles. The subjects of the two works can already be found in the very first pictures he painted in the studio

in rue Douail, *On the Boulevard* (1893) and *People in the Street* (*Personnages dans la rue*, circa 1894).
In 1898 Bonnard worked on the series of color lithographs, *Aspects of Parisian Life*, commissioned by Vollard, and they were to play a role in the development of iconographic genre elements in the two later works in the Morozov Collection. For example, *A Street Corner* displays some motifs later repeated in *Morning in Paris*: women, children, a little dog, a cart. Part of the background landscape in the picture is recognizable in another work of 1911, *Fog on Boulevard Batignolles*. Bonnard had already painted this intersection on boulevard Batignolles twice before in *The Cart* (1909, Barnes Foundation, Merion) and in *The Ragpickers* (*Les chiffonières*, early 1910; Salz Collection, New York).
In the background of the small picture *The Cart* there is exactly the same landscape as the one in the Hermitage canvas, but the foreground shows a junk dealer with an overloaded cart. In returning to this motif in the more monumental canvas of the *Ragpickers*, the artist changes the arrangement in the foreground.
The bottom lefthand corner is occupied by young women moving towards the spectator, in the center there is a coalman's donkey and cart, which indicates the time of day, since the coalman delivered in the early morning.
In the later painting *Morning in Paris* Bonnard abandons the subject of the *Ragpickers* (who, on their way back from Les Halles, force the coalman to walk along the edge of the road) and simply hints at the sunrise, thus changing the main elements into easily recognizable forms.

36. *Le soir à Paris*, 1911
Evening in Paris
Oil on canvas, 30 × 47¾ in.
Signed bottom right: "Bonnard"
Inv. no. 9105
(companion piece to inv. no. 9107)

Provenance: acquired from the GMNZI in 1948.
Formerly:
from 1912 I.A. Morozov Collection;
from 1918 GMNZI

The idea of painting two pictures of street life in Paris, at different times of day, had been the aim of all Bonnard's previous production. The location of his studio in rue Douail, which led into place Clichy, where the boulevards Clichy and Batignolles intersected was essential for this purpose. This neighborhood was already very busy even then and Bonnard, in constantly returning to the motifs of bustling street life in the late 1890s and after 1900, never abandoned the idea of a composition in sections capable of containing more impressions than a single canvas. In 1896 and 1900 he executed two triptychs depicting place Clichy (J. and H. Dauberville, *Bonnard, Catalogue raisonné de l'oeuvre peint*, Paris, 1967, pp. 136, 237). The first of these is entitled *Les âges de la vie*. This idea can also be seen in the two canvases in the Morozov Collection, since each picture features figures representing the three different ages of man.
The pictures from which *Evening in Paris* developed were *Les Batignolles* or *The Fiacre Horse* (*Les Batignolles*

or *Le cheval de fiacre*, 1895; National Gallery of Art, Washington) and the lithographs in the series *Aspects of Parisian Life* (*Boulevard, The Square at Night, Street in the Evening in the Rain*) dating from the same period. Japanese influences are evident both in the lithographs and in *Evening in Paris*. The frieze-like elements in the composition owe something to Kiyonaga's techniques and the evening street scene is reminiscent of the color xylograph by Hirosighe *Evening Scene at Saruwakacho* in the series *Famous Views of Edo* (1856). The idea of *Evening in Paris* is very similar to *The Flower Seller* painted by Bonnard six years earlier (J. and H. Dauberville, *op. cit.* p. 322), depicting an old woman with a cart full of flowers and little girls on the right.

Ker Xavier Roussel
1867-1944

37. *Sujet mythologique*, circa 1903
Mythological Scene
Oil on canvas, 18½ × 24½ in.
Inv. no. 9065

Provenance: acquired from the GMNZI in 1948.
Formerly:
Galerie Bernheim-Jeune;
from 1911 Nekrasov Collection, Moscow;
S.A. Polyakov Collection, Moscow;
from 1917 Tretyakov Gallery;
from 1925 GMNZI

This picture does not depict a specific myth, but is a variation on the arcadian theme. In portraying nudes in a natural landscape the artist deli-

berately chooses a mythological vein. His admiration for seventeenth-century painting has influenced the poses of the figures. The animals at play represent the Dionysian theme; Dionysus was worshipped in Greece, the Romans identified him with Bacchus, and he was clothed in the skin of a black goat. Within the context of this composition the female nudes represent Bacchantes.
Roussel began to paint mythological themes in 1900. Before then his pictures of people and animals were modern renderings of everyday life (*Boy with Goat*, circa 1890; private collection, Paris). The artist's mythological compositions, probably inspired by Cross, display a sense

of humor characteristic of the Nabis. This can be seen in the hairstyles in this painting that are typical of the early twentieth century.

The mythological subject suggests that Roussel is depicting the Mediterranean coast. In fact, the picture has been dated to 1906, which means that it was executed during the artist's journey to Provence with Denis. However this took place in winter, while the colors of the landscape in *Mythological Scene* are definitely autumnal. The artist had already been to the Mediterranean coast; in 1899 he had visited Cannes with Vuillard and from there they had gone on to Venice. The pictorial style and rendering of the female figures are similar to the painting *Before the Sea* (*Devant de la mer*, circa 1903; Musée du Petit Palais, Paris) and to *Bathers* (1903; Bernheim-Jeune Collection, Paris), but above all to the studies that preceded this composition. This similarity allows *Mythological Scene* to be dated to around 1903.

Félix Vallotton
1867-1925

38. *Une dame au piano*, 1904
A Lady at the Piano
Oil on canvas, 17 × 22½ in.
Signed and dated
bottom right:
"F. Vallotton 04"
Inv. no. 4860

Provenance: acquired from the GMNZI in 1948.
Formerly:
from 1911 G.E. Haasen Collection, St. Petersburg;
from 1921 Hermitage;
from 1930 GMNZI

This painting depicts Vallotton's wife, Gabrielle, in their house in the country at Varangeville where they spent the summer of 1904 (since 1899 the artist had been accustomed to spending the summer months in Normandy). In his *Inventory* Vallotton described no. 527 as *Woman Playing the Piano in a Country Interior. Varangeville* (*Femme jouant du piano dans un intérieur de campagne. Varangeville. Salon d'Automne*). This picture was exhibited at the Salon d'Automne in 1904. No. 528 in the *Inventory* is *Dining Room in a House in the Country* (*La Salle à manger dans une maison de campagne*, 1904; Galerie Paul Vallotton, Lausanne) in which the artist's wife is seen in the same pose and wearing the same robe. Probably Vallotton was thinking of *A lady at the Piano* when he wrote a letter to his brother on 30 December 1909 about sending some pictures that were in his possession to Haasen: "...You can take, for example...the *Lady at the Piano*." (F. Vallotton, *Documents pour une biographie et pour l'histoire d'une oeuvre*, introduced, edited and annotated by G. Gaison and D. Jacubec, vol. II: *1900-1914*, Lausanne, Paris, 1974, letter 241).

39. *Jeune femme au chapeau noir*, 1908
Young Woman with a Black Hat
Oil on canvas, 32 × 25¾ in.
Signed and dated
top right:
"F. Vallotton 08"
Inv. no. 5108

Provenance: acquired from the GMNZI in 1948.

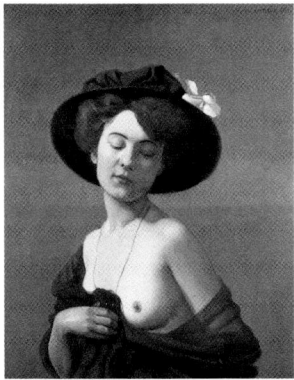

Formerly:
from 1911 G.F. Haasen Collection, St. Petersburg;
from 1921 Hermitage;
from 1930 GMNZI

In Vallotton's *Inventory* this picture is no. 637 and is entitled *Bust of a Woman with Bare Breast Draped in a Black Shawl, with a Black Hat and Pink Ribbon*. This painting is mentioned in the letter to his brother written on 30 December 1909: "If you want to send Haasen the pictures you have, you can take for example... the *Woman with a Black Hat* (F. Vallotton, *Documents pour une biographie et pour l'histoire d'une oeuvre*, introduced, edited and annotated by G. Gaison and D Jacubec, vol. II: *1910-1914*, Lausanne, Paris, 1974, letter 241).

In 1908 the *Young Woman with a Black Hat* was exhibited at the "Golden Fleece" exhibition in Moscow together with two other pictures executed at the same time, in which a similar technique is used, *Woman with a Green Hat* and *Female Nude*. In the first of these the shawl is thrown over the model's shoulders in a similar way, leaving the breast bare (*Golden Fleece*, Moscow, 1908, pp. 20, 61, nos. 7-9).

40. *Portrait de Georges E. Haasen*
Portrait of Georges E. Haasen
Oil on canvas, 32 × 39½ in.
Signed and dated top left:
"F. Vallotton 1912 +1"
Inv. no. 4901

Provenance: acquired in 1921.
Formerly:
from 1913 G.E. Haasen Collection, St. Petersburg

Georges E. Haasen, who collected modern paintings, particularly by French artists including Bonnard, Vallotton, Marquet and Manguin, was also an art dealer and partner of Félix Vallotton's brother Paul. He was the representative of the Swiss chocolate factory Cailler in St. Petersburg and he moved there before 1906. At the beginning of 1913 Haasen invited Vallotton to visit him in St. Petersburg. On 5 March he wrote to his brother, giving Haasen's address as Kamennoostrovsky prospekt 59/1: "I'm happy to be here and today I begin the portrait, unfortunately the weather is very overcast... Haasen and his wife are well; they are both extremely kind and can't do enough for me." (F. Vallotton, *Documents pour une biographie et pour l'histoire d'une oeuvre*, introduced, edited and annotated by G. Gaison and D. Jacubec, vol. II: *1914-1910*, Lausanne, Paris, 1974, letter 271). In the following letter that is undated but was sent no later than the middle of March he writes: "The portrait is nearly finished; it has turned out well and is full of amusing chromatic elements, because it includes nearly the whole apartment that is quite colorful." (F. Vallotton, *op. cit.* letter 272).

In the letter sent from Paris on 29 March, the artist again mentions the painting: "The portrait of Haasen is a good piece, a little severe as usual, but I am the problem because I don't take life lightheartedly." (F. Vallotton, *op. cit.*, letter 273).

Judging from the date the artist wrote on the painting ("1912 +1") it seems likely that he began the work, perhaps from a photograph, in Paris in 1912.

Louis Valtat
1869-1952

41. *Une réunion de jeunes femmes*, circa 1898
A Gathering of Young Women
Oil on canvas, 25½ × 31½ in.
Signed bottom right: "L. Valtat"
Inv. no. 7722

Provenance: acquired from the GMNZI in 1934.
Formerly:
Galerie Vollard;
from 1907 I.A. Morozov Collection;
from 1918 GMNZI

Experts are not in agreement on the date of this painting or that of the whole group of pictures depicting women

and children in Parisian parks to which it belongs. Cogniat attributes two very similar canvases *People in the Bois de Boulogne* and *Young Women in the Bois de Boulogne* to 1898 (R. Cogniat, *Louis Valtat*, Neuchâtel, 1963, pp. 49, 122). The figures in the foreground in *People in the Bois de Boulogne*, the little girl with the white hat and the woman in a light colored dress adjusting her hair, are to be found, with slight alterations in the Hermitage picture.
The fact that *A Gathering of Young Women* was probably executed in 1898 is confirmed by paintings similar in theme and style depicting walks and games in Parisian parks, for example *Elegant Walk* (*La promenade des élégants*), *Walk in the Luxembourg Gardens* (*Promenade au Luxembourg*) and *Children's Games* (*Jeux d'enfants*), which the artist's son Jean attributed to 1898.

42. *La barque*, 1899
The Boat
Oil on canvas, 32 × 39¾ in.
Signed and dated bottom right: "Valtat 99"
Inv. no. 5108

Provenance: acquired from the GMNZI in 1948.
Formerly:
Galerie Vollard;
from 1906 I.A. Morozov Collection;
from 1918 GMNZI

When I.A. Morozov purchased the painting Vollard's records stated that it had been

executed at Bagnoles-sur-Mer. Valtat had, in effect, worked there and at nearby Collioure, on the Mediterranean during that period. The organizers of the artist's retrospective in Bordeaux (1995), however, reject the possibility that it was executed at Bagnoles, and insist that it is one of the series of canvases painted at Agay, where Valtat worked at the beginning of 1899 ("Louis Valtat, Exposition Retrospective", Musée des Beaux-Arts, Bordeaux, 1995, no. 39). In actual fact, the subject of the picture (children playing on the sand) and the landscape suggest no grounds for believing that it was painted in winter. Finally, in the catalog of the artist's painting compiled by Jean Valtat, a variant of the composition in the Hermitage (J. Valtat, *Catalogue de l'oeuvre peint. 1869-1952*, vol. I, Neuchâtel, 1977, p.121) is entitled *La barque à Anthéor* and mistakenly dated 1891. It has the same landscape in the background though the boat and the people are arranged a little differently. The hypothesis that the whole group was painted at Agay is confirmed by the canvas *Mother and Children on the Beach* (*Mère et enfants sur la plage*), dated and signed by the artist "Agay / 99" (Musée des Beaux-Arts, Bordeaux). This composition depicts the family of the local fisherman Bompart and it is reasonable to suppose that the same people feature in the Hermitage picture. Probably Valtat painted *Children in the Boat* (*Les enfants sur la barque*, circa 1899; private collection; "Louis Valtat" exhibition, Petit Palais, Geneva, 1969, no. 16) at the same time. The subject of the woman and children in the boat drawn up on the sand is repeated in the small picture *The Boat* (*Le bateau*, 1899; Musée des Beaux-Arts, Bordeaux), in which the woman is seated and wearing a red dress, and there is the sea in the background instead of mountains.

43. *Les falaises violettes*
The Purple Cliffs
Oil on canvas, 25¾ × 32 in.
Signed and dated bottom left: "Valtat 19[00]"
Inv. no. 8961

Provenance: acquired from the GMNZI in 1948.
Formerly:
M.A. Morozov Collection;
from 1903 M.K. Morozova Collection;
from 1910 Tretyakov Gallery (gift of M.K. Morozova);
from 1925 GMNZI

This picture is better known as *The Undertow*.
The original title the artist gave it *Les falaises violettes* is

on a card attached to the frame.
These are obviously the same cliffs, painted from the opposite side, as those depicted in the *Seascape* exhibited at the Salon d'Automne in 1905 and reproduced on the famous page in *L'Illustration* of 4 November the same year, devoted to the Fauves.
This picture is also similar to the landscape *The Red Rocks of Anthéor* (*Les Rochers rouges d'Anthéor*, circa 1901; formerly in the Georges Besson Collection, Paris).
Besson, who knew Valtat very well, insisted that his masterly handling of color was at its height at Anthéor. It is also very likely that the landscape in the Hermitage was painted at Anthéor.

44. *Le golfe d'Anthéor*,
circa 1906-1907
The Gulf of Anthéor
Oil on canvas, 29 × 36¾ in.
Signed bottom left: "L. Valtat"
Inv. no. 8887

Provenance: acquired from the GMNZI in 1948.
Formerly:
Galerie Vollard; from 1907 I.A. Morozov Collection;
from 1918 GMNZI

This picture was traditionally dated 1907, the year in which it was exhibited for the first time at the Salon d'Automne. However, it may have been painted a little earlier. The subject and style are similar to the *Sailing Boat* (1906: private collection), which also depicts the Gulf of Anthéor with rocky mountains in the distance.

Albert Marquet
1875-1947

45. *Vue de la Seine et le monument de Henri IV,* circa 1906
View of the Seine and the Monument to Henri IV
Oil on canvas, 25¾ × 32 in.
Signed bottom left: "marquet"
Inv. no. 9151

Provenance: acquired from the GMNZI in 1948.
Formerly: Galerie Druet, Paris; from 1906 I.A. Morozov Collection; from 1918 GMNZI

After moving to the bank of the Seine, Gds-Augustins, 25, in 1905, Albert Marquet painted a series of views from the window of his studio including the *Gds-Augustins Bank of the Seine* (Centre Georges Pompidou, Paris), the *Pont Neuf* (1906; National Gallery Washington), and *Pont Neuf in the Sun* (1906; Museum Boymans-van Beuningen, Rotterdam.
The upper section of this last painting reproduces the same view as the one in the Hermitage canvas, though the landscape in Rotterdam was painted at the end of summer, while the one in St. Petersburg was probably executed at the end of autumn. The lower righthand portion of the picture shows the square near the Pont Neuf with the monument to Henri IV by Lemot (1818) and a part of the Île de la Cité, in the distance the Pont des Arts and, on the right, the Louvre.

46. *Le port de Hambourg,* 1909
The Port of Hamburg
Oil on canvas, 26¼ × 31½ in.
Signed bottom right: "marquet"
Inv. no. 8907

Provenance: acquired from the GMNZI in 1948.
Formerly: Galerie Druet, Paris; from 1913 I.A. Morozov Collection; from 1918 GMNZI

Marquet lived in Hamburg in the winter of 1909 and painted a series of landscapes of the port. The exhibition of his works at the Galerie Druet in 1910 included thirteen views of the port of Hamburg. In some of them, like the picture in the Hermitage, the central motif is the tug, especially in *Tug at Hamburg* (two variants: 1909, private collection; 1910, M. Marquet Collection, Paris). The same area of the port with the tug on the right can be seen in *Port of Hamburg* (private collection, USA). The drawing *The Tug, Hamburg* (*Le remorqueur, Hambourg,* 1909; private collection, France; "Marquet" exhibition, Musée de Lodeve, 1908, no. 89) can be considered a preliminary study for the canvas in the Hermitage.

This picture depicts the right arm of the Elbe, the rose colored warehouses along the Customs canal can be seen in the distance, and in the center the bell towers of two medieval churches, St. Catherine's on the right and St. Michael's on the left.
Probably the composition in the Hermitage was exhibited at the 1909 Salon d'Automne with the title *Hamburg in the Winter Sun* (Druet Collection; no. 1132).

47. *Naples,* 1909
The Gulf of Naples
Oil on canvas, 24½ × 31¾ in.
Signed bottom right: "marquet"; dated below in ink: "1909"
Inv. no. 9150

Provenance: acquired from the GMNZI in 1948.

Formerly: Galerie Druet, Paris; from 1913 I.A. Morozov Collection; from 1918 GMNZI

After visiting Naples for the first time in 1908, Albert Marquet spent the summer of 1909 there. At the exhibition held at the Galerie Druet in May 1910 he showed eleven landscapes he had brought back from the Italian city a few months earlier. Most of the pictures in this series depict the Gulf of Naples with Vesuvius in the background and rowboats, sailboats or barges. The paintings that bear the greatest resemblance to the Hermitage canvas as regards composition and style are *Naples. The Sailboat* (*Naples. Le Voilier,* 1909; Musée de Beaux-Arts, Bordeaux) and *Naples. Oarsman* (1909; private collection, Paris). *Vesuvius* (1909; GMII) was also painted from the same vantage point.

48. *Notre-Dame sous la pluie,* 1910
Notre-Dame in the Rain
Oil on canvas, 32 × 26 in.
Signed bottom right: "marquet"
Inv. no. 6256

Provenance: acquired from the GMNZI in 1930.
Formerly: Galerie Druet, Paris, from 1911 I.A. Morozov Collection; from 1918 GMNZI

Marquet painted the cathedral of Notre-Dame in Paris several times, in different light and weather conditions, from 1901 onwards.
After moving to quai St-Michel in 1908, the artist could see Notre-Dame from his window.
The series of views of the bank of the Seine with the cathedral in the background dates from 1908-1910.
The same composition as the Hermitage painting is repeated in *Notre-Dame. Snow*

(early 1910; private collection, Paris).
The card on the frame gives the precise date of this painting, in fact it reads "Inondation janvier. Notre-Dame. 1910".
The picture depicts the end of the flood after the waters of the Seine have subsided leaving the lower banks of the river visible.

49. *Vue aux environs de Rouen,* 1927
View in the Environs of Rouen
Pen, Indian ink and pencil on paper, 8½ × 12¼ in.
Signed bottom left: "marquet"
Inv. no. 44969

Provenance: acquired in 1959 (gift of the artist's widow).
Formerly: M. Marquet Collection, Paris

This drawing was executed in 1927, when Marquet lived in Rouen. The composition of the drawing, with the broad stretch of water occupying the whole of the foreground, gives the impression that the original sketch from life was made in a boat. Later the drawing was finished with pen and Indian ink in his studio.

Henri Manguin
1874-1949

50. *Paysage à Saint-Tropez*, 1905
Landscape at Saint-Tropez
Oil on canvas, 20 × 24 in.
Signed bottom right: "Manguin"
Inv. no. 4854

Provenance: acquired from the G.E. Haasen Collection in 1921. Formerly: from 1905 Galerie Vollard; from March 1905 Haasen Collection, St. Petersburg.

In 1905 Manguin rented Villa Demière, near Saint-Tropez, where he also painted *Path at Saint-Tropez* (Hermitage).
Probably these works were among the hundred and fifty canvases that Vollard, who "discovered" the artist, bought from him en bloc for 5,000 francs.
The motif of the knotty trees recurs frequently in Henri Manguin's paintings from his Fauve period. The house in the center of the landscape is the so-called Château Martin. Painted in the summer of 1905, the *Landscape at Saint-Tropez* was shown that same year in the exhibition held at the Galerie Berthe Weill with the title *Le bois, soir* ("Exposition de groupe", Galerie Berthe Weill, Paris, 1905, no. 30).

51. *Matin (Au bord du golfe de Cavalière)*, 1906
Morning (On the Shore of the Gulf of Cavalière)
Oil on canvas, 32 × 25½ in.

Signed bottom right: "Manguin"
Inv. no. 8956

Provenance: acquired from the GMNZI in 1948. Formerly: from 1906 S.I. Shchukin Collection (purchased at the Salon d'Automne exhibition); from 1918 GMNZI

This picture, which is one of the artist's most successful works, is also known as *Woman on the Seashore*, *Woman Sitting on the Shore of the Gulf of Cavalière* and *Morning*. The last title indicates that when Manguin spent the spring and summer months on the Mediterranean coast, during his Fauve period, he usually painted in the early morning and often depicted a female figure in a landscape. This picture was executed in the spring or summer of 1906 and is one of the Cavalière series. Two of these works, like the Hermitage composition, feature Manguin's favorite model, his wife Jeanne, with the same parasol (private collection, Germany; *Jeanne à l'ombrelle, Cavalière*, Kunsthalle, Bielefeld).

Maurice de Vlaminck
1876-1958

52. *Une vue de la Seine*, circa 1906
A View of the Seine
Oil on canvas, 21½ × 25¾ in.
Signed bottom right: "Vlaminck"
Inv. no. 9112

Provenance: acquired from the GMNZI in 1930. Formerly: from 1909 Galerie Kahnweiler; S.I. Shchukin Collection; from 1918 GMNZI

This picture was executed in the Parisian suburb of Chatou where the artist worked with André Derain. Chatou Bridge, often painted by Maurice de Vlaminck in 1905-1907, can be glimpsed on the right in the distance.
A similar subject is to be found in the landscapes *Boats at Chatou* (1906; Mayer Collection, Geneva) and *Bridge at Chatou* (1907; Neue National Galerie, Berlin).

53. *Bourg*, circa 1908-1909
Market Town
Oil on canvas, 29 × 36½ in.
Signed bottom right: "Vlaminck"
Inv. no. 6539

Provenance: acquired from the GMNZI in 1930. Formerly: from 1909 Galerie Kahnweiler; S.I. Shchukin Collection; from 1918 GMNZI

This picture dates from between the end of 1908 and the beginning of 1909, when it was purchased by the Galerie Kahnweiler. However, it differs in style from the works of the first half of 1908. Probably the *Landscape* depicting the same place was painted at the same time as *Market Town*. The former was auctioned by Christie's on 1 December 1967 and dated 1909.
It is thought that the picture is of Valmondois, a town in the Seine et Oise département, not far from Paris.

Maurice Utrillo
1883-1955

54. *Rue Custine à Montmartre*, 1909-1910
Rue Custine in Montmartre
Tempera on paperboard, 21½ × 25¾ in.
Signed bottom right: "Maurice Utrillo-V"
Inv. no. 10598

Provenance: acquired in 1997. Formerly: Lepoutre Collection, Paris; private collection, Lyons; private collection, Paris

This work was executed to be published on the title-page of the book by A. Basler, *Maurice Utrillo* (Paris, 1931), one of the first volumes on the artist. The prominent position given to *Rue Custine in Montmartre* implies that it was probably Utrillo himself who chose to place it here. At the time this picture was in

the Lepoutre Collection.
It is a view of rue Custine, seen from the intersection with rue Caulaincourt. In the same period, circa 1909, Utrillo painted another view of this street (formerly in the Petrides Collection, Paris; P. Petrides, *L'oeuvre complet de Maurice Utrillo*, vol. I, Paris, 1959, no. 411). This variant does not have the street lamp in the foreground and the vantage point has changed so that the righthand side and not the lefthand side of the street is visible.

Kees Van Dongen
1877-1968

55. *Printemps*, 1908
Spring
Oil on canvas, 31¾ × 39½ in.
Signed towards the bottom right: "Van Dongen"
Inv. no. 9130

Provenance: acquired from the GMNZI in 1948.
Formerly:
from 1908 Galerie Bernheim-Jeune; S.I. Shchukin Collection; from 1918 GMNZI

Though the influence of works by Henri Matisse, for example his studies for *Bonheur de vivre* (1905-1906; Barnes Foundation, Merion) is evident, the canvas cannot have been painted before 1908, in other words, before the first Cubist landscapes by Picasso, whom the painter was close to in this period. A 1909 photograph of Van Dongen in his studio shows a landscape in the center of which there is the same cube-shaped house that appears in *Spring*. The exhibition held at the Galerie Bernheim-Jeune at the end of 1908 included a picture entitled *Spring*. It is very likely that this was the canvas in the Hermitage, since there are no other works with this title in the exhibition catalogs.

56. *Lucie et son danseur*, 1911
Lucie and Her Dancer
Oil on canvas,
51¼ × 38 in.
Signed bottom left: "Van Dongen"
Inv. no. 9087

Provenance: acquired from the GMNZI in 1948.
Formerly:
from 1908 Galerie Bernheim-Jeune;
M.O. Cetlin Collection, Moscow;
Poryvkina Collection, Moscow;
from 1939 GMNZI.

The other title of this picture is *The Dancer and the Negro*. Its subject belongs both to the genre of cabaret improvisations and to portraiture. It expresses an ambiguous attitude towards reality. Van Dongen was an acute and ironical observer, as he had already demonstrated in his many drawings for satirical magazines, yet he evidently satisfies his models' desire to appear more dignified, a talent that explains why he was later to become a successful high society portraitist.
In December 1911 this picture was shown at the exhibition held at the Galerie Bernheim-Jeune (the gallery card on the back gives the date when it was executed as 1911).
The year before Lucie had posed nude for Van Dongen in *Lucie the Mulatta* (*Lucie la Mulatresse*) and her companion, the negro Ginnadu Tairu, nicknamed Charlie, had posed for *Portrait of Ginnadu Tairu* (both works are published in the book *Van Dongen*, Paris, 1925, nos. 11, 16).

Georges Rouault
1871-1958

57. *Filles*, 1907
Girls
Tempera, watercolor and pastel on paper, 28½ × 22½ in.
Signed and dated top right (twice):
"G. Rouault 907"
Inv. no. 43783

Provenance: acquired from the GMNZI in 1948.
Formerly:
from 1908 Galerie Druet;
from 1908 N.P. Ryabushkinsky Collection, Moscow;
Nosov Collection, Moscow;
from 1918 First Proletarian Museum, Moscow;
from 1923 GMNZI

The brothel is one of the most tragic and recurrent themes in Rouault's work between 1903 and 1914. Bodies misshapen by the "profession", women aggressive in their vulgarity, more like torturers than "high priestesses of love" are to be found in many of his pictures. This composition is very similar to the watercolors bearing the same title, dating from 1905 and 1906 (Musée de Grenoble; Musée d'Art Moderne de la Ville de Paris), and to *Girls in the Mirror* (*Filles au miroir*; Musée National d'Art Moderne, Centre Georges Pompidou, Paris). Probably the Hermitage picture was also begun in 1906. A variant of this work is an oil painting in the Kunstmuseum, Bern (1910).

58a. *Le printemps*, 1911
Spring
Watercolor and pastel on paper, 28½ × 22¾ in.
Signed and dated bottom right: "G. Rouault 1911"
Inv. no. 42157

Provenance: acquired from the GMNZI in 1934.
Formerly:
from 1911 I.A. Morozov Collection (purchased at the Salon des Indépendants exhibition, no. 5278);
from 1918 GMNZI

The oval, almost round shape of this composition, reminiscent of the rose windows in Gothic cathedrals, the bold

brushwork and lines that model the shapes of the landscape and the figures, the border that acts as a frame, are all elements that reflect Rouault's great interest in medieval stained glass windows. The artist, however, does not imitate stained glass work, which he considered a long lost art. The bright patches of watercolor among the dark outlines of the landscape are intended to create filtered light effects. The flowing, transparent tints are handled in a masterly way to render the fresh, damp atmosphere of the spring landscape, a subject extremely rare in Rouault's oeuvre.

58b. *Esquisse de vase* (verso de *Le printemps*), circa 1910-1911
Sketch of Vase (back of *Spring*)
Tempera and watercolor on paper, 28½ × 22¾ in.
Inv. no. 42157

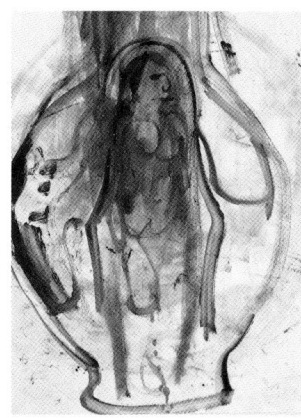

This tempera from the Hermitage is a rare example of a preliminary study by the artist for the decoration of a vase. Judging from the date on the back, which coincides with the period in which he was in close contact with the ceramist André Metthey, the sketch was executed in 1910-1911, when Rouault showed large groups of ceramic works at his exhibitions at the Galerie Druet in Paris (fifty-four in 1910, fifty-eight in 1911). Evidently he also exhibited some sketches of decorations for ceramics, as can be seen from the following not very flattering comment by Guillaume Apollinaire, who was certainly not an admirer of Rouault's talent: "...M. Georges Rouault is exhibiting designs for the decoration of ceramics in which one perceives a tumultuous sense of grandeur and a kind of aversion to beauty." (G. Apollinaire, *Chroniques d'art - 1902-1918*, Paris, 1960, p. 152).

André Derain
1880-1954

59. *Le bois*, 1912
The Wood
Oil on canvas, 46 × 32 in.
Signed on the back:
"a. derain"
Inv. no. 9085

Provenance: acquired from the GMNZI in 1948.
Formerly: Galerie Kahnweiler; from 1913 S.I. Shchukin Collection; from 1918 GMNZI

This picture was painted in Paris at the end of 1912, after spending the summer at Martigues (Provence). In the environs of Martigues Derain found similar motifs connected with woods, which he rendered in a stylized manner. This painting is reminiscent of the landscapes *In the Wood* and *Wood* (Both in the Rupf Collection, Bern), and also of *Trees* (GMII). The homonymous canvas in the Rupf Collection can be considered a preliminary study for this picture. It shows the same part of the wood with three trees in the foreground, however the forms in the composition under examination here are more static. The same subject is depicted in an Indian ink drawing (Hirschland Collection, New York), perhaps executed from life, however, the trunks and branches are arranged differently. *Wood at Sausset-les-Pins* (1913; Statens Museum for Kunst, Copenhagen) is also similar to the Hermitage landscape.

60. *Table et chaises*, 1912
Table and Chairs
Oil on canvas, 34¾ × 34 in.
Signed on the back:
"a. derain"
Inv. no. 9127

Provenance: acquired from the GMNZI in 1948.
Formerly:
Galerie Kahnweiler;
from 1913 I.A. Morozov Collection; from 1918 GMNZI

This picture was probably executed in the second half of 1912, since it was already in the I.A. Morozov Collection at the beginning of 1913. At the Galerie Kahnweiler (no. 2044) it was dated 1912. The works of this period are characterized by a concentric composition.
The vase in the foreground in this still life, occupies the same central position in *The Game-Bag* (*La Gibecière*, 1913; Musée de l'Orangerie, Paris). *Still Life with Pitcher* (Národni Galeri, Prague) is similar in composition to the picture held by the Hermitage.

61. *Nature morte*, circa 1913
Still Life. Basket with Bread, Jug and a Glass of Red Wine
Oil on canvas, 39½ × 46½ in.
Signed bottom right:
"a. derain"
Inv. no. 6542

Provenance: acquired from the GMNZI in 1930.
Formerly:
Galerie Kahnweiler;
from 1913 S.I. Shchukin Collection;
from 1918 GMNZI

This picture was probably executed at the beginning of 1913 (it is in the 1913 catalog of the Shchukin Collection with the title *Still Life. Fish*). The same pitcher, glass, and basket appear in *The Game-Bag* (*La Gibecière*, 1913; Musée de l'Orangerie, Paris).

62. *Portrait d'une jeune fille en noir*, 1913-1914
Portrait of a Young Girl in Black
Oil on canvas, 46 × 35 in.
Signed on the back:
"a. derain"
Inv. no. 9125

Provenance: acquired from the GMNZI in 1948.
Formerly:
Galerie Kahnweiler;
from 1914 S.I. Shchukin Collection;
from 1918 GMNZI

This picture was painted in Paris at the end of 1913 or the beginning of 1914. In the album of photographs in the Kahnweiler archive it is date 1913. It is one of the first works that shows the tendency to start out from the observation of life, which was to become dominant in Derain's work from the end of World War I. This is a very true likeness of the young girl, as can be noted by comparing *Young Girl in Black* (Hermitage) with *Portrait of a Young Girl* (1914; Musée Picasso, Paris).
The artist's particular irony is also expressed here in the choice of a format that is generally used for official portraits. Miriam Simon's suggestion that by portraying the motionless figure in a frontal position wearing an enormous white lace collar Derain was alluding to Ingres' hieratic *Napoleon* (1806; Musée de l'Armée, Paris), seated on a throne wearing a cloak of

white ermine, does not seem so far-fetched (*André Derain. Le peintre du "trouble" moderne*, Musée d'Art Moderne de la Ville de Paris, Paris, 1994, p. 24).

Henri Matisse
1869-1954

63. *Jeu de boules*, 1908
Game of Bowls
Oil on canvas,
45¼ × 58 in.
Initialed and dated bottom left:
"H.M. 08"
Inv. no. 9154

Provenance: acquired by the GMNZI in 1948.
Formerly:
Galerie Bernheim-Jeune;
from 1909 S.I. Shchukin Collection;
from 1918 GMNZI

This picture was painted very quickly at the beginning of summer 1908, and by the middle of the season it was already in Moscow. It is one of the cycle of works linked to the theme of the "golden age", which began with *Joy of Life* (*Bonheur de vivre*, 1905-1906; Barnes Foundation, Merion) and continued with two variants of *Luxury* (*Luxe*, 1907; Centre Georges Pompidou, Paris; Statens Museum for Kunst, Copenhagen).
The next step was the creation of compositions with three figures: *Bathers with a Turtle* (*Baigneuses à la tortue*, 1908; Art Museum, Saint Louis) and *Game of Bowls*. The poses of the figures in *Luxury* and *Game of Bowls* are very similar. The *Bathers* canvas also resembles the Hermitage picture in the arrangement of the landscape and figures.
The symbolic setting of *Game of Bowls* and the immense green meadow with a stretch of blue water are repeated in *Bathers with a Turtle*, a canvas as imposing as *Joy of Life*, the same size format was also used later for *The Red Room*. The powerful symbolism of the *Bathers* and the *Game of Bowls* is expressed through the stylized landscape, the number of figures,

and their nudity that is reminiscent of the original condition of man.
In painting *Game of Bowls* as the "male" pendant for the *Bathers*, the artist went well beyond the primitivism he had intended. According to Picasso, who was a close friend of Matisse at the time, the artist's style was influenced by his sons Pierre and Jean who had just begun to draw. Their rough outlines and clumsy, childish brushstrokes gave their father the idea of how to introduce simplifications and yet preserve the essentials.

64. *La chambre rouge (Harmonie rouge)*, 1908
The Red Room (Harmony in Red)
Oil on canvas,
71 × 86¾ in.
Signed and dated bottom left:
"Henri-Matisse 1908"
Inv. no. 9660

Provenance: acquired from the GMNZI in 1948.
Formerly:
from 1909 S.I. Shchukin Collection;
from 1918 GMNZI

In the spring of 1908, Matisse began *Harmony in Blue*,

using as his starting point a decorative Jouy fabric with blue arabesques that he loved and kept in his studio until he died.
Earlier he had painted the same fabric in the picture *Vase, Bottle and Fruit* (1906; Hermitage) and a little later it was to return in *Still Life with Blue Tablecloth* (1909; Hermitage).
In repeating the compositional scheme he had already used in the realist work *The Breton Servant Girl* (*La Serveuse bretonne*, 1896; this picture remained in the artist's collection) and then in the Impressionist picture *The Sideboard* (*La Desserte*, 1897; Niarchos Collection, Paris), Matisse handled color in a completely new way.
We have an idea of what *Harmony in Blue* was like from the greenish-blue lines that have remained from the former painting on the edge of the canvas and from the color slide of the first version of the picture.
On the eve of the 1908 Salon d'Automne, where the painting was to be exhibited, since Matisse already planned to take it to S.I. Shchukin in Moscow, he suddenly completely repainted it.
Thus *Harmony in Blue* became *Harmony in Red* better known in Russia as *The Red Room*.
On 6 August he wrote a letter to Shchukin, which, like the others addressed to him, was lost in the post-revolution turmoil.
However, there is a draft of it in the Matisse Archive in Paris: "A month had passed since I considered the L.S.L. [large still life. AK] finished, and I had hung it on the wall in my studio to study it better. At the time Druet photographed it. Then I began to think it wasn't decorative enough and I couldn't help putting my hand to it again, which I'm now pleased about. In fact, even those who initially said it was good, find it far more beautiful now. I personally am not very satisfied with the scheme. I shall send you a photograph of it and try to give you an idea of the color in a watercolor sketch. Its price is 4,000 fr... ."
(A. Kostenevich, 'La correspondance de Matisse avec les collectionneurs russes' in A. Kostenevich, N. Semionova, *Matisse et la Russie*, Moscow-Paris, 1993, p. 92).
The watercolor sketch enclosed with the letter has been lost.

65. *La nymphe et le satyre*, 1908-1909
The Nymph and the Satyr
Oil on canvas, 35 × 46 in.
Signed and dated bottom right:
"Henri-Matisse 09"
Inv. no. 9053

Provenance: acquired from the GMNZI in 1948.
Formerly:
from 1909 S.I. Shchukin Collection;
from 1918 GMNZI

In spring 1907, Matisse executed a ceramic triptych depicting a dancing nymph in each side panel and a satyr and a nymph in the central panel, for Hagen's Villa Osthaus.
Unlike the later version held by the Hermitage, the satyr is depicted with a hairy skin and goat's hooves. The nymph's feet are half hidden by drapery.
The model for the ceramic panel was Correggio's *Antiope* in the Louvre. Matisse was certainly familiar with other variants of this theme, particularly Watteau's *The Nymph and the Faun*, also in the Louvre.
Commissioned by S.I. Shchukin, who evidently knew the Hagen triptych, to execute a painting of this subject, the artist abandoned the mythological elements and altered the poses of the figures.
The Nymph and the Satyr is not only more monumental than the similar ceramic composition, but also far more dynamic, thanks to the extraordinarily vibrant colors.
The expressionistic vivacity of the tone and the overtly sensual quality make this picture unique in Matisse's oeuvre, and it reflects the attraction the artist felt for his Russian pupil Olga Meerson.
The golden-haired nymph, despite her stylized features, bears a great resemblance to the model in the *Portrait of Olga Meerson* (Museum of Fine Arts, Houston).
The canvas was painted at the Hôtel Cendrillon in Cas-

sis, in January 1909.
On 7 February Matisse wrote to Fénéon: "I must tell you that I have finished the picture you have sold to Mr. Shchukin, 'A Faun Surprising a Nymph'. I think it ought to be dry, but since the color has not yet had the time to set, please will you give him only the photograph that I have had framed... Permit me to remind you that Mr. Shchukin is eagerly awaiting the picture and that he has made me promise that I will send it to him as soon as possible, in great haste to Moscow... ." (*Henri Matisse*, Galerie Bernheim-Jeune, Paris, 1977).
The picture was begun in 1908 (Matisse writes this in a letter to Fénéon on 26 November). Probably the photograph of the early stages of the composition was also taken at that time.
The original green outlines are still visible and it can be seen that the figures' movements must initially have been even more dynamic.

66. *Fruits, fleurs, panneau "La Danse"*, 1909
Fruit, Flowers, Panel "The Dance"
Oil on canvas,
35¼ × 46¼ in.
Signed and dated bottom right:
"Henri-Matisse 1909"
Inv. no. 9042

Provenance: acquired from the GMNZI in 1948.
Formerly:
from 1910 I.A. Morozov Collection;
from 1918 GMNZI

In this picture, also known as *Still Life with "The Dance"*, Matisse returns to the study of still lifes in interiors, already experimented in *Corner of a Studio* (1900; private collection, Paris).
In the painting under examination, however, he depicts one of his own works, the first variant of *The Dance* (1909; Museum of Modern Art, New York). In some texts it is sometimes mistakenly indicated that this is *The Dance* executed for S.I. Shchukin.
When Shchukin wrote to the artist that he was enthusiastic about the panel *The Dance*,

he was referring to the first variant, which can be seen, in its initial stages (the outlines of the figures are barely sketched) in the photo by the great American photographer Steichen, who photographed

Matisse in his studio. Later work on the two canvases proceeded simultaneously. Therefore the picture does not depict the studio in Issy-les-Moulineaux, as has sometimes been said, but the one on boulevard des Invalides, which Shchukin visited before 31 March 1909, the date when he sent Matisse a letter including a contract for a new *Dance*.

67. *Statuette rose et pot d'étain sur commode rouge*, 1908
Pink Statuette and Pewter Tankard on Red Chest of Drawers
Oil on canvas, 35½ × 46 in.
Signed and dated bottom right:
"Henri-Matisse 10"
Inv. no. 6520

Provenance: acquired from the GMNZI in 1930.
Formerly:
from 1910 S.I. Shchukin Collection;
from 1918 GMNZI

This picture, also known as *Still Life with Pewter Tankard* (*Nature morte au pot d'étain*), was painted at Issy-les-Moulineaux; the same paneled wall in the background appears in *The Pink Studio* (*L'Atelier rose*, 1911; GMII), the chest of drawers is depicted in *The Red Studio*

(*L'Atelier rouge*, 1911; Museum of Modern Art, New York). Between 1908 and 1912 Matisse painted a terracotta statuette of a reclining woman in *Sculpture and Persian Vase* (*Sculpture et vase persane*, 1908; Nasjonaalgalleriet, Oslo), *Goldfish* (*Les Poissons rouges*, 1909-1910; Statens Museum for Kunst, Copenhagen), *Goldfish and Sculpture* (1911; Museum of Modern Art, New York), *Goldfish. Interior* (1912; Barnes Foundation, Merion). This statuette by Matisse, known above all in its bronze versions, was executed in 1907 and reproduces the pose of one of the nudes in *Joy of Life* (*Bonheur de vivre*, 1905-1906; Barnes Foundation, Merion); it also inspired *Blue Nude. Memory of Biskra* (*Nu bleu. Souvenir de Biskra*, 1907; Baltimore Museum of Arts, Baltimore).

68. *Jeune fille aux tulipes*, 1910
Girl with Tulips
Oil on canvas,
36¼ × 29 in.
Signed and dated bottom left:
"Henri-Matisse 10"
Inv. no. 9056

Provenance: acquired from the GMNZI in 1948.
Formerly:
Galerie Bernheim-Jeune;
from 1910 S.I. Shchukin Collection;
from 1918 GMNZI

This picture depicts Jeanne Vaderin, whom Matisse and his wife called Jeanette. She lived at Clamart, near Issy-les-Moulineaux, where she was convalescing after an illness.
That year she posed for the two bronze heads *Jeanette I* and *Jeanette II*, the first of which resembles this picture. The subsequent three sculptures of Jeanette were not executed from life and the artist concentrated on solving plastic problems, and was not concerned with physical likeness.
There is also a charcoal drawing similar to this picture (Museum of Modern Art, New York), probably executed some time earlier.
Here Jeanne Vaderin is depicted standing by a table on which there is a vase of tulips. The everyday quality, great "naturalism" and true-to-life rendering which characterize the New York drawing make it likely that this was a preliminary study for the picture.

Girl with Tulips was probably painted in February 1910. This is borne out by the presence of the tulips that indicate the coming of spring, and by the fact that this was the only painting by Matisse to be exhibited at the Salon des Indépendants in the middle of March.

69. *La Danse*, 1910
The Dance
Oil on canvas,
102½ × 154 in.
Signed and dated bottom right:
"Henri-Matisse 1910"
Inv. no. 9673

Provenance: acquired from the GMNZI in 1948.
Formerly:
from 1910 S.I. Shchukin Collection;
from 1918 GMNZI

The basic idea of *The Dance*, like that behind *Music*, which is closely linked to this picture, took shape over the space of five years. The composition goes back to *Joy of Life* (*Bonheur de vivre*, 1905-1906: Barnes Foundation, Merion) with the ring of figures in the background. In 1906, Matisse executed the wooden bas-relief *The Dance* (Musée Matisse, Nice) depicting the ecstatic movements of dancing nymphs. The same motif is also found on the artist's decorated vases.
At the beginning of 1909, while Matisse was working on the first version of *The Dance* (Museum of Modern Art, New York), S.I. Shchukin, who must have seen it, commissioned another panel the same size, which was far more dynamic, for his house in Moscow. In mid-March he wrote to Matisse that he had received his letters "with the sketches of the large pictures." (A. Kostenevich, 'La correspondance de Matisse avec les collectionneurs russes', in A. Kostenevich, N. Semionova, *Matisse et la Russie*, Moscow-Paris, 1993, p. 163). He was referring to the two watercolor

sketches *Composition I* and *Composition II* (GMII). The first is a draft of *The Dance*. There also exist other drawings of this composition, in pencil (Museum of Modern Art, New York) and in charcoal (Musée de Grenoble). Unlike *Music*, *Composition II*, originally proposed to Shchukin, would have been a completely different pendant for *The Dance* (this idea was realized later in *Girls at the River* [*Demoiselles à la rivière*, Art Institute of Chicago]). It is evident that when *The Dance* was commissioned, Matisse and Shchukin considered all three subjects.

According to Hans Purmann, who had watched the painting of *The Dance* that is now in New York, the picture was painted extremely rapidly in the space of one or two days. Evidently *The Dance II*, unlike *Music*, was also painted very rapidly.
Having finished the panel for Shchukin, Matisse abandoned the theme of the dance and only returned to it in 1932-33, when he worked on a decorative composition for Barnes, closely linked to architecture (Barnes Foundation, Merion; the two earlier variants are in the Musée de l'Art Moderne de la Ville de Paris).
The artist also used the compositional scheme of the Shchukin panel in his illustrations for Ronsard's *Florilège des amours* (1948).
In 1938 Matisse executed a gouache replica of this panel (Davis Collection, New York), which served as a model for the lithograph in the *Verve* almanac (1938).
There is another replica in the form of a gouache *découpée* with red figures, a greenish-yellow hill, and a black sky, executed during the last years of his life (auctioned at Sotheby's on 17 November 1986; private collection, Japan).

70. *Nature morte d'Espagne*, 1910
Spanish Still Life
Oil on canvas,
35¼ × 45¾ in.
Signed bottom right:
"Henri-Matisse"
Inv. no. 9043

Provenance: acquired from the GMNZI in 1948.
Formerly:
from 1911 S.I. Shchukin Collection;
from 1918 GMNZI

The "Spanish" and "Sevillian" still lifes (cf. no. 71 in the present catalog) were painted at the same time, or

one immediately after the other, and have sometimes been considered companion pieces; however, despite the fact they have elements in common, the intention differs and they do not constitute a pair.
The tendency in Western art criticism to entitle both works *Sevillian Still Lifes*, the "Spanish" one being the first and the "Sevillian" the second, often creates confusion and has led to the *Spanish Still Life* being considered the first in order of execution.
In actual fact, we do not know the order in which they were executed and the artist may even have worked on them simultaneously.
The two pictures were Matisse's response to Shchukin's letter of 14 November 1910: "... Now I beg you to paint me two still lifes the same size as the Munich one and approximately the same kind. I offer you 5,000 francs for each canvas. Meanwhile I beg you to give me priority over any other commissions."
(A. Kostenevich, 'La correspondance de Matisse avec les collectionneurs russes', in A Kostenevich, N. Semionova, *Matisse et la Russie*, Moscow-Paris, 1993, p. 167).
Matisse, who was in Spain at the time, returned to France immediately and took the commission very seriously, seeking to execute it virtually to the letter.
For the "Spanish" and "Sevillian" still lifes he chose approximately the measurements of "the Munich one", which was the *Still Life with a Geranium* (*Nature morte au geranium*, 1910; Neue Pinakothek, Munich), painted for Hugo von Tschudi, director of the Neue Staatliche Galerie, Munich.
Even more importantly he repeated the same motif of a geranium in a pot and decorative fabrics.

71. *Nature morte de Séville*, 1910
Sevillian Still Life
Oil on canvas,
35½ × 46 in.
Signed bottom right:
"Henri-Matisse"
Inv. no. 6570

Provenance. acquired from the GMNZI in 1931.
Formerly:
from 1911 S.I. Shchukin Collection;
from 1918 GMNZI

The *Sevillian Still Life* shows more decorative fabrics, that the artist had brought back from his trip, than the *Spanish Still Life*.
It is hardly surprising that this picture, painted in the sa-

me hotel room in Seville, is also known as *Interior with Spanish Shawls* and *The Pink Room*.
Matisse started work on the two paintings immediately after receiving Shchukin's letter of 14 November 1910.
A week later the Moscow collector replied to a letter from Spain, thanking the artist and asking him to send the works as soon as possible and with great haste. Shchukin's letters permit us to date both canvases, formerly attributed to 1910-11or 1911, more precisely.

72. *Portrait de la femme de l'artiste*, 1913
Portrait of the Artist's Wife
Oil on canvas,
57½ × 38½ in.
Signed bottom right:
"Henri Matisse"
Inv. no. 9053

Provenance: acquired from the GMNZI in 1948.
Formerly:
from 1913 S.I. Shchukin Collection;
from 1918 GMNZI

This picture was painted in the artist's garden at Issy-les-Moulineaux in the summer of 1913.
That year Matisse executed few works and one of the reasons for this was the *Portrait* (this was the title of the only work he exhibited at the 1913 Salon d'Automne), a painting that took him a long time to complete.
To the critic Walter Pach, who had stated that the free handling was the result of rapid execution, the artist replied that the *Portrait* had taken over a hundred sittings.
On 15 September he wrote to Camoin: "At the moment I am very tired and I need to forget all my preoccupations. Moreover I have not worked much this summer, but I have gone ahead with my large picture of the Bathers, the Portrait of my wife, and also

my Bas-Relief... ."
(D. Giraudy, 'Corréspondance Henri Matisse-Charles Camoin' in *Revue de l'Art*, no. 12, 1971, p. 15).
In another letter Matisse wrote to Camoin: "Among other things my picture (the portrait of my wife) has met with success among the progressives. But I am not very satisfied, it is the start of a great effort." (D. Giraudy, *op. cit.*, p. 16).
On 10 March 1914, Shchukin wrote to Matisse that he hoped to receive the "portrait" as soon as possible, and according to the news he had received it had already crossed the frontier ("Moreover I hope to receive the portrait as soon as possible, the shipping agent has told me it has already crossed the frontier." A. Kostenevich, 'La correspondance de Matisse avec les collectionnaires russes', in A. Kostenevich, N. Semionova, *Matisse et la Russie*, Moscow-Paris, 1993, p. 176).
The *Portrait of the Artist's Wife* was the last picture by Matisse to enter the Shchukin Collection.

73. *Etude de modèle*, 1934
Study of a Model
Graphite on paper,
9¾ × 13 in.
Signed bottom right with the initials: "H.M."
Inv. no. 46061

Provenance: acquired in 1968 (gift of L.N. Delektorskaya).
Formerly:
L.N. Delektorskaya Collection (gift of the artist)

According to the memoirs of Lydia Nikolaevna Delektorskaya, this drawing was executed in Nice in 1934.
On entering his wife's bedroom to take a rest, Matisse found Lydia Delektorskaya, who was her companion at the time. The naturalness of the woman's pose attracted his attention: "...while I was absent-mindedly listening to the conversation, he unexpectedly said: Don't move! And opening his sketchbook he drew me in a favorite pose of mine, with my head resting on my arms, leaning on the back of a chair... That first drawing was later the model for the canvas 'Les Yeux Bleus', his first painting of me."
(L.N. Delektorskaya, *Matis-*

se...l'apparente facilité, Paris, 1986, p. 16).
His new model (from February of the following year Lydia began to pose regularly for the artist) led to the creation of a series of works on the same theme.
In 1935 he painted two pictures: *Blue Eyes* (*Les Yeux Bleus*, in late February-March; Baltimore Museum of Art, Baltimore) and *The Dream* (*La Rêve*, April-May; Centre Georges Pompidou, Paris).
At the same time, and also later, he made drawings of the same subject.
Two pencil drawings are dated 1935, one was published in R. Fry, *Henri Matisse*, Paris, 1935, plate 58; the other is cited in the book by Delektorskaya (*op. cit.*, p. 44).
The position of the head and arms, similar to the one in the original drawing, is also repeated in the charcoal studies, one of which – *Nude on a Yellow Chair* (*Nu à la chaise jaune*) – was begun in April 1935 and, after a series of reworkings, finished in 1936 (L.N. Delektorskaya, *op. cit*. pp. 49-51).

74. *Nu couché*, 1935
*Reclining Nude
(The Artist and the Model)*
Pen and Indian ink
on paper, 15 × 20 in.
Signed and dated
bottom left:
"Henri Matisse 1935"
Inv. no. 46047

Provenance: acquired
in 1968 (gift of L.N.
Delektorskaya).
Formerly:
L.N. Delektorskaya
(gift of the artist)

This is one of the finer series of large ink drawings, executed at the end of 1935 after the paintings *Large Reclining Nude* (*Grand nu couché*; Baltimore Museum of Art, Baltimore) and *Pink Nude* (*Nu rose crevette*), destroyed by the artist himself.
In this series of drawings (the first part of which was reproduced in *Cahiers d'Art*, nos. 3-6, 1936), his research, which began in the above-mentioned works, evolved more

independently. Techniques and subjects were developed differently, and the very nature of the composition changed. One of the most important elements in the theme of the reclining female nude in an interior is the reflection in the mirror both of the model and of the artist depicting her, so that each component appears twice in the work. In the lower righthand portion of the drawing the artist's hand is seen resting on his drawing board. Top left, in the mirror, the artist's head is seen diagonally above the barely sketched outline of the model.
According to Delektorskaya, Matisse had not planned to include the detail of the drawing board; it just happened. In sitting almost behind the model and covering her with a corner of the drawing board, Matisse automatically took in the whole scene: the girl, part of the drawing board, and his own hand holding the pen.
Thus the artist becomes part of the composition, but is also outside it, among the spectators, who for their part are witnesses to his creative act. The significance of this composition, which cannot have escaped Matisse himself (in fact, he repeated it in other drawings in the series), does not merely consist in the complex echoes of the unusual dialogue between the artist and the model.
This compositional arrangement creates particular spatial relations between the individual components, determines their rhythmic structure, and seems to expand the interior.

75. *Portrait de jeune femme*, 1935
Portrait of a Young Woman
Pencil on paper,
10 × 12¾ in.
Dedicated, dated and signed bottom left:
"à Lydia Delektorskaya / 6 juillet 1935 Henri Matisse"
Inv. no. 46058

Provenance: acquired
in 1968 (gift of L.N.
Delektorskaya).
Formerly:
from 1935 L.N.
Delektorskaya
Collection
(gift of the artist)

In this study the model's facial features are a new source of attraction for the artist, probably because of the hairstyle. Her personality emerges in the rendering of the

traits of the portrait, as does the detail in the taut lines, the drawing of the stiff curls, the shape of the face, the eyebrows, the eyelids, the shadows under the eyes, and the shape of the lips, whose fullness is accentuated by the subtle outline.
A slightly larger variant, also dating from 1935 (Musée Matisse, Cateau-Cambrésis), despite its similarity to the work held by the Hermitage, is different in character.
It was probably executed later, when the first strong and very concrete impression, had faded and become more lyrical.
Hence the pencil lines also differ: while in the study in the Hermitage the dark graphite is reminiscent of charcoal, in the later variant the pencil seems to barely touch the paper, the lines are smooth and less harsh.

76. *Portrait de femme en capuchon*, 1939
Portrait of a Woman with a Hood
Graphite on paper,
12¾ × 10 in.
Dedicated, dated and signed bottom left:
"à Lydia Delektorskaya / Henri Matisse / 9/39"
Inv. no. 46045

Provenance: acquired
in 1968 (gift of L.N.
Delektorskaya).
Formerly:
from 1939 L.N.
Delektorskaya
Collection (gift of the artist)

This drawing of a woman with a hood is one of the numerous portraits of Lydia Delektorskaya.
The subtle line of the arabesque flows softly combining with the outline of the hood and the gentle shape of the face, finishing in the strange motif of the ribbon tied under her chin on which her hand rests, thus becoming a single ornament.
The artist's statement that the arabesque possesses a musical structure and reveals its own original timbre each time, is visibly confirmed here.
Here the timbre of the drawing is intimate, toned down, without a single strident note, and conceals a kind of reticence.
This drawing was executed at Rochefort-en-Yvelines (near Paris), where the artist spent the first three weeks of the war, in September 1939.

He stayed at the local Hôtel Saint-Pierre, and at the same time as the drawing in the Hermitage he also painted two oil portraits, one of which (Matisse Family Collection) is a repetition of the pencil drawing, while the other – *Young Woman in a Blue Blouse* (a portrait of L.N. Delektorskaya) – is now in the Hermitage.

77. *Nature morte.
La cruche et les pommes*, 1940
Still Life. Pitcher and Apples
Graphite on paper,
17¾ × 13½ in.
Signed and dated bottom right:
"Henri Matisse 40"
Inv. no. 46055

Provenance: acquired
in 1968 (gift of L.N.
Delektorskaya).
Formerly:
L.N. Delektorskaya
Collection (purchased from Matisse)

The subject of this *Still Life* is similar to that of the A series, which is part of the collection *Thèmes et variations* (ed. 1943). The same apples or peaches, leafy branch and Spanish pitcher (sometimes replaced by a pitcher with only one handle), appear in different combinations with other elements, for example, in *Persian Dress, Flowers and Fruit* (*La Robe persane, fleurs et fruits*, private collection), in some drawings of 1939-41 (Musée Matisse, Nice), and in a series of other works. The rendering of the objects has been reduced to a simple outline. However, in simplifying his graphic language, Matisse chooses the most expressive features that model the plastic form. Here the leading role is played by the pitcher, one of the objects that continually "posed" for Matisse. By slightly altering the proportions, he introduces life and irony to the "still life", by making the pitcher look as if it has its hands on its hips,

78. *Profil de femme (Portrait de Lydia Delektorskaya)*, 1942
Profile of a Woman (Portrait of Lydia Delektorskaya)
Graphite on paper,
21 × 16 in.
Signed and dated bottom left:
"016 / Henri-Matisse 42"
Inv. no. 46052

Provenance: acquired in 1968 (gift of L.N. Delektorskaya).

Formerly:
from 1942 L.N. Delektorskaya Collection (purchased from Matisse)

This portrait is one of the works published in *Thèmes et variations*, which includes one hundred and fifty-eight reproductions of various drawings, grouped in series, and chosen for this publication by Matisse himself. Each of the seventeen series is distinguished by a letter of the alphabet and opens with a drawing of the "theme", in charcoal in most cases, which is followed by variations in pencil or ink.
This drawing in the Hermitage is no. 16 in the "O" series. In actual fact, the theme and type of model in the series examined here have nothing in common with many other drawings of the same face. Many variants are frequently far-removed from the original image.
"When I execute my 'Variations' drawings", writes Henri Matisse, "the path my pencil follows on the sheet of paper is somewhat similar to the gesture of a man feeling his way in the dark. I mean that my way is not planned: I do not lead, I am led. I go from one point of the object, of my model, to another point, which I always see exclusively alone, isolated from the other points towards which my pen will move later. I am not merely driven by an inner urge that I translate as it takes shape, but rather by the outer form that I am contemplating...." (Matisse/Fourcade, 1972, p. 164).

79. *Jeune femme aux seins nus*, 1948
Young Woman with Bare Breasts
Charcoal on paper,
23¾ × 16 in.
Dedicated, dated and signed bottom left:
"à L. Delektorskaya / Henri Matisse avril 48"
Inv. no. 46046

Provenance: acquired in 1968 (gift of L.N. Delektorskaya).

Formerly:
from 1948 L.N. Delektorskaya (gift of the artist)

On the basis of the date of the dedication and the reproduction in the 1948 portfolio, this drawing must have been executed no later than April 1948.
In 1950, it was printed in five hundred copies by the Maison de la Pensée Française, where a major exhibition of Matisse's paintings, drawings, gouaches *découpées*, and sculptures was held in July-September 1950.

80. *Tête de femme*, 1948
Head of a Woman
Charcoal on paper,
20½ × 16¾ in.
Dedicated, dated and signed bottom left:
"à Lydia / H. Matisse 48"
Inv. no. 46051

Provenance: acquired in 1968 (gift of L.N. Delektorskaya)
Formerly:
from 1948 L.N. Delektorskaya Collection (gift of the artist)

Henri Matisse designed the cover of his book *Jazz*, the graphics, and wrote by hand the text that was reproduced in facsimile (*Henri Matisse, Jazz*, Paris, 1947).
Matisse dedicated a copy to Lydia Delektorskaya and for the occasion executed a drawing, to which this work is linked. According to her, he was not satisfied with the first rapid sketch (now in a private collection) and in three sittings he executed the charcoal study of a woman's head now in the Hermitage. This study was the starting point for the linear, graphite drawing dashed off on a blank page of an originally unbound copy (no. XV) of the book (Hermitage). This female portrait in pencil, with

the dedication "à Lydia Delektorskaya H. Matisse avril 48", was drawn after the publication of the book, in 1948, as was the earlier charcoal study given to Lydia Delektorskaya.

81. *Face de femme*, 1935
Woman's Face
Pencil on paper,
15 × 20 in.
Signed and dated bottom left:
"Henri Matisse 1935"
Inv. no. 46047

Provenance: acquired in 1968 (gift of L.N. Delektorskaya)

Formerly:
from 1948 L.N. Delektorskaya Collection (gift of the artist)

Matisse's late drawings include depictions of faces without outlines. By cutting out the shape of the head and only using fragments, the face becomes a group of conventional, yet easily recognizable signs that indicate the eyes, nose, and mouth. The perfect rhythm of the lines makes one forget the lack of an outline and creates an impression of refined beauty.
In the typology of the face and technique of execution this drawing is very similar to one of Matisse's lithographs illustrating Pierre de Ronsard's *Florilège des amours* (Paris, 1948, p. 18). The artist worked on the drawings for this publication from 1941 to 1947. It is possible, as often happened, that the artist returned to the same theme after the book was published. As Lydia Delektorskaya noted, the drawing shows a certain affinity with two later depictions of faces in ceramic and in a gouache *découpée* that once decorated one of the walls of Henri Matisse's studio.

82. *Tête de femme*, 1935
Head of a Woman
Pencil on paper,
20¾ × 16 in.
Dedicated, dated and signed top left:
"à Lydia / 1r juin 1952 / H. Matisse 49"
Inv. no. 46050

Provenance: acquired in 1968 (gift of L.N. Delektorskaya).
Formerly:
from 1952 L.N. Delektorskaya Collection (gift of the artist)

By reducing the figurative technique to a minimum, the artist often makes the face resemble a mask, on which the eyes are traced lightly in pen, the nose is marked by a curved line, and nothing seems to be definite. And yet, despite this, the effect is recognizable. All he needs is a very or-

dinary pretext – the head of his usual model wrapped in a towel after washing her hair – to fire his creative imagination. The second drawing in the Hermitage with the face depicted frontally was inspired by similar circumstances. The series of drawings dated 1952, including fifteen variations of portraits with turbans (Claude Duthuit Collection, Paris) was executed in the same manner.

Pablo Picasso
1881-1973

83a. *La buveuse d'absinthe*, 1901
The Absinthe Drinker
Oil on canvas, 28¾ × 21¼ in.
Signed bottom right: "Picasso"
Inv. no. 9045

Provenance: acquired from the GMNZI in 1948.
Formerly:
Galerie Kahnweiler;
from 1911 S.I. Shchukin Collection;
from 1918 GMNZI

From the iconographic viewpoint this picture is similar to works like *Dry Throat* (*Gueule de Bois*) by Toulouse-Lautrec (1889, Musée Toulouse-Lautrec, Albi) and *Café in Arles* by Gauguin (1888; GMII), who was staying with Vollard when *The Absinthe Drinker* was being painted and Picasso evidently knew him. Moreover, paintings of women sitting alone at a table in a bar were also done by other Barcelona artists who frequented the café "El Quatre Gats" with Picasso and who in their turn had taken this theme from French artists at the end of the nineteenth century.
The theme of a woman in a café appears in Picasso's Barcelona works of 1899-1900. In the summer of 1901 he exhibited *Absinthe* (Jaffe Collection, New York) at Vollard's, from which *The Absinthe Drinker* was to develop.
He soon went beyond the Impressionist elements that determined the style of *Absinthe* and the figure's bold gesture disappeared.
In the pastel *Absinthe* held by the Hermitage (formerly Otto Krebs Collection, Holzdorf), which is midway between the picture in the Jaffe Collection and *The Absinthe Drinker*, the woman's gesture has altered and there appears an element that was to become of crucial importance: the left hand cupping her chin. The style here is characterized by sharp outlines.
Picasso repeats the gesture of the earlier pastel in *The Absinthe Drinker*, but the model is different.
He also deliberately accentuates her chignon so that it becomes reminiscent of a Phrygian cap or the hat worn by the prostitutes in the prison hospital of Saint-Lazare; a motif he was to return to several times a year later. This is a very clear allusion to the drinker's profession.
The identity of the woman in the picture is not known, but the same model is portrayed in *Woman with a Chignon* (*Femme au chignon*; Fogg Art Museum, Harvard University, USA), *Girl with her Arms Folded* (Obersteg Collection, Geneva), and perhaps *Woman with a Cigarette* (*Femme à la cigarette*; Barnes Foundation, Merion).
In each of these canvases of 1910 and in *The Absinthe Drinker*, there is part of a picture in the background, which seems to indicate the art world, which for Picasso is associated with the theme of loneliness.

83b. Verso de *La buveuse d'absinthe*
Back of *The Absinthe Drinker*
Oil on canvas, 28¾ × 21¼ in.

The back of this picture shows the beginning of a work that was then covered with thick layers of blue and yellow paint. Probably it depicted dancers, and was perhaps a variant of *French Cancan* (Barbey Collection, Geneva). Evidently these pictures were executed around the same time as the pastel *Absinthe* formerly in the Krebs Collection, where a wild dance that is the drunken prostitute's hallucination is depicted in the background.
Picasso was not satisfied with this work and erased it almost immediately, though the layers covering it look like an example of Action Painting, which was to become the fashion fifty years later. Because of the straitened circumstances in which he lived, during these years the artist often used both sides of the canvases or sheets of cardboard.
When he turned over the canvas to paint a new variant of the *Absinthe Drinker*, Picasso did not cover it with primer but simply with a layer of glue, thus obtaining a rough effect that left the texture of the canvas visible.

84. *Portrait de Benet Soler*, 1903
Portrait of Benet Soler
Oil on canvas, 39½ × 28 in.
Signed and dated top left: "Picasso 1903"
Inv. no. 6528

Provenance: acquired from the GMNZI in 1930.
Formerly:
from 1903 Soler Collection, Barcelona;
from 1913 Galerie Kahnweiler;
from 1913 S.I. Shchukin Collection;
from 1918 GMNZI

For a long time it was thought that the person depicted here was José Maria Soler. Palau y Fabre states that the model's real name was Benet Soler (Palau y Fabre, *Picasso: Life and Work of the Early Years, 1881-1907*, Oxford, 1981). His full name was Benet Soler Vidal and he was a fashionable tailor who set himself up as a patron of young painters and writers. His apartment was near the café "El Quatre Gats", the favorite haunt of avant-garde artists in Barcelona. Picasso often dined at Soler's, he was a friend of his, and it is said he paid for the clothes he made for him in pictures. Max Jacob insisted that even in the years of poverty the artist was always very concerned about his appearance. The *Portrait of Mrs. Soler* (1903; Neue Pinakothek, Munich) is a pendant to this portrait in the Hermitage. Picasso also executed a large *Portrait of the Soler Family* (1903; Musée d'Art Moderne, Liège), in which Benet is depicted sit-

ting on the grass with his daughter on his lap. Though they are not a triptych, these three pictures formed a group with the portrait of the wife on the left and that of the husband on the right. Picasso remained close friends with Soler for some years. A drawing of him in colored pencils (The Metropolitan Museum of Art, New York) dates from around 1900.

85a. *Garçon au chien*, 1905
Boy with a Dog
Gouache and pastel on paperboard, 22½ × 16¼ in.
Signed and dated top left: "Picasso. 05"
Inv. no. 41158

Provenance: acquired from the GMNZI in 1934.
Formerly:
S.I. Shchukin Collection;
from 1918 GMNZI

This study is linked to a work depicting a group of *saltimbanques*, or circus people, begun at the end of 1904 (Ch. Zervos, *Pablo Picasso*, Paris, 1932-1978, vol. I, p. 285), and particularly to the variant with the two acrobats, one of which repeats the figure of the boy in this picture with the same dog.
The study in New York was executed no later than mid-February 1905, since from 25 February to 6 March it was exhibited at the Galerie Sérurier and was reproduced in the article by Guillaume Apollinaire in the magazine *La Plume* of 15 May 1905. The tempera in the Hermitage was probably executed shortly before the study now in New York.
The artist reworked the picture several times and also changed the original figures in the composition. The characters in the above-mentioned studies do not appear in the definitive version, *The Family of Acrobats* (National Gallery of Art, Washington). The original idea of the two acrobats and the dog was revealed in an X-ray examination of the picture in Washington, in which these figures are still visible under subsequent layers of paint.

85b. *Deux figures et tête d'homme en profil*
(verso de *Garçon au chien*), 1904-1905
Study of Two Figures and Man's Head in Profile
(back of *Boy with a Dog*)
Oil on paperboard, 16¼ × 22½ in.
Inv. no. 41158

This sketch dates from the end of 1904 or the beginning of 1905, since the drawing on the front of the sheet of paperboard can be dated to no later than mid-February 1905. Probably the artist had invented two compositions with *saltimbanques* at the sa-

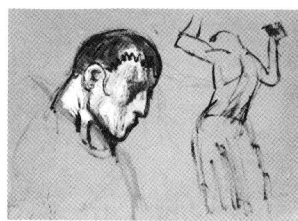

me time and he developed them into a series of variants. The one with the boy and the dog was never executed, while the other, connected with the sketch described here, represents the initial stage of the work on this theme that was to become *Young Acrobat on a Ball* (GMII).
This sketch is a first study from life of the arrangement of the figures.
The torsion and the position of the arms of the figure on the right (evidently a boy) indicate that he is balancing with difficulty on an uneven surface.
Later, in departing from the sketches from life, Picasso replaced the clumsy figure of the boy with a slender, graceful girl set in a vertical instead of a horizontal composition.
But the idea of the contrast between the uncertain, fleeting pose of the graceful figure balancing on the ball and the strong, muscular, motionless athlete can already be clearly perceived in the sketch.
The gradual development of the composition is reflected in two ink drawings (Ch. Zervos, *Pablo Picasso*; Paris, 1932-1978; vol. VI, pp. 603, 604) and in two watercolors (Ch. Zervos, *op. cit.*, vol. XXII, p. 159).

86a. *Garçon nu*, 1906
Nude Boy
Gouache on paperboard, 26¾ × 20½ in.
Signed top right: "Picasso"
Inv. no. 40777

Provenance: acquired by the GMNZI in 1934.
Formerly:
from 1914 S.I. Shchukin Collection;
from 1918 GMNZI

This study is typical of the end of the Rose period, marked by a return to classical forms and rhythms. Picasso abandons the unsettled, emaciated, melancholy world of the circus people, for strong nudes that are reminiscent of ancient heroes.
The artist had already pain-

ted athletic figures earlier, but they served to heighten the frailty of the other characters, whose nudity was the result of poverty.
This picture, by contrast, displays the natural, healthy nudity of youth.
It is one of the first studies in a series of sketches of Paris (spring 1906) and of Gosol (summer 1906) that are unfinished compositions of boys leading horses to water (Ch. Zervos, *Pablo Picasso*, Paris, 1932-1978: vol I, pp. 264, 266; vol. XXII, pp. 266, 267, 269, 270 etc.).

86b. *Femme couchée et garçon nu* (verso de *Garçon nu*), 1904-1905
Reclining Woman and Nude Boy
(back of *Nude Boy*)
Gouache and charcoal on paperboard, 20½ × 26¾ in.
Inv. no. 40777

The style and subject of this picture are characteristic of the Rose period.
The objects in the scene, though rendered sketchily, and the kitten nestling close to the woman reflect the circumstances of the artist's meeting with Fernande Olivier, and suggest that it depicts Picasso's home at the Bateau-Lavoir.
Many years later, after she and Picasso had separated, Fernande described the episode that probably inspired this sketch.
In July 1904, she had returned to the Bateau-Lavoir soaked to the skin after being caught in a storm and had bumped into Picasso in the dark corridor.
He was so overwhelmed, he handed her a kitten he had found on the sidewalk.
He showed Fernande into a room with a bed and a chest that served as a table, a chair and a container for magazines and drawings.
The figure of the boy was probably added later, when he was developing the theme of the *saltimbanques*, which, however, did not go beyond the initial phase.

87. *Composition avec tête de mort*, 1908
Composition with a Skull
Oil on canvas, 45½ × 34¾ in.
Inv. no. 9162

Provenance: acquired from the GMNZI in 1948.
Formerly:
Galerie Kahnweiler;
from 1911 S.I. Shchukin Collection;
from 1918 GMNZI

The motif of the skull appears in the original idea for *Les demoiselles d'Avignon*. Picasso had intended to set the figure of a student holding a skull, a kind of symbol of *memento mori*, against the sailor surrounded by nude women, flowers and fruit.
It was probably then, in the spring of 1907, that the artist did the three Indian ink drawings depicting a skull

and an inkstand (Ch. Zervos, *Pablo Picasso*, Paris, 1932-1978, vol. XXVI, pp. 191-193).
The picture in the top righthand corner of the *Composition with a Skull* also bears some relation to *Les demoiselles d'Avignon*.
The canvas *Female Nude* in the Museum of Fine Arts, Boston, is very similar to this work.
For a long time the *Composition with a Skull* was dated 1907, but this has been revised. Since the *Female Nude* in Boston is dated to spring 1908, the still life in the Hermitage cannot have been painted earlier.
The formal structure of the picture resembles that of the painting from the spring or early summer of 1908, though the colors are unusually vivid for that period.
The tones and subject of this picture can be satisfactorily explained if we accept T. Reff's version of the facts.
He connected *Composition with a Skull* with the suicide of Karl-Heinz Wiegels, Picasso's neighbor at the Bateau-Lavoir (T. Reff, 'Themes of Love and Death in Picasso's Early Work', in *Picasso in Retrospect*, New York, 1980).
Wiegles' funeral took place at the beginning of June 1908. It was probably then that Picasso painted a rapid sketch (GMII) and shortly afterwards the picture.
Composition with a Skull can be interpreted in two different ways, either as a work in the traditional genre of *vanitas* or as a *sui generis* funeral oration linked to an event that had really happened.
The palette and the picture in the gilded frame are symbols of art and of the supreme values of life.
They are also reminiscent of the profession and vocation of the man to whom this "epitaph" is dedicated.
The nude woman refers to one of the traditional "joys of

life", but in this particular case it can be read as an allusion to prostitutes (Wiegels' relationships with them actually disguised his homosexual tendencies).
The pipe, the traditional element of *vanitas* in still lifes could be understood here to refer to the use of hashish or other drugs that led Wiegels to commit suicide.
In the sketch the pipe and wineglass are more accentuated. By contrast there are no panels and the palette is barely visible.
Wiegels had come to Paris from Düsseldorf and knew many leading figures in the avant-garde movement including Matisse, Braque, Derain, Jacob and Apollinaire.
After Picasso invited him to stay at the Bateau-Lavoir, the young German could not fit into the artistic milieu of Montparnasse.
Having a rather weak personality he soon turned to drugs after Picasso had initiated him, since at the time, the artist and Fernande Olivier took them regularly.
As time passed he became more and more obsessed by terrifying hallucinations and began to often talk of suicide. In fact, Picasso's closest friend, Manolo, went to stay in the German artist's studio for a time to keep an eye on him.
When he left Wiegels, took an overdose of opium or ha-

shish and killed himself.
The postman found his body the next morning.
Picasso, who was painting a female nude at the time, rushed into his neighbor's studio and found he had hung himself.
Fernande Olivier remembered that for some time the studio where he had died seemed like a chamber of horrors, and they kept imagining they saw the man who had hung himself (J. Richardson, *A Life of Picasso*, vol. II, *1907-1917*, New York, 1996, p. 87).
In remembering the shock of Wiegels' death, Fernande added that from that moment on she and Picasso stopped taking drugs.

88. *Femme assise*, 1908
Seated Woman
Oil on canvas,
59 × 39½ in.
Signed on the back: "Picasso"
Inv. no. 9163

Provenance: acquired from the GMNZI in 1934.
Formerly:
Galerie Kahnweiler;
from 1911 S.I. Shchukin Collection;
from 1918 GMNZI

This picture was painted in Paris in the spring of 1908. The model for the prelimi-

nary drawing that appeared in *Carnet 15* (B. Leal, *Musée Picasso Carnets: Catalogue des dessins*, 2 vols., Paris, 1996, vol. I, p. 210; Musée Picasso, Paris) was probably Fernande Olivier, and the artist used this when he was working from summer 1907 to summer 1908.
There are also another three studies for this painting (Ch. Zervos, *Pablo Picasso*, Paris, 1932-1978, Vol. XXVI, pp. 299-301).
The woman's pose is not very clearly defined, but an explanation for this can be found in the preliminary sketch.
It appears she had fallen asleep sitting on the edge of the bed.
After *Seated Woman*, Picasso painted another smaller version entitled *Rest* (*Repos*, spring 1908; Museum of Modern Art, New York) this time depicting only a bust.
According to Rubin, this was probably because he was not satisfied with the bust and head of the figure in the Hermitage (W. Rubin, *Picasso in the Collection of the Museum of Modern Art*, New York, 1972, p. 46).
However, this explanation is not convincing. Despite the fact that the subject is the same, each picture is imbued with its own particular atmosphere.
Perhaps this time Picasso wanted to paint a version without erotic overtones.

89. *Femme à l'éventail*, 1907-1908
Woman with a Fan
Oil on canvas, 59 × 39½ in.
Inv. no. 7705

Provenance: acquired from the GMNZI in 1934.
Formerly:
Galerie Kahnweiler;
from 1911 S.I. Shchukin Collection;
from 1918 GMNZI

In the Shchukin Collection the title of this painting was

After the Ball and it was probably chosen by the Moscow collector (Picasso was not in the habit of using this kind of title).
Here we perceive one of the psychological motifs common in Salon painting.
In 1904, in the first drawing *Far from the Ball* (Ch. Zervos, *Pablo Picasso*, Paris, 1932-1978, vol. XXII, p. 86), Picasso had painted a languid woman beside a mustachioed Don Juan.
However, this picture cannot be simply seen as a parody. By depicting a psychological subject in a geometric style Picasso gives it a new vitality and makes the situation itself somewhat grotesque.
An X-ray examination of the picture (*Picasso and Portraiture: Representation and Transformation*, ed. W. Rubin, Museum of Modern Art, New York, 1996, p. 270) has revealed that the woman's head was mostly reworked (initially her eyes were wide open).
This original variant (which probably dates from spring 1908) is linked to the *Portrait of Fernande* (pencil, 1908; Musée Picasso, Paris), folio 7 of *Carnet 15* (B. Leal, *Musée Picasso: Catalogue des dessins*, 2 vols., Paris, 1996, vol. I, p. 203).
Stylistically this drawing should be included among the

works of 1907, when the artist began this portfolio.
The portrait of Fernande came before the sheet of paper with four sketches for the future picture: three with the design of the whole composition and one (perhaps the first) with the bust of a woman in which the turn of the shoulders is only hinted at (Ch. Zervos, *op. cit.*, vol. II, p. 67). The portrait is followed by three drawings of a figure (ff. 8R, 9R, 11R; B. Leal, *op. cit.*, vol. I, pp. 203-204; Ch. Zervos, *op. cit.*, vol. II, pp. 701, 702). Folio 11, which is more finely executed, echoes the works of 1907, when the picture was probably begun. It has the same format as the canvas, but it is far more true to life, the shoulders are more sloping, and the sketch reproduces the natural chiaroscuro. In this drawing the breast is not bare. At a certain point Picasso decided to depict the woman with a fan full length and standing, as can be seen from the sketch on folio 40 of *Carnet 15* (B. Leal, *op. cit.*, vol. I, p. 208).

90. *Maisonnette dans un jardin*, 1908
Cottage in a Garden
Oil on canvas,
28¾ × 24¾ in.
Signed on the back: "Picasso"
Inv. no. 6533

Provenance: acquired from the GMNZI in 1930.
Formerly:
Galerie Kahnweiler;
S.I. Shchukin Collection;
from 1918 GMNZI

This picture was painted at La Rue-de-Bois near Créteil, where Picasso went when he was on the verge of a nervous breakdown in August 1908. La Rue-de-Bois, on the road that ran along the River Oise near the Forêt d'Halatte, was a small village of only about a dozen cottages.
It was nothing special, yet

from the standpoint of transposing reality into a Cubist form it was probably a fortunate choice. The artist lived there alone for a month (which turned out to be an incredibly productive period), although he originally planned to stay longer.
Of the five landscapes painted at La Rue-de-Bois the one that bears the greatest resemblance to the canvas in the Hermitage is the work with the same title at the GMII. Probably both paintings were executed soon after Pablo Picasso arrived in the village.

91. *Vase avec fruits*, 1909
Vase with Fruit
Oil on canvas, 35¾ × 28½ in.
Signed on the back: "Picasso"
Inv. no. 9160

Provenance: acquired from the GMNZI in 1948.
Formerly:
Galerie Kahnweiler;
S.I. Shchukin Collection;
from 1918 GMNZI

This picture, also known as *Fruit Dish with Pears* (*Compotier aux poires*) and *Vase, Fruit and Wineglass*, was painted in Paris at the beginning of 1909. During that period Picasso executed a series of still lifes that were less monumental and more rhythmic than the similar works painted in the summer and autumn of 1908. The works in this group that most resemble the composition in the Hermitage are *Le Compotier* (Museum of Modern Art, New York) and *Vase, Gourd and Fruit on a Table* (*Vase, gourde et fruits sur une table*; Whitney Collection, New York). The small watercolor *The Fruit Dish* (*Le Compotier*) in the Musée de Grenoble was evidently painted at the same time as the picture in the Hermitage. It depicts a very similar, though less distinct, fruit dish with apples and pears. The strange vase in Picasso's possession, whose shape is reminiscent of the corolla of a flower, which is repeated in all these works, sometimes faithfully depic-

ted, as in the picture in the Hermitage, sometimes more stylized, is an Art Nouveau piece (circa 1890). The same vase with pears can be seen in the background of *Queen Isabeau* (*La reine Isabeau*, 1909; GMII).

92. *L'homme aux bras croisés*, 1909
Man with Arms Folded
Tempera and watercolor on paper, 25½ × 19¾ in.
Signed on the back: "Picasso"
Inv. no. 43481

Provenance: acquired from the GMNZI in 1934.
Formerly:
Galerie Kahnweiler;
from 1914 S.I. Shchukin Collection;
from 1918 GMNZI

This picture is one of a large group of works that were executed in Paris in the spring of 1909.
They are based on the same model, whose features were probably created by the artist himself, who juggled with them to produce numerous variants, by changing the angle of the bust, the inclination of the head, and the proportions of the face.
Those that bear the closest resemblance to the picture held by the Hermitage are *Man with Arms Folded* (Ch. Zervos, *Pablo Picasso*, Paris, 1932-1978: vol. XXVI, p.

411) and the studies of a male head (Ch. Zervos, *op. cit.*, vol. II, pp. 141, 166, 715, 747, 748; vol. VI, pp. 1113, 1152).
The artist is not interested in portraying a real person, but in bringing to light the hidden structure of the form, its dynamism, the possibilities of geometric simplification, of new linear, spatial, and plastic relations.
Picasso returned to the same theme at Horta de Ebro in the summer of 1909.

93. *La briqueterie à Tortosa*, 1909
The Brick Factory at Tortosa
Oil on canvas,
20 × 23¾ in.
Signed on the back: "Picasso"
Inv. no. 9047

Provenance: acquired by the GMNZI in 1948.
Formerly:
from 1909 Haviland Collection, Paris;
Galerie Kahnweiler;
S.I. Shchukin Collection;
from 1918 GMNZI

Until quite recently this picture was known as *Factory at Horta de Ebro*.
Picasso was at Horta de Ebro (now Horta de San Juan) from June to September 1909.
In the past it was thought that all the works the artist brought back with him from Spain were painted at Horta. Dex notes, however, that some of them were executed during his stay in Barcelona. This picture is not, in fact, of Horta de Ebro, though it was probably painted there.
Palau y Fabre points out that there are palm trees in the painting, which do not grow at Horta de Ebro, yet critics have generally been of the opinion that Picasso invented this element.
However, this explanation is not convincing, because in all his distortions Picasso's starting point was always real life.

His tendency to crystallize that culminated in the landscapes of summer 1909 was triggered by the Tarragona countryside and architecture. In the photographs he took and sent to the Steins in Paris, the "Cubist" style of the villages is evident: the whitewashed houses are arranged exactly like cubes.
A comparison with the pho-

tographs shows that Picasso did not depict the village of Horta realistically, nor did he limit himself to simplifying the details or rendering them geometric.
He followed the example of El Greco, who freely played with perspective in his views of Toledo; he respected the requirements of rhythm and composition rather than topographical accuracy.
Yet the true character of the place clearly emerges, and this is confirmed once again by the photographs.
He did not have to imagine the palms, because they grow at Tortosa, the administrative center of the district where Horta de Ebro is located.
At the beginning of July, on his way to Horta, Picasso stopped in this town on the banks of the Ebro, and sent a postcard with a view of it on 5 July.
Maria Luisa Borras has stated that Tortosa was the place depicted in the picture in the Hermitage.
The town is still famous for its brick factories.
These were traditionally built with a central core similar to a warehouse, roofing to cover the stacks of bricks, and a chimney that was generally square.
One of these factories is depicted in the Hermitage painting.
Executed in the same manner, the landscapes of Horta de Ebro, *Houses on the Hill* (Museum of Modern Art, New York) and *Reservoir* (David Rockefeller Collection, New York) feature the hilly terrain.
These together with *The Brick Factory at Tortosa* constitute a group of stylistically similar architectural landscapes, governed by the principle of inverse perspective.

94. *Violon et guitare*,
circa 1912-1913
Violin and Guitar
Oil on canvas, 25¾ × 21¼ in.

Signed on the back: "Picasso"
Inv. no. 9048

Provenance:
acquired from the GMNZI in 1948.
Formerly:
from 1913 Galerie Kahnweiler;
from 1913 S.I. Shchukin Collection;
from 1918 GMNZI

During 1912 Picasso painted a whole series of pictures and did a large number of drawings on the "guitar-violin" theme.
In December he executed some vertical compositions about the same size as the picture in the Hermitage.
The central vertical axis dominates, and it is accentuated by the violin strings, the top is marked by the curling end of the instrument, and in the center the holes in the sound box are the point of junction of the whole composition.
Composition with a Violin (private collection), *Violin* (Centre Georges Pompidou, Paris) and others follow this scheme.
Most of them are newspaper collages. The canvas in the Hermitage is likely to have been painted at the same time or at the beginning of 1913. The composition of *Violin on the Wall* (1913; Kunstmuseum, Bern) closely resembles this work.

95. *Composition.*
Compotier et poire coupée, 1914
Composition.
Fruit Dish and Cut Pear
Gouache, graphite and collage of wallpaper on paperboard,
13¾ × 12¾ in.
Signed and dated top right: "Picasso 4/1914"
Inv. no. 42159

Provenance: acquired from the GMNZI in 1934.
Formerly:
from 1914 Galerie Kahnweiler;
from 1914 S.I. Shchukin Collection;
from 1918 GMNZI

This still life is one of Picasso's more formal compositions painted in 1913-14, in which the link with real objects is reduced to a minimum. Apart from the leafy branches and the cut pear (which is barely perceptible in the brown collage streaked with yellow, glued onto white

paper in the center of the composition, which is somewhat enigmatic and may represent a wineglass or a carafe), no object can be clearly distinguished. All the elements of this still life are abstract and reduced to lightly colored surfaces. Often the titles of the two collages with the cut pear held by the Hermitage create a certain confusion. Both are also referred to as still lifes with books, though this is misleading.

96. *Vase à fruits et grappe de raisin*, 1914
Vase with Fruit and Grapes
Gouache, graphite and collage on brown paper, vinyl paint and sawdust on paperboard,
26¾ × 20½ in.
Signed and dated bottom right: "Picasso 4/1914"; another signature is part of the composition
Inv. no. 43789

Provenance: acquired from the GMNZI in 1948.
Formerly:
from 1914 Galerie Kahnweiler;
from 1914 S.I. Shchukin Collection;
from 1918 GMNZI

This is a variant of the numerous still lifes dating from 1914, based on the motif of the cut pear and bunch of grapes, sometimes depicted together and sometimes separately. This is very similar both in composition and style to the still life in the D. Millot Collection (Ch. Zervos, *Pablo Picasso*, Paris, 1932-1978: vol. II-2, p. 476) and to the still life with a bunch of grapes, pears and a pipe (Ch. Zervos, *op. cit.*, vol. II-2, p. 497). The composition in the Hermitage is also known as *Books, Still Life with a Plate of Fruit and a Bunch of Grapes, Composition with a Bunch of Grapes and a Cut Pear*. This is hardly surpri-

sing, since the lines that divide the surface into rectangles, triangles and semicircles from which a vertical figure emerges that is evidently supposed to be a vase, do not accentuate but rather conceal the concrete forms, turning the composition into a kind of brainteaser. But the less objectively realistic the representation, the more physical and tactile the media adopted: real elements such as sawdust, sand, and wallpaper acquire objectivity.

97. *Scènes du ballet "La Boutique fantasque"*, 1919
Scenes from the Ballet "La Boutique fantasque"
Pen and dark brown ink on paper, 11¾ × 16 in.
Inscribed, signed and dated bottom right:
"A Léonide Massine / Artiste que j'aime / son ami / Picasso / Londres 1914"
Inv. no. 48155

Provenance: acquired in 1991 (gift of M.I. Baryshnikov, received through the International Telemarathon of St. Petersburg).
Formerly:
from 1919 L.F. Miasin Collection, Paris
(gift of the artist);
private collection, New York;
M.I. Baryshnikov Collection, New York

In May-July 1919, Picasso was in London designing the sets and costumes for the ballet *Tricorne* with music by Manuel de Falla and choreography by Leonid Miasin.
Here, in the meantime, he finished work on the staging of

the one-act ballet *La Boutique fantasque*, with music by Gioacchino Rossini, arranged and orchestrated by Ottorino Respighi, and sets by Derain. The choreographer and leading dancer was Miasin. Since de Falla was behind with the score of *Tricorne*, the ballet *La Boutique fantasque* opened first on 5 June 1919 and the première of *Tricorne* came a month and a half later.

Picasso always attended the rehearsals and did many pencil and ink drawings of Derain, Diaghilev, Miasin, Lopuchova, Nemichinova and other members of the Russian Ballet, including Felix Fernandez.

Diaghilev and Miasin had seen the young Spanish dancer dancing the flamenco in a small café in Madrid the previous year, and they were so enthusiastic about his talent they invited him to join their company, in the hope that he would give the ballet a genuine Spanish flavor.

They did not succeed in including Felix in the performance of the ballet itself, but he proved to be a mine of information on traditional Spanish dancing for Miasin and the Russian Ballet. The fact that Miasin danced in the high-heeled shoes typical of the flamenco showed that the lessons Felix had given him had become incorporated in *La Boutique fantasque*.

The drawing in the Hermitage reflects various aspects of Picasso's view of classical ballet including the somewhat grotesque "leap" of the ballerina with exaggeratedly fat calves and Miasin's rather comic pose as he catches her and sits her on his knee. By contrast, the Spanish dance by Miasin and Lopuchova is rendered faithfully without the slightest touch of humor.

In this sketch, which appears to have been executed rapidly, the large, strong hands draw the spectator's attention and are reminiscent of the picture *Italian Woman* (1919, Marina Picasso Collection) and the later neoclassical compositions.

Sonia Delaunay Terk
1885-1979

Blaise Cendrars
(pseudonym
of Frederik Sauser Halle)
1887-1961

98. *La prose du transsibérien et de la petite Jeanne de France*, 1913
The Prose of the Trans-Siberian and of Little Jeanne of France
Paper and watercolor
on a cutout shape,
78 × 14½ in. (complete);
75 × 7 in. (painted part on left, without head)
Alongside the description of the work, the dedications of both artists:
"à mon vieil cher ami simultane Sacha Sonia Delaunay-Terk";
left, in black ink:
"Blaise Cendrars à Smirnov le premier qui sur les ailes simultanées apporta le disque synchrome en Russie / 1 janv. 1914"
Inv. no. 46011

Provenance: acquired
in 1966.
Formerly:
A.A. Smirnov, Leningrad

The planned run of one hundred and fifty copies was not completed and many of those that were printed were not colored. Though the painting was printed from the block held by the Centre Georges Pompidou, each copy can be considered a replica *d'auteur*. *La prose du transsibérien* is a poem written by Cendrars after traveling through Russia for four years and going by train from Moscow to Habin. The aim of this painting by Sonia Terk – whose emotional and creative life was closely bound to Robert Delaunay's – was to accompany the text with parallel, color harmonies, which through the effect of light generated new forms, giving the impression of continual motion and crea-

ting the so-called "simultaneous contrast". The *Deckchair*, to be looked at and read from top to bottom of its two-meter length, was declared a new artistic genre and the first simultaneous book. The person named in the dedication, Alexander Alexandrovich Smirnov (1863-1962), the eminent Russian philologist, took upon himself the task of making the theory of simultaneity and the *Premier libre simultané* known to the Russian public. He went to Paris in 1911 and was a frequent guest at the Delaunay home. He spent the following summer at their house in the country and took part in discussions on the constructive role of light and color, and on simultaneity.

After his return to St. Petersburg "sur les ailes simultanées", on 22 December 1913 Smirnov gave a lecture on the theme "Simultané – a New Passion in French Art", showing "photographs and originals", according to the poster, at the "Stray Dog Cellar", the club of the Artistic Society of the Intimate Theater. Sonia Delaunay's name did not appear on the program, but Smirnov certainly spoke of her art during the lecture, since he showed a copy of the *Prose du transsibérien*.

Fernand Léger
1881-1955

99. *Violon et guitare*, 1924
Violin and Guitar
Oil on canvas, 28¾ × 36¼ in.
Signed and dated
bottom right: "F. LEGER-24"
Inv. no. 9146

Provenance: acquired
from the GMNZI in 1948
Formerly:
from 1927 B.N. Ternovec
Collection (purchased from
the artist);
from 1927 GMNZI (gift of
B.N. Ternovec)

The meaning of this painting does not only lie in the decorative arrangement of planes of color but in the creation of a "machine image". The different colored squares are arranged in such a way as to make the spectator aware of a series of red circles that turn into a revolving wheel. A series of abstract canvases following the same principle were painted in 1924.
In the same period *Mechanical Ballet*, a performance without a script, based on a play of geometric forms, was staged. In some canvases executed at the same time the artist introduced the human figure consisting of "mechanical components". Their role is evident if a comparison is made between *Violin and Guitar* and *Man in a Sweater* (*L'homme au chandail*, 1924; Israel Museum, Jerusalem; a second version is in the Maleng Collection, Paris), in which the background is similar in rhythm and in the arrangement of the planes of color to the work in the Hermitage. A sketch with the same title was auctioned at Christie's in London on 25 June 1984 (no. 23).

100. *La Carte postale*, 1932-1948
The Postcard
Oil on canvas, 36½ × 25¾ in.
Signed and dated
bottom right: "F. LEGER";
inscribed and dated
on the back:
"La carte postale. 2-me etat. 1932-1948"
Inv. no. 9726

Provenance: acquired
from the GMNZI in 1953.
Formerly:
14 December 1949 gift of a group of Léger's pupils to Marshal Stalin on the occasion of his seventieth birthday;
from 1949 "Exhibition of the Gifts to I.V. Stalin", Moscow;
from 1953 GMII

This picture owes its title to the postage stamp depicted in the top lefthand corner and to the motif of the woman holding a flower, a recurrent one on greetings cards. *The Postcard* is similar in style to the compositions of the early 1930s, which the artist himself described as "vertical" works of art: depth and perspective were reduced to a minimum. It is difficult to say how long this work remained unfinished at the beginning of the 1930s and how it changed after Léger's return to France after World War II, when the final date was added.
In 1929 the artist devoted himself to depicting two women "floating" in space with a rose, and the picture was sometimes called *The Two Graces* or *The Dance*. The following year he painted a brown, almost monochrome canvas with two figures, a rose and sheet of paper entitled *The Postcard* (*La Carte postale*, Boffa Collection, Italy). The replica of this work, in a shade of green, is dated 1931. These two *Postcards* are the first stage of this composition. The second stage is the picture in the Hermitage and another smaller canvas from the same period, dated 1932 (private collection, Paris). The details in this *Postcard* differ slightly from those of the Hermitage painting. The general color is somewhat different, the outlines are not so strong, there is no large yellow flower in the center linking the whole composition, and the postage stamp is more clearly defined.
The theme of *The Postcard* was probably inspired by his correspondence with Simone Herman. The artist's passionate, secret affair with this much younger woman began in 1931 and continued until Léger was forced to leave France in 1940 (cf. F. Léger, *Une correspondance poste restante*, Les Cahiers du Musée National d'Art Moderne, Centre Georges Pompidou, Paris, 1997).

This volume has been printed by Elemond spa
at the plant in Martellago (Venice), 1999